EVOLVE

STUDENT'S BOOK

with Digital Pack

Ben Goldstein and Ceri Jones

6

CAMBRIDGE
UNIVERSITY PRESS

CAMBRIDGE
UNIVERSITY PRESS & ASSESSMENT

Shaftesbury Road, Cambridge CB2 8EA, United Kingdom

One Liberty Plaza, 20th Floor, New York, NY 10006, USA

477 Williamstown Road, Port Melbourne, VIC 3207, Australia

314–321, 3rd Floor, Plot 3, Splendor Forum, Jasola District Centre, New Delhi – 110025, India

103 Penang Road, #05–06/07, Visioncrest Commercial, Singapore 238467

Cambridge University Press & Assessment is a department of the University of Cambridge.

It furthers the University's mission by disseminating knowledge in the pursuit of education, learning and research at the highest international levels of excellence.

www.cambridge.org
Information on this title: www.cambridge.org/9781009237581

First published with Digital Pack 2022

20 19 18 17 16 15 14 13 12 11 10 9 8 7 6

Printed in Great Britain by Ashford Colour Press Ltd.

A catalogue record for this publication is available from the British Library

ISBN 978-1-009-23088-9 Student's Book with eBook
ISBN 978-1-009-23758-1 Student's Book with Digital Pack
ISBN 978-1-009-23759-8 Student's Book with Digital Pack A
ISBN 978-1-009-23760-4 Student's Book with Digital Pack B
ISBN 978-1-108-40909-4 Workbook with Audio
ISBN 978-1-108-40885-1 Workbook with Audio A
ISBN 978-1-108-41196-7 Workbook with Audio B
ISBN 978-1-108-40520-1 Teacher's Edition with Test Generator
ISBN 978-1-108-41077-9 Presentation Plus
ISBN 978-1-108-41206-3 Class Audio CDs
ISBN 978-1-108-40802-8 Video Resource Book with DVD
ISBN 978-1-009-23070-4 Full Contact with Digital Pack

Additional resources for this publication at www.cambridge.org/evolve

ACKNOWLEDGMENTS

The *Evolve* publishers would like to thank the following individuals and institutions who have contributed their time and insights into the development of the course:

Antonio Machuca Montalvo, **Organización The Institute TITUELS**, Veracruz, Mexico; Asli Derin Anaç, **Istanbul Bilgi University**, Turkey; Claudia Piccoli Díaz, **Harmon Hall**, Mexico; Professor Daniel Enrique Hernández Cruz, **Fundación Universitaria Unimonserrate**, Colombia; Daniel Martin, **CELLEP**, Brazil; Daniel Nowatnick, USA; Daniel Valderrama, **Centro Colombo Americano de Bogota**, Colombia; Diego Ribeiro Santos, **Universidade Anhembri Morumbi**, São Paulo, Brazil; Isabela Villas Boas, **Casa Thomas Jefferson**, Brasília, Brazil; Ivanova Monteros, **Universidad Tecnológica Equinoccial**, Ecuador; Lenise Butler, **Laureate Languages**, Mexico; Lillian Dantas; Professor Lizette Antonia Mendoza Huertas, **Fundación Universitaria Unimonserrate**, Colombia; Maria Araceli Hernández Tovar, **Instituto Tecnológico Superior de San Luis Potosí**, Capital, Mexico; Ray Purdey, **ELS Educational Services**; Roberta Freitas, **IBEU**, Rio de Janeiro, Brazil; Rosario Aste Rentería, **Instituto De Emprendedores USIL**, Peru; Verónica Nolivos Arellano, **Centro Ecuatoriano Norteamericano**, Quito, Equador.

To our speaking competition winners, who have contributed their ideas:

Ana Netto, Brazil; Andressa Zanfonatto Slongo, Brazil; Betsi García Alonso, Mexico; Carlos Alfredo Reyes, Honduras; Daniela Estefanía Mota Silva, Mexico; Katherine, Ecuador; Marcelo Piscitelli, Brazil; Renata Lima Cardoso Mendes, Brazil; Stephanie, Honduras; Victoria Rueda Leister Pinto, Brazil.

To our expert speakers, who have contributed their time:
Andrea Mendoza, Audrey Decker, Eric Rodriguez, João Glauber Barbosa, Ryoko Mathes, Susanne Gutermuth.

And special thanks to Wayne Rimmer for writing the Pronunciation sections, and to Laura Patsko for her expert input.

Authors' Acknowledgments

A special thanks to all the editorial team, particularly Dena Daniel, whose patience and professionalism helped make this project a pleasure to work on.

The authors and publishers acknowledge the following sources of copyright material and are grateful for the permissions granted. While every effort has been made, it has not always been possible to identify the sources of all the material used, or to trace all copyright holders. If any omissions are brought to our notice, we will be happy to include the appropriate acknowledgements on reprinting and in the next update to the digital edition, as applicable.

Key: REV = Review, U = Unit.

Text

U5: Project Remote for the text about 'Project Remote'. Reproduced with kind permission of Ryan Means; **U8**: CNBC LLC. for the text from '6 tips for putting together the perfect elevator pitch' by Elizabeth Schulze, 05.12.2017. Copyright © CNBC LLC. Reproduced with permission; **U10**: Text about EXO. Copyright © EXO. Reproduced with kind permission; bio-bean Ltd for the text about 'bio-bean Ltd'. Reproduced with kind permission of Jessica Folkerts; **U12**: Michael Hauge for the article 'The Five Key Turning Points Of All Successful Movie Scripts' by Michael Hauge. Copyright © Michael Hauge. Reproduced with kind permission.

Photography

All photographs are sourced from Getty Images.

U1–U12: Tom Merton/Caiaimage; **U1**: Westend61; wonry/E+; Javier Pierini/The Image Bank/Getty Images Plus; Alliya23/iStock/Getty Images Plus; Charly Triballeau/Stringer/AFP; TPG/Getty Images Entertainment; Bloomberg; baloon111/iStock/Getty Images Plus; Leren Lu/The Image Bank/Getty Images Plus; Dennis Bernardo/EyeEm; olgalngs/iStock Editorial/Getty Images Plus; **U2**: Image Source; Plume Creative/DigitalVision; Juanmonino/E+; Lane Oatey/Blue Jean Images; Fancy/Veer/Corbis; Mint Images RF; Westend61; Ian Ross Pettigrew; Magone/iStock/Getty Images Plus; undefined undefined/iStock/Getty Images Plus; Viorika/E+; BraunS/E+; Yevgen Romanenko/Moment; NYS444/iStock/Getty Images Plus; numbeos/E+; **U3**: Cliff Philipiah/Photolibrary/Getty Images Plus; avid_creative/E+; Westend61; Delmaine Donson/E+; simonkr/iStock/Getty Images Plus; bowdenimages/iStock/Getty Images Plus; Fiona McAllister Photography/Moment; **U4**: thanes satsutthi; Power And Syred/Science Photo Library/Getty Images Plus; Steve Gschmeissner/Science Photo Library/Getty Images Plus; Steve Gschmeissner/Science Photo Library/Getty Images Plus; JoSon/DigitalVision; zazamaza/iStock/Getty Images Plus; Micro Discovery/Corbis Documentary/Getty Images Plus; Clouds Hill Imaging Ltd./Corbis NX/Getty Images Plus; ER Productions Limited/DigitalVision; ArminStautBerlin/iStock/Getty Images Plus; Mariia Romanchuk/EyeEm; Dimitri Otis/DigitalVision; Danielle Hogan/FOAP; Blend Images - JGI; Jena Ardell/Moment; d3sign/Moment; **U5**: Seth K. Hughes/Image Source; Evgeny Tchebotarev/500px Prime; Cavan Images; DaniloAndjus/E+; Hero Images; AndreyPopov/iStock/Getty Images Plus; **U6**: skynesher/E+; Oliver Furrer/Photographer's Choice/Getty Images Plus; Bill Heinsohn/Photographer's Choice/Getty Images Plus; Graiki/Moment; Robert Riger/Getty Images Sport; HEX; JohnnyGreig/E+; Maskot; Brand X Pictures/Stockbyte/Getty Images Plus; Ilya Rumyantsev/iStock/Getty Images Plus; kahramaninsan/E+; Frank Gaglione/Photolibrary/Getty Images Plus; **REV2**: migin/iStock/Getty Images Plus; **U7**: valentinrussanov/E+; Inti St Clair; asiseeit/E+; Alfred Pasieka/Science Photo Library; Tek Image/Science Photo Library/Getty Images Plus; uschools/E+; rodho/iStock/Getty Images Plus; View Stock; Copyright Xinzheng. All Rights Reserved./Moment; Adriana O./Moment Open; kitamin/iStock/Getty Images Plus; Wibowo Rusli/Lonely Planet Images/Getty Images Plus; Pinghung Chen/EyeEm; Fernando Trabanco Fotografía/Moment; Manuel Breva Colmeiro/Moment; nrqemi/iStock/Getty Images Plus; FG Trade/E+; IgorKovalchuk/iStock/Getty Images Plus; ROMEO GACAD/AFP; Kylie McLaughlin/Lonely Planet Images/Getty Images Plus; **U8**: Dirk Anschutz/Stone/Getty Images Plus; Navaswan/Taxi/Getty Images Plus; Mike Harrington/Stone/Getty Images Plus; Punsayaporn Thaveekul/EyeEm; Tinpixels/E+; BanksPhotos/E+; Bertrand Demee/Photographer's Choice RF; **U9**: Artyom Geodakyan/TASS; Hero Images; Westend61; Caiaimage/Tom Merton; skynesher/E+; Cultura RM Exclusive/Frank and Helena/Getty Images Plus; westphalia/E+; Spondylolithesis/iStock/Getty Images Plus; RODGER BOSCH/AFP; Cultura Exclusive/WALTER ZERLA/Getty Images Plus; stevecoleimages/E+; Ariel Skelley/DigitalVision; Foodcollection GesmbH; filadendron/E+; Eva-Katalin/E+; mapodile/E+; Slavica/E+; Thomas Northcut/DigitalVision; Alfaproxima/iStock/Getty Images Plus; **U10**: Fernando Trabanco Fotografía/Moment; Waitforlight/Moment Unreleased; Krit of Studio OMG/Moment; Kryssia Campos/Moment; grandriver/E+; Jef_M/iStock/Getty Images Plus; Juanmonino/E+; Thomas Imo/Photothek; Francesco Perre/EyeEm; Chee Siong Teh/EyeEm; Accessony/iStock/Getty Images Plus; Premyuda Yospim/iStock/Getty Images Plus; Tracy Packer Photography/Moment; andresr/E+; Michael Burrell/iStock/Getty Images Plus; Monika Ribbe/Photographer's Choice/Getty Images Plus; carlosalvarez/E+; Jutta Kuss; B&M Noskowski/E+; deimagine/E+; Tadamasa Taniguchi/Taxi/Getty Images Plus; DjelicS/E+; Chesnot/Getty Images News; **U11**: altrendo images/Juice Images; Andreas Korth/EyeEm; Abd Rahman Fahmi Mat Hasan/EyeEm; Tai Heng Leong/EyeEm; Neil Setchfield/Lonely Planet Images/Getty Images Plus; Andrey Nyrkov/EyeEm; quisp65/DigitalVision Vectors; Donato Sardella/Getty Images Entertainment; James Baigrie/Photodisc; photosindia; Elena_Danileiko/iStock/Getty Images Plus; Anikona/iStock/Getty Images Plus; NoirChocolate/iStock/Getty Images Plus; Clive Mason/Getty Images Sport; GREGG NEWTON/AFP; Icon Sportswire; John Russel/National Hockey League; BOLDG/iStock/Getty Images Plus; chelovek/iStock/Getty Images Plus; **U12**: DawidKasza/iStock/Getty Images Plus; Compassionate Eye Foundation/DigitalVision; sturti/E+; De Agostini/Archivio J. Lange/Getty Images Plus; Daniel Kreher; Anton Petrus/Moment; Bjorn Holland/Photodisc; by Edward Neyburg/Moment; Monica Rodriguez/The Image Bank/Getty Images Plus; Neil Mockford/GC Images; Barcroft Media; wabeno/iStock/Getty Images Plus; Car Culture; DNY59/E+; by wildestanimal/Moment; Colin Anderson Productions pty ltd/DigitalVision; vandervelden/E+; 3DMAVR/iStock/Getty Images Plus; **REV4**: Kikor.

The following photographs are sourced from other libraries/sources.

U1: RM Studio/Shutterstock; Courtesy of Consequential Robotics; **U3**: Paul Christian Gordon/Alamy Stock Photo; **U4**: thanes satsutthi/Shutterstock; **U5**: © Automattic Inc. Reproduced with kind permission of Matt Mullenweg; Courtesy of Ryan Means; **U9**: Courtesy of LifeStraw; © Larry Fisher/Quad-City Times via ZUMA Wire; **U10**: © A photograph of Viva Technology 2018. Reproduced with kind permission of Stacey Binnion; © bio-bean Ltd.

Front cover photography by Hans Neleman/The Image Bank/Getty Images Plus/Getty Images.

Illustration

U2: Pete Ellis (D'Avila Illustration); **U3**: Gavin Reece (New Division); **REV1, U9**: Robert Filip (Good Illustration); **U11**: Ben Swift (NB Illustration); **U12**: 411 Jo (KJA Artists).

Audio production by CityVox, New York.

EVOLVE

SPEAKING MATTERS

EVOLVE is a six-level American English course for adults and young adults, taking students from beginner to advanced levels (CEFR A1 to C1).

Drawing on insights from language teaching experts and real students, EVOLVE is a general English course that gets students speaking with confidence.

This student-centered course covers all skills and focuses on the most effective and efficient ways to make progress in English.

Confidence in teaching.
Joy in learning.

Better Learning WITH EVOLVE

Better Learning is our simple approach where insights we've gained from research have helped shape content that drives results. Language evolves, and so does the way we learn. This course takes a flexible, student-centered approach to English language teaching.

Meet our expert speakers

Our expert speakers are highly proficient non-native speakers of English living and working in the New York City area.

Videos and ideas from our expert speakers feature throughout the Student's Book for you to respond and react to.

Scan the QR codes below to listen to their stories.

Andrea Mendoza
from Colombia
Financial analyst

Eric Rodriguez
from Ecuador
Graphic designer

Ryoko Mathes
from Japan
Academic advisor

Audrey Decker
from France
Co-founder of a non-profit organization

João Glauber Barbosa
from Brazil
Works in finance for an insurance company.

Susanne Gutermuth
from Germany
Real estate agent

INSIGHT

Research shows that achievable speaking role models can be a powerful motivator.

CONTENT

Bite-sized videos feature expert speakers talking about topics in the Student's Book.

RESULT

Students are motivated to speak and share their ideas.

Student-generated content

EVOLVE is the first course of its kind to feature real student-generated content. We spoke to more than 2,000 students from all over the world about the topics they would like to discuss in English and in what situations they would like to be able to speak more confidently. Their ideas are included throughout the Student's Book.

"It's important to provide learners with interesting or stimulating topics."

Teacher, Mexico (Global Teacher Survey, 2017)

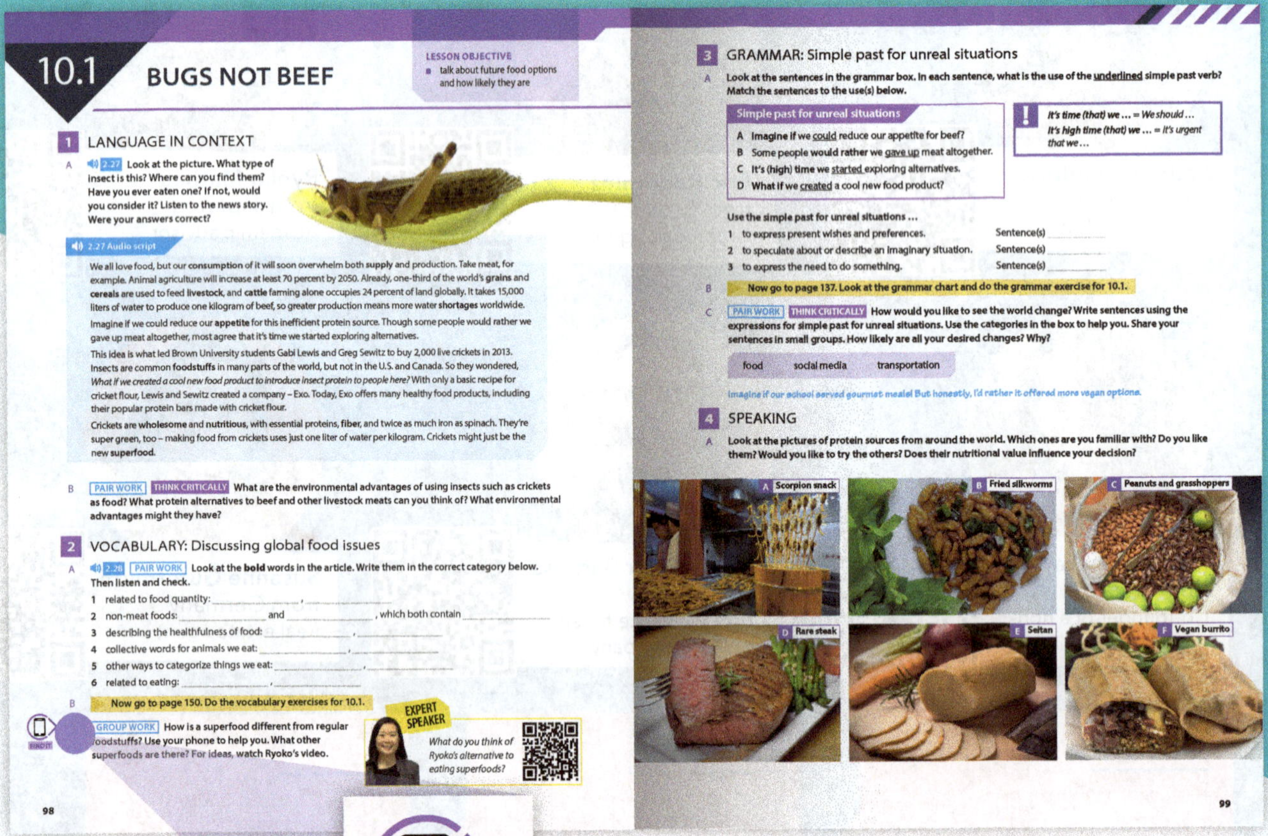

10.1 **BUGS NOT BEEF**

LESSON OBJECTIVE
- talk about future food options and how likely they are

1 LANGUAGE IN CONTEXT

A 2.27 **Look at the picture. What type of insect is this? Where can you find them? Have you ever eaten one? If not, would you consider it? Listen to the news story. Were your answers correct?**

2.27 Audio script

We all love food, but our **consumption** of it will soon overwhelm both **supply** and production. Take meat, for example. Animal agriculture will increase at least 70 percent by 2050. Already, one-third of the world's **grains** and **cereals** are used to feed **livestock**, and **cattle** farming alone occupies 24 percent of land globally. It takes 15,000 liters of water to produce one kilogram of beef, so greater production means more water **shortages** worldwide.

Imagine if we could reduce our **appetite** for this inefficient protein source. Though some people would rather we gave up meat altogether, most agree that it's time we started exploring alternatives.

This idea is what led Brown University students Gabi Lewis and Greg Sewitz to buy 2,000 live crickets in 2013. Insects are common **foodstuffs** in many parts of the world, but not in the U.S. and Canada. So they wondered, *What if we created a cool new food product to introduce insect protein to people here?* With only a basic recipe for cricket flour, Lewis and Sewitz created a company – Exo. Today, Exo offers many healthy food products, including their popular protein bars made with cricket flour.

Crickets are **wholesome** and **nutritious**, with essential proteins, **fiber**, and twice as much iron as spinach. They're super green, too – making food from crickets uses just one liter of water per kilogram. Crickets might just be the new **superfood**.

B PAIR WORK THINK CRITICALLY **What are the environmental advantages of using insects such as crickets as food? What protein alternatives to beef and other livestock meats can you think of? What environmental advantages might they have?**

2 VOCABULARY: Discussing global food issues

A 2.28 PAIR WORK **Look at the bold words in the article. Write them in the correct category below. Then listen and check.**

1 related to food quantity: ____________, ____________
2 non-meat foods: ____________ and ____________, which both contain ____________
3 describing the healthfulness of food: ____________, ____________
4 collective words for animals we eat: ____________, ____________
5 other ways to categorize things we eat: ____________, ____________
6 related to eating: ____________, ____________

B **Now go to page 150. Do the vocabulary exercises for 10.1.**

FIND IT

C GROUP WORK **How is a superfood different from regular foodstuffs? Use your phone to help you. What other superfoods are there? For ideas, watch Ryoko's video.**

EXPERT SPEAKER

What do you think of Ryoko's alternative to eating superfoods?

98

3 GRAMMAR: Simple past for unreal situations

A **Look at the sentences in the grammar box. In each sentence, what is the use of the underlined simple past verb? Match the sentences to the use(s) below.**

Simple past for unreal situations

A **Imagine if we could reduce our appetite for beef?**
B **Some people would rather we gave up meat altogether.**
C **It's (high) time we started exploring alternatives.**
D **What if we created a cool new food product?**

! *It's time (that) we ... = We should ...*
It's high time (that) we ... = It's urgent that we ...

Use the simple past for unreal situations ...

1 to express present wishes and preferences. Sentence(s) ____
2 to speculate about or describe an imaginary situation. Sentence(s) ____
3 to express the need to do something. Sentence(s) ____

B **Now go to page 137. Look at the grammar chart and do the grammar exercise for 10.1.**

C PAIR WORK THINK CRITICALLY **How would you like to see the world change? Write sentences using the expressions for simple past for unreal situations. Use the categories in the box to help you. Share your sentences in small groups. How likely are all your desired changes? Why?**

food social media transportation

Imagine if our school served gourmet meals! But honestly, I'd rather it offered more vegan options.

4 SPEAKING

A **Look at the pictures of protein sources from around the world. Which ones are you familiar with? Do you like them? Would you like to try the others? Does their nutritional value influence your decision?**

A Scorpion snack
B Fried silkworms
C Peanuts and grasshoppers
D Rare steak
E Seitan
F Vegan burrito

99

Find it

INSIGHT

Research with hundreds of teachers and students across the globe revealed a desire to expand the classroom and bring the real world in.

CONTENT

Find it are smartphone activities that allow students to bring live content into the class and personalize the learning experience with research and group activities.

RESULT

Students engage in the lesson because it is meaningful to them.

Designed for success

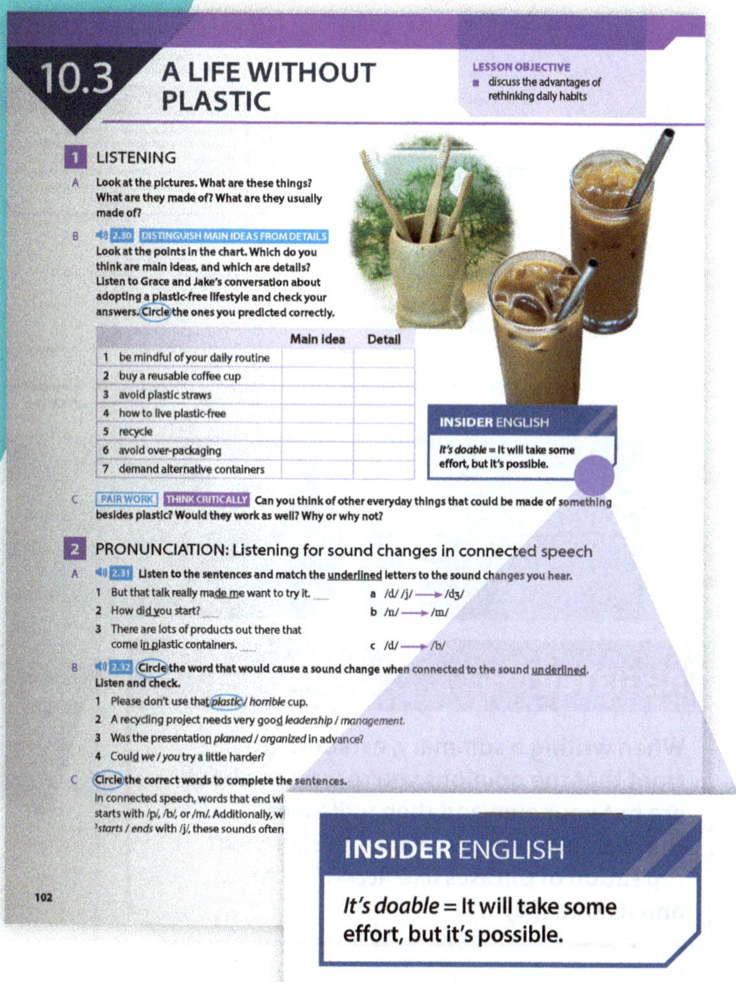

10.3 A LIFE WITHOUT PLASTIC

LESSON OBJECTIVE
- discuss the advantages of rethinking daily habits

1 LISTENING

A Look at the pictures. What are these things? What are they made of? What are they usually made of?

B 2.30 DISTINGUISH MAIN IDEAS FROM DETAILS
Look at the points in the chart. Which do you think are main ideas, and which are details? Listen to Grace and Jake's conversation about adopting a plastic-free lifestyle and check your answers. Circle the ones you predicted correctly.

	Main idea	Detail
1 be mindful of your daily routine		
2 buy a reusable coffee cup		
3 avoid plastic straws		
4 how to live plastic-free		
5 recycle		
6 avoid over-packaging		
7 demand alternative containers		

INSIDER ENGLISH
It's doable = It will take some effort, but it's possible.

C PAIR WORK THINK CRITICALLY Can you think of other everyday things that could be made of something besides plastic? Would they work as well? Why or why not?

2 PRONUNCIATION: Listening for sound changes in connected speech

A 2.31 Listen to the sentences and match the underlined letters to the sound changes you hear.

1 But that talk really made me want to try it. ___
2 How did you start? ___
3 There are lots of products out there that come in plastic containers. ___

a /d/ /j/ → /dʒ/
b /n/ → /m/
c /d/ → /b/

B 2.32 Circle the word that would cause a sound change when connected to the sound underlined. Listen and check.

1 Please don't use that *plastic / horrible* cup.
2 A recycling project needs very good *leadership / management*.
3 Was the presentation *planned / organized* in advance?
4 Could *we / you* try a little harder?

C Circle the correct words to complete the sentences.
In connected speech, words that end wi…
starts with /p/, /b/, or /m/. Additionally, w…
starts / ends with /j/, these sounds often…

102

INSIDER ENGLISH
It's doable = It will take some effort, but it's possible.

Pronunciation

INSIGHT

Research shows that only certain aspects of pronunciation actually affect comprehensibility and inhibit communication.

CONTENT

EVOLVE focuses on the aspects of pronunciation that most affect communication.

RESULT

Students understand more when listening and can be clearly understood when they speak.

Insider English

INSIGHT

Even in a short exchange, idiomatic language can inhibit understanding.

CONTENT

Insider English focuses on the informal language and colloquial expressions frequently found in everyday situations.

RESULT

Students are confident in the real world.

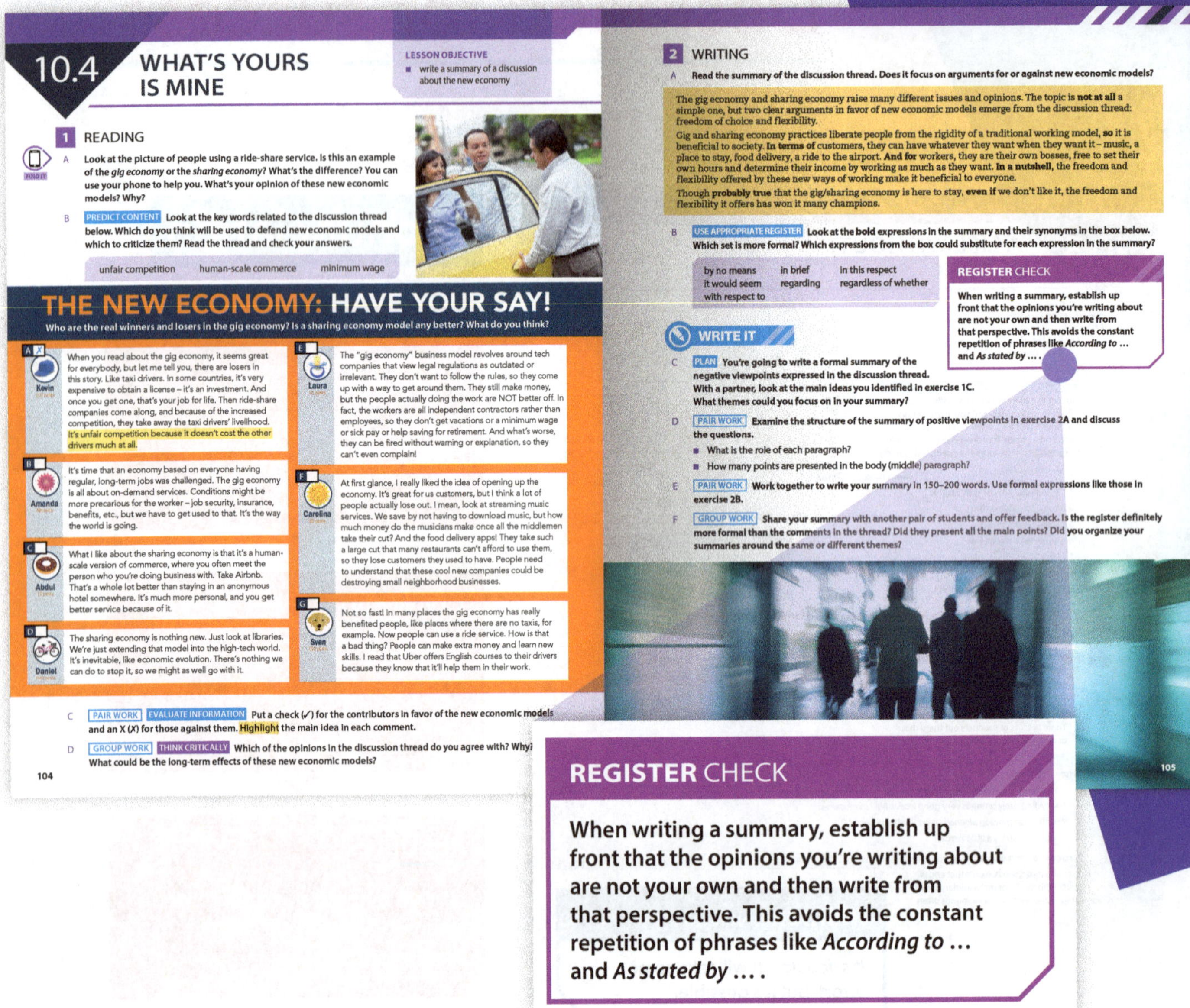

10.4 WHAT'S YOURS IS MINE

LESSON OBJECTIVE
- write a summary of a discussion about the new economy

1 READING

A Look at the picture of people using a ride-share service. Is this an example of the *gig economy* or the *sharing economy*? What's the difference? You can use your phone to help you. What's your opinion of these new economic models? Why?

B PREDICT CONTENT Look at the key words related to the discussion thread below. Which do you think will be used to defend new economic models and which to criticize them? Read the thread and check your answers.

unfair competition | human-scale commerce | minimum wage

THE NEW ECONOMY: HAVE YOUR SAY!

Who are the real winners and losers in the gig economy? Is a sharing economy model any better? What do you think?

A ✗ Kevin: When you read about the gig economy, it seems great for everybody, but let me tell you, there are losers in this story. Like taxi drivers. In some countries, it's very expensive to obtain a license – it's an investment. And once you get one, that's your job for life. Then ride-share companies come along, and because of the increased competition, they take away the taxi drivers' livelihood. It's unfair competition because it doesn't cost the other drivers much at all.

B Amanda: It's time that an economy based on everyone having regular, long-term jobs was challenged. The gig economy is all about on-demand services. Conditions might be more precarious for the worker – job security, insurance, benefits, etc., but we have to get used to that. It's the way the world is going.

C Abdul: What I like about the sharing economy is that it's a human-scale version of commerce, where you often meet the person who you're doing business with. Take Airbnb. That's a whole lot better than staying in an anonymous hotel somewhere. It's much more personal, and you get better service because of it.

D Daniel: The sharing economy is nothing new. Just look at libraries. We're just extending that model into the high-tech world. It's inevitable, like economic evolution. There's nothing we can do to stop it, so we might as well go with it.

E Laura: The "gig economy" business model revolves around tech companies that view legal regulations as outdated or irrelevant. They don't want to follow the rules, so they come up with a way to get around them. They still make money, but the people actually doing the work are NOT better off. In fact, the workers are all independent contractors rather than employees, so they don't get vacations or a minimum wage or sick pay or help saving for retirement. And what's worse, they can be fired without warning or explanation, so they can't even complain!

F Carolina: At first glance, I really liked the idea of opening up the economy. It's great for us customers, but I think a lot of people actually lose out. I mean, look at streaming music services. We save by not having to download music, but how much money do the musicians make once all the middlemen take their cut? And the food delivery apps! They take such a large cut that many restaurants can't afford to use them, so they lose customers they used to have. People need to understand that these cool new companies could be destroying small neighborhood businesses.

G Sven: Not so fast! In many places the gig economy has really benefited people, like places where there are no taxis, for example. Now people can use a ride service. How is that a bad thing? People can make extra money and learn new skills. I read that Uber offers English courses to their drivers because they know that it'll help them in their work.

C PAIR WORK EVALUATE INFORMATION Put a check (✓) for the contributors in favor of the new economic models and an X (✗) for those against them. Highlight the main idea in each comment.

D GROUP WORK THINK CRITICALLY Which of the opinions in the discussion thread do you agree with? Why? What could be the long-term effects of these new economic models?

104

2 WRITING

A Read the summary of the discussion thread. Does it focus on arguments for or against new economic models?

The gig economy and sharing economy raise many different issues and opinions. The topic is **not at all** a simple one, but two clear arguments in favor of new economic models emerge from the discussion thread: freedom of choice and flexibility.

Gig and sharing economy practices liberate people from the rigidity of a traditional working model, **so** it is beneficial to society. **In terms of** customers, they can have whatever they want when they want it – music, a place to stay, food delivery, a ride to the airport. **And for** workers, they are their own bosses, free to set their own hours and determine their income by working as much as they want. **In a nutshell**, the freedom and flexibility offered by these new ways of working make it beneficial to everyone.

Though **probably true** that the gig/sharing economy is here to stay, **even if** we don't like it, the freedom and flexibility it offers has won it many champions.

B USE APPROPRIATE REGISTER Look at the **bold** expressions in the summary and their synonyms in the box below. Which set is more formal? Which expressions from the box could substitute for each expression in the summary?

by no means | in brief | in this respect
it would seem | regarding | regardless of whether
with respect to

REGISTER CHECK

When writing a summary, establish up front that the opinions you're writing about are not your own and then write from that perspective. This avoids the constant repetition of phrases like *According to …* and *As stated by … .*

WRITE IT

C PLAN You're going to write a formal summary of the negative viewpoints expressed in the discussion thread. With a partner, look at the main ideas you identified in exercise 1C. What themes could you focus on in your summary?

D PAIR WORK Examine the structure of the summary of positive viewpoints in exercise 2A and discuss the questions.
- What is the role of each paragraph?
- How many points are presented in the body (middle) paragraph?

E PAIR WORK Work together to write your summary in 150–200 words. Use formal expressions like those in exercise 2B.

F GROUP WORK Share your summary with another pair of students and offer feedback. Is the register definitely more formal than the comments in the thread? Did they present all the main points? Did you organize your summaries around the same or different themes?

105

REGISTER CHECK

When writing a summary, establish up front that the opinions you're writing about are not your own and then write from that perspective. This avoids the constant repetition of phrases like *According to …* and *As stated by … .*

Register check

INSIGHT

Teachers report that their students often struggle to master the differences between written and spoken English.

CONTENT

Register check draws on research into the Cambridge English Corpus and highlights potential problem areas for learners.

RESULT

Students transition confidently between written and spoken English and recognize different levels of formality as well as when to use them appropriately.

"The presentation is very clear, and there are plenty of opportunities for student practice and production."

Jason Williams, Teacher, Notre Dame Seishin University, Japan

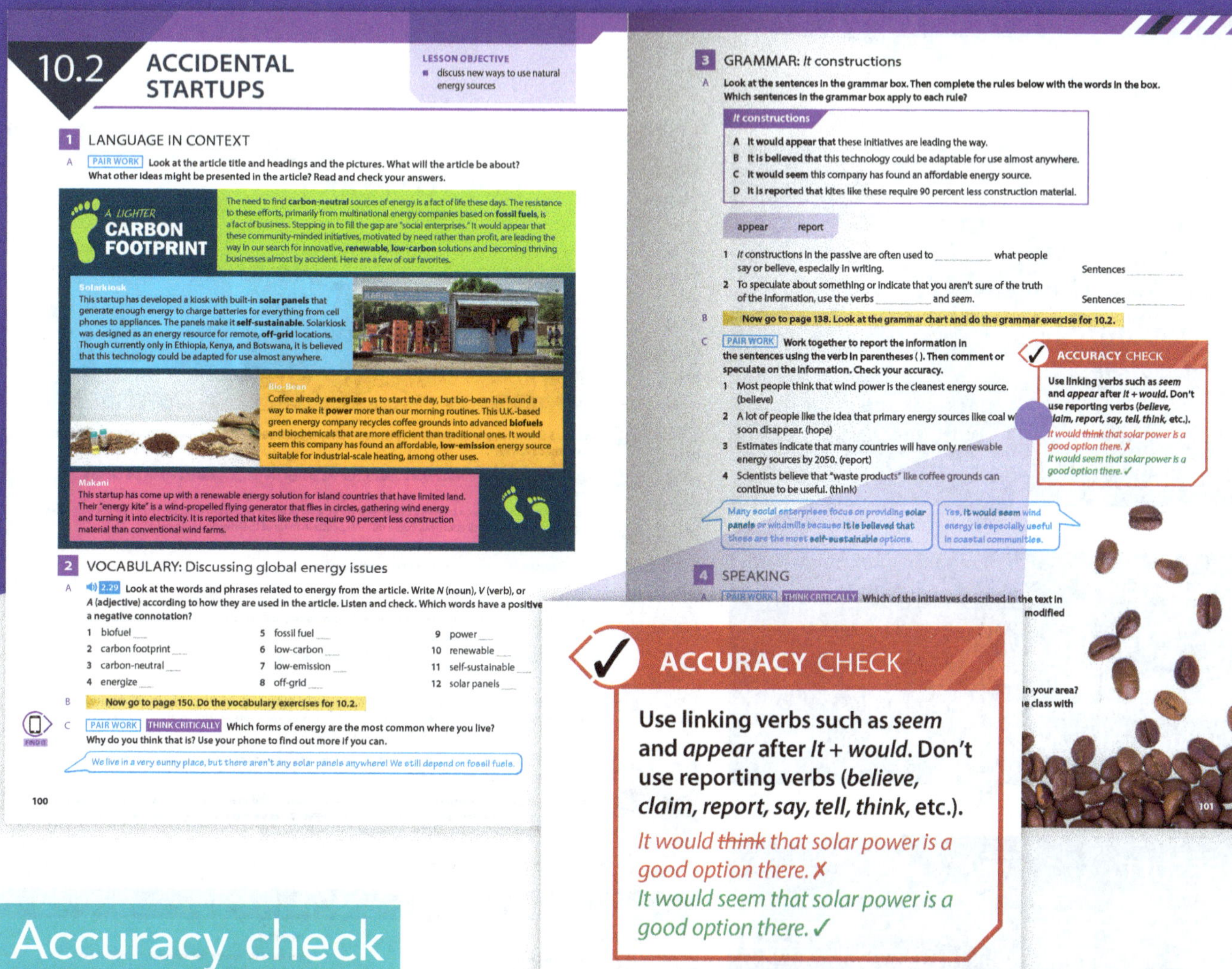

10.2 ACCIDENTAL STARTUPS

LESSON OBJECTIVE
- discuss new ways to use natural energy sources

1 LANGUAGE IN CONTEXT

A PAIR WORK Look at the article title and headings and the pictures. What will the article be about? What other ideas might be presented in the article? Read and check your answers.

A LIGHTER CARBON FOOTPRINT

The need to find **carbon-neutral** sources of energy is a fact of life these days. The resistance to these efforts, primarily from multinational energy companies based on **fossil fuels**, is a fact of business. Stepping in to fill the gap are "social enterprises." It would appear that these community-minded initiatives, motivated by need rather than profit, are leading the way in our search for innovative, **renewable**, **low-carbon** solutions and becoming thriving businesses almost by accident. Here are a few of our favorites.

Solarkiosk
This startup has developed a kiosk with built-in **solar panels** that generate enough energy to charge batteries for everything from cell phones to appliances. The panels make it **self-sustainable**. Solarkiosk was designed as an energy resource for remote, **off-grid** locations. Though currently only in Ethiopia, Kenya, and Botswana, it is believed that this technology could be adapted for use almost anywhere.

Bio-Bean
Coffee already **energizes** us to start the day, but bio-bean has found a way to make it **power** more than our morning routines. This U.K.-based green energy company recycles coffee grounds into advanced **biofuels** and biochemicals that are more efficient than traditional ones. It would seem this company has found an affordable, **low-emission** energy source suitable for industrial-scale heating, among other uses.

Makani
This startup has come up with a renewable energy solution for island countries that have limited land. Their "energy kite" is a wind-propelled flying generator that flies in circles, gathering wind energy and turning it into electricity. It is reported that kites like these require 90 percent less construction material than conventional wind farms.

2 VOCABULARY: Discussing global energy issues

A 2.29 Look at the words and phrases related to energy from the article. Write N (noun), V (verb), or A (adjective) according to how they are used in the article. Listen and check. Which words have a positive or a negative connotation?

1 biofuel ___	5 fossil fuel ___	9 power ___
2 carbon footprint ___	6 low-carbon ___	10 renewable ___
3 carbon-neutral ___	7 low-emission ___	11 self-sustainable ___
4 energize ___	8 off-grid ___	12 solar panels ___

B Now go to page 150. Do the vocabulary exercises for 10.2.

C PAIR WORK THINK CRITICALLY Which forms of energy are the most common where you live? Why do you think that is? Use your phone to find out more if you can.

We live in a very sunny place, but there aren't any solar panels anywhere! We still depend on fossil fuels.

100

3 GRAMMAR: *It* constructions

A Look at the sentences in the grammar box. Then complete the rules below with the words in the box. Which sentences in the grammar box apply to each rule?

It constructions
A It would appear that these initiatives are leading the way.
B It is believed that this technology could be adaptable for use almost anywhere.
C It would seem this company has found an affordable energy source.
D It is reported that kites like these require 90 percent less construction material.

appear report

1 *It* constructions in the passive are often used to ___ what people say or believe, especially in writing. Sentences ___
2 To speculate about something or indicate that you aren't sure of the truth of the information, use the verbs ___ and *seem*. Sentences ___

B Now go to page 138. Look at the grammar chart and do the grammar exercise for 10.2.

C PAIR WORK Work together to report the information in the sentences using the verb in parentheses ( ). Then comment or speculate on the information. Check your accuracy.
1 Most people think that wind power is the cleanest energy source. (believe)
2 A lot of people like the idea that primary energy sources like coal w... soon disappear. (hope)
3 Estimates indicate that many countries will have only renewable energy sources by 2050. (report)
4 Scientists believe that "waste products" like coffee grounds can continue to be useful. (think)

Many social enterprises focus on providing solar panels or windmills because it is believed that these are the most self-sustainable options.

Yes, it would seem wind energy is especially useful in coastal communities.

ACCURACY CHECK
Use linking verbs such as *seem* and *appear* after *It* + *would*. Don't use reporting verbs (*believe, claim, report, say, tell, think*, etc.).
It would ~~think~~ that solar power is a good option there. ✗
It would seem that solar power is a good option there. ✓

4 SPEAKING

A PAIR WORK THINK CRITICALLY Which of the initiatives described in the text in ... modified ... in your area? ... class with

101

ACCURACY CHECK

Use linking verbs such as *seem* and *appear* after *It* + *would*. Don't use reporting verbs (*believe, claim, report, say, tell, think*, etc.).

It would ~~think~~ that solar power is a good option there. ✗

It would seem that solar power is a good option there. ✓

Accuracy check

INSIGHT

Some common errors can become fossilized if not addressed early on in the learning process.

CONTENT

Accuracy check highlights common learner errors (based on unique research into the Cambridge Learner Corpus) and can be used for self-editing.

RESULT

Students avoid common errors in their written and spoken English.

You spoke. We listened.

Students told us that speaking is the most important skill for them to master, while teachers told us that finding speaking activities that engage their students and work in the classroom can be challenging.

That's why EVOLVE has a whole lesson dedicated to speaking: Lesson 5, *Time to speak*.

Time to speak

INSIGHT

Speaking ability is how students most commonly measure their own progress but is also the area where they feel most insecure. To be able to fully exploit speaking opportunities in the classroom, students need a safe speaking environment where they can feel confident, supported, and able to experiment with language.

CONTENT

Time to speak is a unique lesson dedicated to developing speaking skills and is based around immersive tasks that involve information sharing and decision making.

RESULT

Time to speak lessons create a buzz in the classroom where speaking can really thrive, evolve, and take off, resulting in more confident speakers of English.

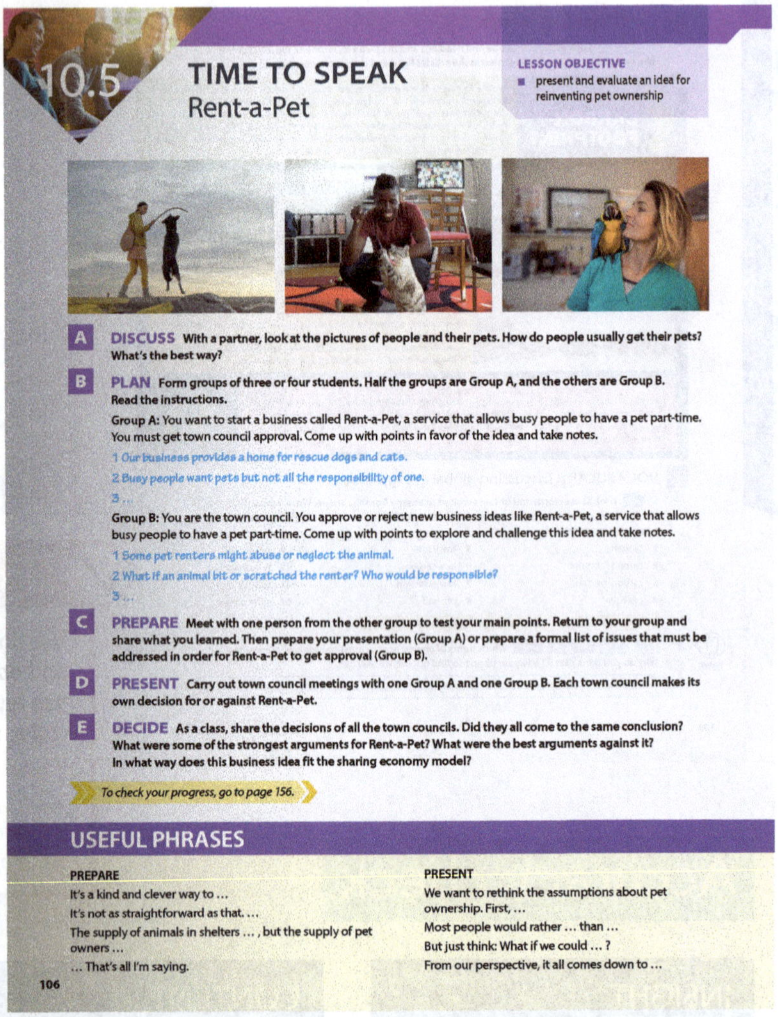
10.5 TIME TO SPEAK
Rent-a-Pet

LESSON OBJECTIVE
- present and evaluate an idea for reinventing pet ownership

A **DISCUSS** With a partner, look at the pictures of people and their pets. How do people usually get their pets? What's the best way?

B **PLAN** Form groups of three or four students. Half the groups are Group A, and the others are Group B. Read the instructions.

Group A: You want to start a business called Rent-a-Pet, a service that allows busy people to have a pet part-time. You must get town council approval. Come up with points in favor of the idea and take notes.

1 Our business provides a home for rescue dogs and cats.

2 Busy people want pets but not all the responsibility of one.

3 ...

Group B: You are the town council. You approve or reject new business ideas like Rent-a-Pet, a service that allows busy people to have a pet part-time. Come up with points to explore and challenge this idea and take notes.

1 Some pet renters might abuse or neglect the animal.

2 What if an animal bit or scratched the renter? Who would be responsible?

3 ...

C **PREPARE** Meet with one person from the other group to test your main points. Return to your group and share what you learned. Then prepare your presentation (Group A) or prepare a formal list of issues that must be addressed in order for Rent-a-Pet to get approval (Group B).

D **PRESENT** Carry out town council meetings with one Group A and one Group B. Each town council makes its own decision for or against Rent-a-Pet.

E **DECIDE** As a class, share the decisions of all the town councils. Did they all come to the same conclusion? What were some of the strongest arguments for Rent-a-Pet? What were the best arguments against it? In what way does this business idea fit the sharing economy model?

To check your progress, go to page 156.

USEFUL PHRASES

PREPARE
It's a kind and clever way to ...
It's not as straightforward as that. ...
The supply of animals in shelters ... , but the supply of pet owners ...
... That's all I'm saying.

PRESENT
We want to rethink the assumptions about pet ownership. First, ...
Most people would rather ... than ...
But just think: What if we could ... ?
From our perspective, it all comes down to ...

106

Experience Better Learning with EVOLVE: a course that helps both teachers and students on every step of the language learning journey.

Speaking matters. Find out more about creating safe speaking environments in the classroom.

EVOLVE unit structure

Unit opening page

Each unit opening page activates prior knowledge and vocabulary and immediately gets students speaking.

Lessons 1 and 2

These lessons present and practice the unit vocabulary and grammar in context, helping students discover language rules for themselves. Students then have the opportunity to use this language in well-scaffolded, personalized speaking tasks.

Lesson 3

This lesson is built around an off-the-page dialogue that practices listening skills. It also models and contextualizes useful speaking skills. The final speaking task draws on the language and strategies from the lesson.

Lesson 4

This is a skills lesson based around an engaging reading. Each lesson asks students to think critically and ends with a practical writing task.

Lesson 5

Time to speak is an entire lesson dedicated to developing speaking skills. Students work on collaborative, immersive tasks, which involve information sharing and decision making.

CONTENTS

	Learning objectives	Grammar	Vocabulary	Pronunciation
Unit 1 Robot revolution	■ Discuss the potential uses of robots in everyday life ■ Talk about developments in artificial intelligence ■ Acknowledge arguments and propose counterarguments ■ Write an essay about AI in our homes ■ Present a proposal for a robot helper	■ Commenting adverbs with future forms ■ Future perfect and future continuous	■ Using adverbs to add detail ■ Talking about developments in technology	■ Listening for contrastive stress ■ Saying expressions to show a counterargument
Unit 2 The labels we live by	■ Discuss assumptions about behavior ■ Talk about assumptions related to age ■ Compare and discuss similar experiences ■ Write a report based on graphs ■ Conduct a survey about consumerism and labels	■ Uses of *will* ■ Uses of *would*	■ Describing personality ■ Using three-word phrasal verbs	■ Listening for the intonation on interactional phrases ■ Saying stressed syllables beginning with /p/, /k/, /t/
Unit 3 In hindsight	■ Discuss past actions and their present results ■ React to past situations ■ Describe a negative experience; offer sympathy and reassurance ■ Write a short story based on a set of facts ■ Discuss and present an alternate history	■ Variations on past unreal conditionals ■ Commenting on the past	■ Thought processes ■ Describing emotional reactions	■ Listening for weak forms in complex verb phrases ■ Using intonation to show emphasis
Review 1 (Review of Units 1–3)				
Unit 4 Close up	■ Discuss the value of changing perspective ■ Talk about how eyes function in humans and animals ■ Discuss problems caused by staring at screens ■ Write a personal profile statement for a résumé ■ Create and present an action plan for a project	■ Quantifiers and prepositions in relative clauses ■ Noun clauses with question words	■ Describing things ■ Eye idioms and metaphors	■ Listening for /t/ between vowels ■ Saying the stressed syllable in related words
Unit 5 Remote	■ Discuss traveling to remote places ■ Comment on loneliness and working in remote places ■ Discuss cause and effect ■ Write a company profile ■ Prepare and present a case for working remotely	■ Participle phrases in initial position ■ Reduced relative clauses	■ Describing remote places ■ Talking about influences	■ Listening for linking between words ■ Saying tense and lax vowels
Unit 6 Surprise, surprise	■ Discuss shocks and surprises ■ Talk about great upsets in sports and other contexts ■ Discuss the differences between local and global brands ■ Write a paragraph drawing from multiple sources ■ Prepare a surprise for somebody	■ Clefts ■ Question words with *-ever*	■ Using adverbs to add attitude ■ Using the prefixes *under-* and *over-*	■ Listening for the pronunciation of foreign words and phrases ■ Saying clefts
Review 2 (Review of Units 4–6)				

Listening	Speaking skills	Reading	Writing	Speaking
I get what you're saying … ■ A conversation about the innovations found in a new app	■ Acknowledge arguments and propose counterarguments	**Robotics to the rescue** ■ An article about robots and humans working together	**An essay** ■ Introduce examples ■ Organize ideas	■ Talk about the tasks best suited to robots ■ Discuss what things you would like AI to do in the future ■ Offer and support your opinion ■ Discuss interesting examples of AI **Time to speak** ■ Present a proposal for a robot helper to address the needs of a particular job
Same here! ■ A conversation about how speaking another language changes the way you interact with the world	■ Discuss similar experiences	**Read the label** ■ An article about product labeling on healthy food products	**A report based on statistics and graphs** ■ Refer to data in graphs ■ Use language for presenting statistical information	■ Talk about common types of social media users ■ Talk about the right age to do different activities ■ Discuss your experience with language learning ■ Draw conclusions about consumer trends based on statistics **Time to speak** ■ Do a survey about the importance of labels on shopping behavior; present your results
A complete disaster! ■ Two conversations about the same story	■ Describe bad experiences ■ Offer sympathy and reassurance	**Too good to be true** ■ News stories about unlikely events	**An anecdote about a strange coincidence** ■ Create cohesion with *both*, *each*, *neither*, etc.	■ Talk about different possibilities for events in the past ■ Discuss how you might handle different problems ■ Create and share the backstory leading up to a bad experience ■ Discuss and question whether a story is believable **Time to speak** ■ Talk about how changing one past event could affect the world today
Look away! ■ A presentation about the effects of screen time on our eyes	■ Clarify a problem	**Attention to detail** ■ A quiz that reveals if you're a big-picture thinker or tend to focus on details	**A personal profile** ■ Use initial descriptive prepositional phrases for concise writing	■ Talk about the esthetics of close-up imagery ■ React to images of animals' eyes ■ Discuss what problems can occur because of excessive screen time ■ Discuss a personal profile statement; offer suggestions for others **Time to speak** ■ Create and present an action plan that involves both big-picture and detail-oriented tasks
Working from home ■ A presentation about current trends in working from home	■ Signal causes and effects	**Remote success story** ■ A news feature story about a business whose employees work virtually	**A profile** ■ Use participle phrases to connect ideas	■ Discuss where and how you seek solitude ■ Discuss the degree of solitude of different jobs ■ Present and discuss ideas about the pros and cons of current topics ■ Discuss the chances of success for different companies to operate virtually **Time to speak** ■ Make a case for working remotely
A surprising comeback ■ A news feature and interview about business revivals	■ Add emphasis	**Jump scare** ■ Different perspectives on being scared	**Summary of a text** ■ Paraphrase without repetition	■ Talk about reactions to surprises ■ Describe famous upsets ■ Compare local and global industries where you live ■ Write short summaries on articles about fear **Time to speak** ■ Plan a surprise for people based on interviews about their interests

	Learning objectives	Grammar	Vocabulary	Pronunciation
Unit 7 Roots	■ Discuss the growing interest in DNA testing and genealogy ■ Talk about celebrations in your family and community ■ Share a story about visiting a place with special significance ■ Summarize information about a topic ■ Present a plan to promote a cultural celebration	■ Negative and limiting adverbials ■ Fronting adverbials	■ Talking about ancestry ■ Talking about customs and traditions	■ Listening for missing /t/ and /d/ sounds ■ Saying diphthongs
Unit 8 Short	■ Discuss distractions and attention spans ■ Talk about instincts and gut reactions ■ Describe the best features and selling points of apps ■ Write presentation slides ■ Pitch a company, an idea, or a product to investors	■ Phrases with *get* ■ Phrases with *as*	■ Talking about attention and distraction ■ Expressions with *get*	■ Listening for long word groups ■ Saying primary and secondary word stress
Unit 9 Health vs. modern life	■ Discuss the effects of a sedentary lifestyle ■ Suggest ways to establish good sleep habits ■ Ask and deflect probing questions ■ Write about a clean-water initiative and how it works ■ Present and explain choices that you have made for other people	■ Referencing ■ Continuous infinitives	■ Discussing health issues ■ Discussing (lack of) sleep	■ Listening for stressed and unstressed grammar words ■ Saying consonant clusters
Review 3 (Review of Units 7–9)				
Unit 10 Reinvention	■ Talk about future food options and how likely they are ■ Discuss new ways to use natural energy sources ■ Discuss the advantages of rethinking daily habits ■ Write a summary of a discussion about the new economy ■ Present and evaluate an idea for reinventing pet ownership	■ Simple past for unreal situations ■ *It* constructions	■ Discussing global food issues ■ Discussing global energy issues	■ Listening for sound changes in connected speech ■ Saying the /ŋ/ sound
Unit 11 True colors	■ Discuss the importance of color for businesses ■ Talk about color expressions and their meaning ■ Respond to questions in different ways ■ Write a short opinion essay ■ Create a flag for a specific group	■ Subject–verb agreement ■ Articles	■ Describing color associations ■ Color expressions	■ Listening for uncertainty ■ Saying vowels before consonants
Unit 12 Things change	■ Answer job interview questions about change ■ Talk about places that have changed drastically ■ Tell a story that you heard from someone else ■ Write a review of a movie or book ■ Create a structured story from pictures	■ The present subjunctive ■ Perfect infinitive	■ Talking about change ■ Describing change	■ Listening for sound changes in colloquial speech ■ Reading aloud
Review 4 (Review of Units 10–12)				

Listening	Speaking skills	Reading	Writing	Speaking
The story of a returnee ■ An interview with someone who has just returned from her ancestral home	■ Comment on your own story ■ Express an opinion ■ Respond to someone else's story	**When a language dies** ■ A graph and text about languages in danger of extinction	**Summary of a story** ■ Parallel structures	■ Discuss the pros and cons of DNA tests ■ Talk about the occasions that bring your family together ■ Tell stories about visiting new places ■ Synthesize the main points in a story **Time to speak** ■ Discuss a local festivity and decide the best way to promote it
It's the app you need ■ A conversation between an app designer and a friend	■ Speak persuasively about a product	**The perfect pitch** ■ An article about developing a pitch for investors	**Presentation slides** ■ Presentation formats	■ Talk about the distractions in your life ■ Talk about how important instinct is in daily life ■ Discuss the apps that make your life easier ■ Compare presentation slides **Time to speak** ■ Present a pitch to investors for an idea or product
Clearing the air ■ An interview with a politician about clean air issues	■ Ask probing questions ■ Buy time to think / deflect questions	**A thirsty world** ■ Three short articles about water crises around the world and water charities that address them	**A short article** ■ Phrases to highlight viewpoint	■ Talk about ways to discourage a sedentary lifestyle ■ Discuss a sleep plan for different people ■ Discuss important local issues in a role-play activity ■ Consider strengths and weaknesses of an initiative **Time to speak** ■ Present choices for other people based on their priorities
A life without plastic ■ A conversation about the challenges and value of going plastic-free	■ Defend an opinion ■ Conclude a turn	**What's yours is mine** ■ Short texts from a forum about new economic models	**A summary of a discussion** ■ Avoiding opinion in a summary ■ Marking opinion in a summary	■ Discuss alternative food options ■ Discuss renewable energy ■ Debate alternative lifestyle choices that benefit the environment ■ Consider the conclusions from a discussion **Time to speak** ■ Debate the pros and cons of a local initiative
It tastes like green! ■ A Q&A session with two experts on the psychology of color	■ Respond to questions for different purposes	**A sense of identity** ■ An article on the significance of colors in sports marketing	**An opinion essay** ■ Express and support opinions with examples	■ Discuss the best color scheme for different products and companies ■ Discuss color expressions ■ Consider what effect color has on taste expectations ■ Discuss the arguments presented by others and offer feedback for improvement **Time to speak** ■ Discuss and present the characteristics that define a group's identity
"And that's when it all changed!" ■ A story about a celebrity impersonator	■ Retell a story ■ Refer to the original story ■ Skip details	**"The next thing you know, …"** ■ An article about the structure of a successful movie script	**Movie review** ■ Write concise descriptions (multi-clause sentences)	■ Practice giving job interview answers ■ Talk about how things have changed dramatically ■ Retell a story ■ Describe plots and turning points **Time to speak** ■ Develop a creative story based on pictures

UNIT OBJECTIVES

- discuss the potential uses of robots in everyday life
- talk about developments in artificial intelligence
- acknowledge arguments and propose counterarguments
- write an essay about AI in our homes
- present a proposal for a robot helper

ROBOT REVOLUTION

1

START SPEAKING

A **Look at the picture. What does it suggest about the future? Do you think it's a realistic vision of the future? Why or why not?**

B **In what ways do you think technology will change our lives in the future? What kinds of things (wearable technology, personal robots, AI, etc.) do you imagine we'll have in the next 20 years? The next 40 years? In 100 years?**

C **What kinds of robots do we already use? Do you think robots are a positive invention in general? Why or why not? For ideas, watch Eric's video.**

EXPERT SPEAKER

What examples can you think of to support Eric's argument and to counter it?

1.1 THE ROBOT TOUCH

LESSON OBJECTIVE
- discuss the potential uses of robots in everyday life

1 LANGUAGE IN CONTEXT

A 1.02 PAIR WORK THINK CRITICALLY **What does the robot in the ad look like? What, and who, do you think it's for? What can it do? What can it probably not do? Listen to the infomercial and check your answers.**

Courtesy of Consequential Robotics

1.02 Audio script

The MiRo robot may look like a toy, but it is far from it. MiRo is a sophisticated piece of robotic engineering, and it is about to **radically** change the field of home health care.

Though still under development, MiRo will **ultimately** be part of a complex system of sensors and communication networks that will **demonstrably** improve the quality of life for elderly people. MiRo robots will live with their owners 24/7, learn their routines, and monitor their movements, which should **drastically** reduce accidents in the home. They will be able to talk to their owners, as well – reminding them to take their medicine and helping them manage appointments and remember visitors' names. And if there's a medical emergency, MiRo will be able to call for help immediately.

Home health care alternatives are **inevitably** going to become a necessity for countries like Japan and the United States, which are facing the challenge of caring for a **progressively** aging population. Social services will certainly not be able to offer human care and companionship for everyone. Although robot companions are bound to be met with resistance initially, robots like MiRo will **undoubtedly** ease the burden on overstretched social services. The greater benefit, however, will be to the elderly people they serve, who often suffer from loneliness and isolation.

MiRo could **feasibly** revolutionize elder care, making the lives of our senior citizens easier, safer, and far more enjoyable.

2 VOCABULARY: Using adverbs to add detail

A 1.03 **Look at the bold adverbs in the script. Which refer to the way something is done (manner)? Which ones are a comment on the action by the speaker (commenting)? Make a chart like the one below and put them in the correct category. Add the other adverbs from the box below. Then listen and check.**

comprehensively	dramatically	gradually	increasingly
markedly	potentially	unquestionably	

Adverbs of manner	Commenting adverbs
radically	ultimately

B **Now go to page 141. Do the vocabulary exercises for 1.1.**

C PAIR WORK THINK CRITICALLY **Apart from the elderly, who might benefit from having a robot companion? Why? What problems could it solve? What problems might it create?**

3 GRAMMAR: Commenting adverbs with future forms

A **Read the sentences in the grammar box. Circle the correct options to complete the rules.**

Commenting adverbs with future forms

MiRo **will undoubtedly ease** the burden on overstretched social services.

Home health care alternatives **are inevitably going to** become a necessity.

Social services **will certainly not be able to** offer human companionship for everyone.

1 Adverbs of manner can be placed in different positions depending on what they modify. Commenting adverbs, when used with future forms, are usually placed …

- [1]**before** / **after** the modal verb *will*.
- [2]**before** / **after** negative words such as *not* and *never*, or negative contractions such as *won't* and *aren't*.
- [3]**before** / **after** the verb *be* in the phrases *be going to*, *be about to*, and *be bound to*.

B **Now go to page 129. Look at the grammar chart and do the grammar exercise for 1.1.**

FIND IT

C PAIR WORK **Look at the commenting adverbs in the box below. Use a dictionary or your phone to look up ones you don't know. Then add commenting adverbs to the sentences so that they reflect your opinion. Compare with your partner.**

certainly	clearly	eventually	evidently
inevitably	surely	undoubtedly	unfortunately

1 This century will become the age of the robot.
2 Robots are going to change the way we live over the next few decades.
3 Robots will never be able to replace the human touch.
4 Robots are bound to take over for humans in a lot of different areas.
5 The robotics industry is about to make life a lot easier for all of us.

4 SPEAKING

A GROUP WORK THINK CRITICALLY **Imagine a robot assistant for the following jobs. What tasks do you think it could feasibly take on? Would it do those tasks better, worse, or as well as a human? What tasks would the human still have to do? Use commenting adverbs to make your attitudes clearer.**

- a clerk in a hotel
- a nurse in a hospital
- a teacher in a kindergarten

As a hotel clerk, a robot **will undoubtedly** *be more accurate than a human. It might even be friendlier!*

B **As a class, share the most interesting uses for a robot assistant that your group came up with. Then discuss whether robot assistants are inevitable. Give reasons to support your opinion.**

1.2 THE WONDERFUL WORLD OF AI

LESSON OBJECTIVE
- talk about developments in artificial intelligence

1 LANGUAGE IN CONTEXT

A **How would you define *artificial intelligence*? Does the idea scare you, worry you, or excite you? Why or why not?**

B 1.04 **Listen to part of a podcast interview in which a tech industry reporter talks about developments in AI. How will AI be used in the near future? How does the host feel about these uses?**

1.04 Audio script

Reporter Industry experts predict that, by the end of the next decade, **chatbots** will have replaced humans in all customer service call centers, but you won't even know you're talking to one. **Computer-generated speech** will have improved so much that chatbots will sound just like humans.

Host We'll be having conversations with computers and not even know it? Impressive.

Reporter Plus, researchers are developing an app to help blind people "see." It will use the camera on their smartphone to capture the area around them. Then, using a combination of **image-recognition** software and **speech to text**, the app will convert the images into speech. Developers are integrating **facial recognition**, too, so the app can announce when a friend is approaching. They have a **working prototype** now, and they're pretty confident they will have developed a **beta version** for testing by the end of next year!

Host What a great use of technology! What other developments can we expect to see soon?

Reporter Facial-recognition glasses – they'll be linked to police databases to help pick out suspects in a crowd.

Host Really? I'm not sure how I feel about that one.

C PAIR WORK THINK CRITICALLY **Why does the host feel nervous about the police using facial-recognition glasses? What are some other possible uses for that technology? What pros and cons can you think of?**

2 VOCABULARY: Talking about developments in technology

FIND IT

A 1.05 PAIR WORK **Look at the technology terms in the box. Write them in the chart for all the things they are associated with. Use a dictionary or your phone to help you. Listen and check.**

artificial intelligence (AI)	beta version	chatbot	facial recognition
computer-generated speech	computer translation	image recognition	operating system (OS)
virtual assistant	voice activation	voice recognition	working prototype
text to speech / speech to text			

Home computers	Smartphones	Airport security	App development	Social media
OS	*chatbot*	*facial recognition*		

B PAIR WORK **Which item from the box above is not yet commonly used? How long do you think it will be until it is part of daily life?**

C Now go to page 141. Do the vocabulary exercises for 1.2.

3 GRAMMAR: Future perfect and future continuous

A **Read the sentences in the grammar box. Circle the correct options to complete the rules.**

Future perfect and future continuous

By the end of the next decade, chatbots **will have replaced** humans in call centers.
We'**ll be having** conversations with computers and not even know it?

1 Use the future perfect and the future continuous to …
 a describe situations in the future.
 b make suggestions for things to do in the future.

2 Use *will* + *have* + past participle (future perfect) to talk about …
 a actions that will be in progress at a given time in the future.
 b actions that will be completed before a given time in the future.

3 Use *will* + *be* + verb + *-ing* (future continuous) to talk about …
 a actions that will be in progress at a given time in the future.
 b actions that will be completed before a given time in the future.

B **Now go to page 129. Look at the grammar chart and do the grammar exercise for 1.2.**

C PAIR WORK **You are going away this weekend to an unfamiliar location. A friend asks you a lot of questions about your trip. Use the prompts to write the questions in either the future perfect or the future continuous, and check your accuracy. Compare with a partner.**

1 **a** How / travel / there ?
 How will you be traveling there?
 b Who / meet / there ?
 c What activities / do ?

2 **a** By the time the weekend is over, who / speak to ?
 b What / see ?
 c What / do ?

ACCURACY CHECK

Remember not to change the form of *be* in future continuous.

It'll ~~is~~ raining by the time we get there. ✗
It'll be raining by the time we get there. ✓

D PAIR WORK **Answer the questions in exercise 3C and create a story about your weekend trip to tell your partner. Share your stories with another pair of students.**

4 SPEAKING

A GROUP WORK **Make a list of ten machines and gadgets you have in your home right now. How does each one help you or make life easier? Which of them do you think you'll still be using ten years from now? Will you be operating them, or will they depend on AI? For ideas, watch Eric's video.**

EXPERT SPEAKER

How similar are your predictions to Eric's?

B **What ordinary tasks or common devices today will have been replaced by AI by the year 2050?**

I think **facial-recognition** technology **will have replaced** house and car keys long before 2050!

1.3 I GET WHAT YOU'RE SAYING ...

LESSON OBJECTIVE

- acknowledge arguments and propose counterarguments

1 LISTENING

A **Read the text message exchange. What is the relationship between the two texters? Why do you think that?**

B 1.06 LISTEN FOR ATTITUDE **Listen to a conversation between two friends, Jeff and Dani. What does Jeff think of Dani's new app?**

C 1.06 LISTEN FOR MAIN POINTS **Listen again and take notes on the positive and negative points they make about chatbots. Compare answers with a partner.**

Positive: ______________________________

____

Negative: ______________________________

____

D PAIR WORK THINK CRITICALLY **Look back at exercise 1A. Are you surprised that this is actually a chatbot conversation? Do you think computers will ever be able to understand and develop emotions? Why or why not?**

2 PRONUNCIATION: Listening for contrastive stress

A 1.07 PAIR WORK **Listen. Pay attention to the underlined words. Why are they stressed?**

Jeff But it looks like a conversation with a <u>friend</u>.

Dani Well, yeah, that's the point. It's a <u>virtual</u> friend.

Jeff You mean a virtual <u>assistant</u>?

B 1.08 **<u>Underline</u> the words that have contrastive stress. Listen and check. Practice saying the sentences with your partner. Focus on word stress.**

1 You have your own, personal talking machine – a learning machine!
2 I mean, why did they design it? Who did they design it for?
3 You can't always be there for me, but my bot can.
4 You're starting to talk about this bot as if it were a real person.

C **Circle the correct words to complete the sentence.**

When we want to clarify or correct what has been said, we often emphasize the word with the [1]*new* / *old* information and use a [2]*lower* / *higher* pitch.

3 SPEAKING SKILLS

A 1.06 **Listen to Jeff and Dani's conversation again. Check (✓) the expressions in the chart that they use.**

Acknowledging arguments and proposing counterarguments

☐ 1 **I can see how** that might be interesting, but …
☐ 2 **I understand what you're saying**, but I still don't get it.
☐ 3 **It's a valid point**, … but consider the other side.
☐ 4 **You have a good point** there.
☐ 5 **I get where you're coming from**, but …
☐ 6 **I hadn't really thought of it like that.** I guess you're right.
☐ 7 **I guess so**, but I'm still not convinced.
☐ 8 **You could look at it that way**, but that doesn't mean …

B **Look at the expressions in the chart. Why does the speaker say the bold words? What purpose do they serve? What word is used to introduce a counterargument?**

C GROUP WORK **One student reads the statement. The person to their left acknowledges it and offers a counterargument. The next person to the left responds, etc. Change roles and start again. Use different phrases.**

Statement: I don't think machines will ever be more intelligent than human beings.

I hear what you're saying, but I think they can be better than us in some specific tasks.

I get where you're coming from, but …

4 PRONUNCIATION: Saying expressions to show a counterargument

A 1.09 **Listen to the expressions and pay attention to the intonation. Then circle the correct words to complete the sentence below.**

I understand what you're saying, but I still don't get it. I know, I know, and it's a valid point.

Use a [1]*fall-rise / falling* intonation to show you question the other speaker's argument and a [2]*fall-rise / falling* intonation to say what you think is true.

B 1.10 **Listen to the expressions. Check (✓) the ones where intonation suggests that the speaker is going to introduce a counterargument.**

☐ 1 I guess so
☐ 2 I get where you're coming from
☐ 3 You could look at it that way
☐ 4 That may be true
☐ 5 I can see how that might work

C GROUP WORK **Does technology always make life easier? Why or why not? Use the phrases in exercise 4B to introduce counterarguments with appropriate intonation in your discussion.**

5 SPEAKING

A PAIR WORK THINK CRITICALLY **Choose one of the statements and argue both sides of it. Acknowledge your partner's arguments and propose counterarguments.**

- A good friend is always there for you.
- We spend far too much time in front of screens.
- Travel broadens the mind.

B **Report back on your discussion. Summarize the arguments you were able to put forward in the time you had.**

1.4 ROBOTICS TO THE RESCUE

LESSON OBJECTIVE

- write an essay about AI in our homes

1 READING

A

B
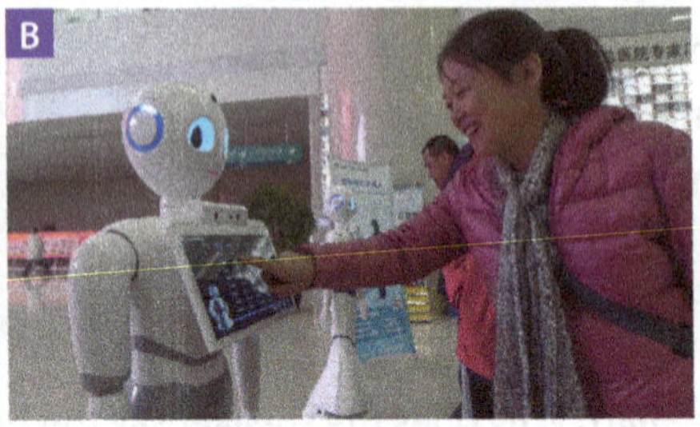

C

A **PREDICT CONTENT FROM PICTURES** **Look at the pictures. Discuss how robots or robotics are being used in each situation to help humans. Read the article. Match the pictures to the correct sections.**

ROBOTS AND HUMANS WORKING TOGETHER

When we think of robots, we often think of movies where humans have lost control and robots have taken over. But in reality, it isn't "us against them." Robots are helpmates in the workplace – more R2D2 than replicant!

Long-distance operations ___

For centuries, the mining industry has been dangerous work. More lives are lost and more workers are injured than in any other private industry. That's why engineers are working with robots to make mining safer. They're bringing the miners up to the surface and sending machines underground. The hope is that the death toll will have been reduced to zero in 20 years.

A great example of this effort is in the searing heat and dust of the red desert of western Australia. Here, robotics, AI, and satellite technology combine to allow engineers to control mining operations from the comfort of an office in Perth – 750 miles away. Driverless trucks, automated drilling machines, and complex logistical programs can all be run from a distance with minimal human intervention on the ground and no risk of injury or death.

They've got our backs ___

In the United States, tens of thousands of manufacturing workers are injured every year. They often perform the same physical tasks over and over, which causes strain to back, neck, and knee muscles and can lead to permanent disabilities. Millions of days of work are lost every year because of injuries. But robots – or more precisely, robotics – are helping reduce these figures.

Exosuits, or robotic vests, are being adopted for jobs that include heavy, repetitive work. In car manufacturing plants, for example, exosuits gently support the necks, backs, and shoulders of workers as they reach up into the engines of cars on the production line overhead. Watching the suit in action is truly amazing. It moves with the wearer and takes all the weight and strain of the manual work. Exosuits allow people to work more comfortably, which means they take fewer breaks and make fewer mistakes. One company estimates that the suits have increased productivity by 85%.

A helping hand ___

The service industry is introducing robots to provide, ironically, more personalized service. In some hotels in Japan, a robot helps out at reception. It greets guests and can translate requests in a number of different languages. It guides guests to their room and delivers messages, leaving human clerks free to deal with more complex transactions.

In the next 10 to 20 years, automation in dangerous jobs will have become the norm. Exosuits will have become common on the factory floor, no one will be left waiting at a hotel reception desk, and manufacturing workers will never again complain of a bad back!

B **READ FOR DETAIL** **Read the article again. What are the three main ways that robots are used? What kind of technology does each one require?**

C **READ FOR ATTITUDE** **The editor of this article wants a new title that introduces the main topic, draws in readers, and also indicates the writer's attitude (skeptical, optimistic, neutral). Share your ideas with the class. Choose the best title.**

D **GROUP WORK** **THINK CRITICALLY** **Can you think what the disadvantages might be for each use? How do you think the article might present the topic differently if it were written by a member of a labor union?**

INSIDER ENGLISH

I've got your back. **= I'm ready and willing to help or defend you.**

2 WRITING

A **Read the essay. Which statement is it responding to? How do you know?**

Robots are stealing our jobs. Robots will make workplaces safer. Robots will eventually do creative work.

Automation is inevitably going to be a feature of most workplaces. Machines are increasingly taking over dangerous jobs in industries **such as** mining and logging. They're already making jobs easier in industries that require a lot of manual labor, **namely** manufacturing and farming. They are also starting to appear in the service industry, helping employees deal with customers in, **for instance**, hotels and airports.

Right now, automation feels good, helpful. But machines are moving from assisting humans to replacing them. **Take, for example**, jobs that consist of repetitive, heavy tasks – loading trucks, stocking shelves in stores, waiting tables in restaurants, **just to name a few**. What will human workers do when machines take over all those jobs?

Optimists say that new jobs will replace these old jobs, that machines will never be as creative and innovative as people, and that the human touch cannot be replaced. I'm not convinced. I see the growth of automation as a direct threat to employment. We should prepare ourselves to face a world without work.

B **EXEMPLIFY ARGUMENTS Look at how the bold expressions in the essay are used to refer to examples. Then write sentences using the prompts below. Use a different expression each time.**

1 robots / dangerous tasks / working underground

Robots will be able to take over dangerous tasks such as working underground.

2 exosuits / different settings / car manufacturing and hardware stores

3 robots / tasks / offering simultaneous translation and greeting guests

4 job loss / in key industries / construction and transportation

REGISTER CHECK

In informal writing and speaking, *like* can also introduce examples.

I use my virtual assistant for stuff ***like*** *reminders, shopping lists, looking something up online, playing music.*

WRITE IT

C **PLAN Read the statement below. Do you agree or disagree with it? What examples can you think of to support your opinion? What counterarguments can you imagine? Take notes.**

Artificial intelligence is going to take over our homes.

D **PAIR WORK Look again at the essay in exercise 2A and match each paragraph with its function.**

Paragraph 1: ____ a Present argument(s)

Paragraph 2: ____ b State a personal opinion

Paragraph 3: ____ c Describe the current situation

Organize the ideas from your notes in the same way. Then work together to write a three-paragraph essay in about 200 words.

E **GROUP WORK In small groups, read each other's essays. What are some of the most interesting examples people used? Which examples do you think are the most effective in supporting their argument? Why?**

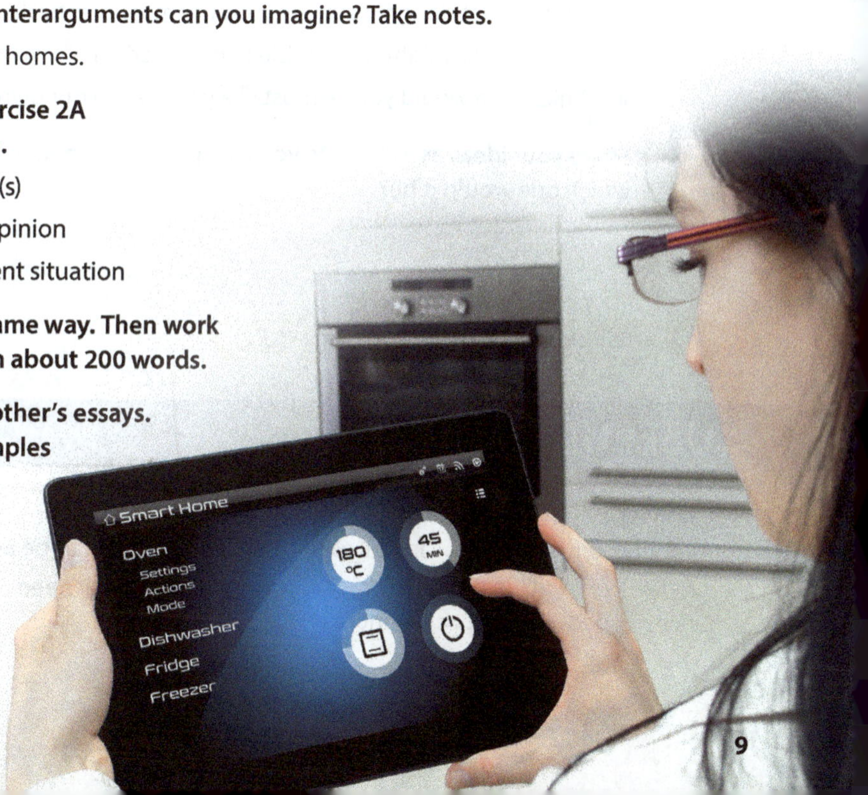

1.5 TIME TO SPEAK
Professor Robot?

LESSON OBJECTIVE

- present a proposal for a robot helper

A **DISCUSS** **With one or two partners, look at the pictures. What is happening in each one? How might a robot helper improve the situation? Could a robot replace the human in any of them?**

B **PREPARE** **Choose one of the scenarios in the pictures (or a similar situation that you know about). Work together to create a proposal for a robot helper. Follow the steps below.**

Step 1 Identify the main problem(s). Outline the tasks your robot will perform to address them and the technology required.

Step 2 Consider the social and psychological effects of a robot helper. What external appearance should the robot have to blend in with the environment?

Step 3 Prepare your proposal. Decide which features to emphasize, the order in which to present them, and who talks about what.

C **PRESENT** **Share your proposal with the class. As you listen to the others, take notes and write at least one question to ask about each proposal.**

D **AGREE** **Discuss the proposals you have heard with students from other groups. Answer the questions.**

- Which robot design do you think is the most practical?
- Which one(s) might be possible to make today?
- Which idea would you be most likely to invest your own money in? Why?

E **Share your ideas as a class. Do you all agree? If you had to choose one of the robot helpers to invest in as a class, which one would it be?**

To check your progress, go to page 153.

USEFUL PHRASES

DISCUSS

A robot could certainly … as well as a person, but maybe not …

Once … , people won't … anymore.

PREPARE

It's going to need to be able to …

In order to … , it'll need …

PRESENT

We believe people will gradually …

With better AI, our robot could feasibly …

UNIT OBJECTIVES

- discuss assumptions about behavior
- talk about assumptions related to age
- compare and discuss similar experiences
- write a report based on graphs
- conduct a survey about consumerism and labels

THE LABELS WE LIVE BY

2

START SPEAKING

FIND IT

A **Describe the people in the pictures in your own words. What can you tell about them from their appearance? Which of the labels in the box would you apply to each of them? Why? Look up any terms you don't know.**

baby boomer	blue collar	conventional	hippie	middle class
millennial	nerd	realist	rebel	upper class

B **Why do we label people? Are labels generally harmless or hurtful? What are labels usually based on? Can you think of a situation where labels might serve a positive purpose? For ideas, watch Ryoko's video.**

EXPERT SPEAKER

What do you think of Ryoko's ideas?

2.1 IS THAT REALLY ME?

LESSON OBJECTIVE
- discuss assumptions about behavior

1 LANGUAGE IN CONTEXT

A PAIR WORK **Look at the quiz results. Do you ever do quizzes like these? Do you share your results? Why or why not?**

B **What do people get out of online personality quizzes? Read the magazine article and check your answers.**

Personality for sale

Personality quizzes are all over social media. By now, most people will have taken quite a few of them and probably shared some of their results. Some people will share quiz results every single day! But will we really learn more about ourselves from *What historical figure are you?* than from *What animal would you be?* Probably not. In fact, personality quizzes won't ever provide any real insights because their real purpose is data mining.

It's easy to imagine the original idea: As a user eagerly takes quiz after quiz and shares the hilarious results across social media, quiz software will be quietly building a detailed profile of their style, tastes, likes, and dislikes. Algorithms will suggest other quizzes in order to fill in gaps. Software companies will then sell the profile to marketing companies.

Personality quizzes are the perfect vehicle because they play on our natural desire to be liked. They will nearly always return positive results. You'll be called **sincere** instead of humorless, fun and **chatty** instead of childish. Labels like **narrow-minded**, **aloof**, and **self-centered** don't exist in quiz world. Choose red as your favorite color, and you'll be labeled "the life of the party." You'll also soon see ads for red clothing, red sports equipment, and red cars!

Maybe a better test of personality is whether any of this matters to you. Now that you've read this article, will you continue to enjoy online quizzes (***open-minded***, *playful*), or will you never take another one (*cautious*, *strong-willed*, *independent*)?

Leo Bradshaw
April 27 •

Hmm, I think this just means I'm boring! 😐

Personality Quiz: What kind of pasta are you?

5 14 2

Jessica Cooke
I got whole wheat penne pasta. lol.

2 VOCABULARY: Describing personality

A 1.11 **Look at the bold adjectives in the article and match them to their synonyms below. Listen and check. Which two adjective pairs are opposites?**

1 talkative ____________
2 genuine ____________
3 antisocial ____________
4 rigid ____________
5 insensitive ____________
6 accepting ____________

B **Now go to page 142. Do the vocabulary exercises for 2.1.**

C PAIR WORK THINK CRITICALLY **Think of a fictional villain (from a book, TV show, movie, etc.). What are they like? Imagine the villain took a personality quiz on social media. How might the results put a positive spin on their negative qualities?**

3 GRAMMAR: Uses of *will*

A **Read the sentences in the grammar box. Match them with the uses below.**

Uses of *will*

A Some people **will share** quiz results every single day!
B But **will** we really **learn** more about ourselves from a quiz?
C They **will** nearly always **return** positive results.
D Now that you've read this article, **will** you **continue** to enjoy online quizzes?

Use *will* …

1 to make predictions, assumptions, or deductions about the future. Sentence B
2 to describe typical behavior or things that are true in general. Sentence ___
3 to express decisions about the future made at the point of speaking. Sentence ___
4 to criticize annoying habits or characteristics. Sentence ___

B **Now go to page 130. Look at the grammar chart and do the grammar exercise for 2.1.**

C PAIR WORK **Read the statements. Respond to them using *will* or *won't*. Check your accuracy. Compare your sentences with a partner.**

1 Personality quizzes on social media aren't meant to provide serious psychological analysis, and most people know that.
Most people won't expect a serious psychological analysis from a social media personality quiz.
2 Advertisers want to target their ads to likely customers. Social media behavior is a good source of information about people's interests.
3 Social media users know more about data mining now and are more careful with their personal information. Software developers are continually working to find new ways to mine user data.
4 People like to be judged positively. They are more likely to click things that seem flattering or positive. App developers know this and consider it in their designs.

✓ ACCURACY CHECK

Use the past participle, <u>not</u> *to* + verb, when talking about something you assume has already happened.

He hates to be late, so I'm sure he'll have ~~to leave~~ the office by now. ✗
He hates to be late, so I'm sure he'll have left the office by now. ✓

4 SPEAKING

A PAIR WORK THINK CRITICALLY **Look at the six types of social media users. What do you think the labels mean? What can you assume, deduce, or predict about the people they're applied to?**

Collectors	Creators	Critics	Inactives	Joiners	Spectators

*Critics **will rate** every restaurant or store they go to, and **they'll be** sincere in their evaluations.*

*Spectators **won't comment** themselves, but **they'll be looking** at everything you post!*

2.2 ACT YOUR AGE

LESSON OBJECTIVE
- talk about assumptions related to age

1 LANGUAGE IN CONTEXT

A 1.12 **Look at the picture. Who do you think the people are, and how are they connected? Listen to the first part of a news interview with one of the men and check your answers.**

1.12 Audio script

Host So, Manuel, would you mind telling us that story you told me earlier?

Manuel Sure. One day, I was talking with a mature student after class when a new supervisor came in and asked if I would leave the room so she could speak to my teacher.

Host What did you say?

Manuel Well, I just told her that, actually, I was the teacher here. She was really shocked. I mean, the student was older than me, so it's natural that she would think he was the teacher, but I could tell that she was **looking down on** me, you know?

Host Does that happen a lot?

Manuel It used to. I started teaching when I was 22. So in the early days, I would **run up against** attitudes like that a lot. There's this impression that millennials are irresponsible, so my colleagues thought a millennial wouldn't make a good teacher, that I just wouldn't **fit in with** the team. That's just ageism. I wouldn't accept it. I had to **stand up for** myself. I'd just tell them, hey, I was *recruited* for this job because I'm really good. Qualifications don't just **come down to** age.

Host But surely your coworkers know that.

Manuel You'd think so. Fortunately, that's all in the past. Now, things are fine.

2 VOCABULARY: Using three-word phrasal verbs

A 1.12 **Listen to the first part of the interview again and read along. Write the bold phrasal verbs next to their definitions below.**

1 feel that you belong ______
2 defend ______
3 experience difficulties ______
4 think you are better than someone ______
5 be the most important part of ______

B 1.13 **Read the definitions below. Then listen to the second part of the interview and complete the three-word phrasal verbs that match the definitions.**

1 deal with face *up to*
2 tolerate put ______
3 make fun of mess ______
4 communicate successfully get ______
5 use something easy or familiar fall ______

C 1.14 **Listen and check your answers to exercises 2A and 2B.**

D **Now go to page 142. Do the vocabulary exercises for 2.2.**

E PAIR WORK THINK CRITICALLY **Think about the interview. What advice does Manuel give to other people who have to fight against a negative label? What example does he give? What qualities do different people associate with millennials? Is that fair? Why or why not?**

3 GRAMMAR: Uses of *would*

A **Read the sentences in the grammar box. Match them with the rules below.**

Uses of *would*

A **Would** you mind telling us that story you told me earlier?

B I **wouldn't** accept it. I had to stand up for myself.

C You'**d** think so.

D She asked if I **would** leave the room.

E In the early days, I **would** run up against attitudes like that a lot.

Use *would* …

1 to refer to past habits or typical, expected behavior. Sentence ___

2 to make a polite request. Sentence ___

3 to express an opinion in a polite way. Sentence ___

4 to report a statement or a question with *will*. Sentence ___

5 to talk about what someone is willing or unwilling to do. Sentence ___

B PAIR WORK **What other ways can you express the ideas in the sentences with *would* from the interview? Restate them without using *would*.**

What's another way to say, "Would you mind telling us that story again?"

"Please tell us that story again." Does that work?

C **Now go to page 130. Look at the grammar chart and do the grammar exercise for 2.2.**

D PAIR WORK **Rewrite the prompts to create questions using *would*. Ask a partner your questions. Answer the questions your partner asks you.**

1 what / do / weekends / childhood ?

2 feel comfortable / tell / something / personal ?

3 what / expectation / strangers / have / you ?

4 what / do / if / stranger / insult / you ?

4 SPEAKING

A GROUP WORK THINK CRITICALLY **Look at the actions in the box. At what age do you think a person is too old or too young to do them? For ideas, watch Ryoko's video.**

take/post a selfie	own a pet	drive
go to music festivals	get a tattoo	vote
start a business	wear jewelry	
ride a skateboard to and from work		

EXPERT SPEAKER

What do you think Ryoko would say about the other actions?

B **Think about your scenarios from exercise 4A. What attitudes might a young or old person run up against? How would you advise them to respond?**

I would tell them to stand up for themselves!

2.3 SAME HERE!

LESSON OBJECTIVE
- compare and discuss similar experiences

1 LISTENING

A PAIR WORK **Look at the picture. What do you think is happening? Who isn't participating? Why not?**

B 1.15 **Listen to a conversation between Adam and Bella. Check (✓) the things they feel the same about.**

☐ **a** Kids aren't affected much by labels.
☐ **b** Learning a language can change the way you see yourself.
☐ **c** People treat you differently when you can speak their language.

C 1.15 LISTEN FOR AGREEMENT **Look at the expressions from the conversation. Write *E* for those that refer to exactly the same experiences and *D* for different experiences that produce the same feelings. Then listen again to check your answers.**

1 I can relate to that. D
2 I know exactly what you mean! ___
3 That reminds me of the time when … ___
4 That's just like the time … ___
5 I know how you feel. ___
6 What a coincidence! ___

D PAIR WORK THINK CRITICALLY **Does learning a foreign language change the way others see you? How might it have an impact on the way you see yourself? What experiences have you had to support your opinion?**

2 PRONUNCIATION: Listening for the intonation on interactional phrases

A 1.16 **Listen. Does the intonation of the underlined phrases rise or fall?**

1 You know, it's weird how you gain more confidence when you start speaking another language.
2 If they label you an introvert, that's how you behave, right?

B 1.17 **Listen. Underline the phrases you hear that have rising intonation.**

1 I was always the quiet kid at school, you know, the one who never had much to say.
2 It's amazing! I'm a more confident person, you know?
3 The best thing is that people respect you more when you can speak their language, don't you think?

C **Circle the correct word to complete the sentence.**

Interactional phrases, which have little real meaning but keep the listener interested and involved, usually have a *rising / falling* intonation.

3 SPEAKING SKILLS

A 1.18 **Complete the expressions that Adam and Bella used in their conversation. Listen and check.**

Discussing similar experiences	
1 I hear ________ .	6 That's ________ like the time (when) …
2 I can ________ to that.	7 I know how you ________ .
3 I know exactly ________ you mean.	8 ________ here, …
4 Has that been the ________ for you?	9 ________ me about it!
5 That ________ me of the time (when) …	10 What a ________ !

B GROUP WORK **One student reads the statement below. The others say whether they share the experience and add their own statements to keep the conversation going.**

Statement: At school, I was the "teacher's pet." All the other kids hated me.

Tell me about it! My aunt was our teacher, so I was definitely the teacher's pet. It can be hard to shake off a label like that.

I know what you mean. I was always the troublemaker. Even when I was good, teachers saw me as "the bad kid."

4 PRONUNCIATION: Saying stressed syllables beginning with /p/, /k/, /t/

A 1.19 **Listen to the /p/, /k/, and /t/ sounds in the sentences. Are the underlined ones different from the circled ones?**

1 My opinion is that most people in this country speak a bit of English.

2 Kids can find it hard to shake off a label like that.

3 Tell me about it! My aunt was my teacher...

B 1.20 PAIR WORK **Underline the /p/, /k/, and /t/ sounds in stressed syllables. Listen and check. Practice the conversation with a partner.**

A What do you think? Could you teach English to kids?

B Tough question! I like children, and I'm quite patient, but the parents can be too demanding at times.

A Tell me about it! You've got to have a really strong character to put up with some of them.

C PAIR WORK **With your partner, add two lines to the conversation above using as many /p/, /k/, and /t/ sounds in stressed syllables as you can. Join another pair of students and read your conversations.**

5 SPEAKING

A PAIR WORK **Read the statements about language learning and explain whether you can relate.**

I have a hard time with humor when I speak another language. I'm funnier in my own language.

I learn a lot by watching TV shows and reading the subtitles.

B GROUP WORK THINK CRITICALLY **Join another pair of students and share your ideas. Create your own statements about language learning based on your discussion.**

C **Share your statements with the class. Is there an experience that you all have in common?**

2.4 READ THE LABEL

LESSON OBJECTIVE
- write a report based on graphs

1 READING

A **PREDICT CONTENT** **Look at the product labels in the article. What do they have in common? Read the headline of the article. What do you think the article will be about? Read it to check your answer.**

IT'S NOT NATURAL

You're in your local grocery store to buy a can of soup. You're looking for a healthy option, so you dutifully read the product labels. But now the choice gets even more confusing. One says that the ingredients are "locally sourced," another says "organic," and another claims it is "100% natural." All that sounds great, but are "free-range" eggs really better for you? Is "grass-fed beef" also "hormone-free"? What is an "artificial color" anyway? In other words, which labels actually represent real nutritional value, and which are just the latest food fad?

In general, the vaguer the term, the more difficult it is to prove. For example, the United States Department of Agriculture (USDA) was recently forced to develop a definition and guidelines regarding the label "organic." To use "organic" on the packaging, a product must have 70% organic ingredients. And to be "100% organic," products should have no added chemicals, synthetics, pesticides, or genetically engineered substances.

The label "natural," however, is a lot trickier, as there is no legal definition, meaning that even obviously unhealthy foods can be marketed as "natural" and nobody can say it isn't true. This has led to many lawsuits, which focus not only on food, but on other products that also carry the "natural" label.

What makes the "natural" label particularly complicated is that it is associated in our minds with the idea of "healthy." It brings to mind simple, unprocessed foods cooked at home and put on the family dinner table by mom. Consumers will pay a lot for that fantasy, so companies want "natural" on their product labels – and they would rather *not* have it legally defined.

The "natural" debate has been with us for a long time, but the latest food fad seems to be "free-from" products. The strange thing is that you now see these labels on products that would never contain the target substance in the first place. You can even buy "sugar-free" water!

Customers are choosing "free-from" products because they assume the product is healthier for them, but actually, the opposite might be true. For example, research shows that following a gluten-free diet when you have no medical need for it can lead to weight gain. Why? Because gluten-free substitutes are often higher in fat and lower in protein. Also, if a food is perceived as healthy, people are likely to eat more of it!

The irony is that in the past we measured the healthfulness of food by the nutrients it contained. Now we measure by what a product claims *not* to have. If all the labels on the supermarket shelves make you dizzy, the best advice is not to go for "fat-free," but "fad-free." You can never go wrong with fresh fruits and vegetables from your local farmers market.

INSIDER ENGLISH

makes me dizzy **= is too much to think about clearly**

B **PAIR WORK** **READ FOR MAIN IDEAS** **Answer the questions.**

1 What is the difference between the labels "organic" and "natural"?
2 What assumption do people make about "free-from" products?
3 What is the writer's general advice about choosing products?

C **PAIR WORK** **IDENTIFYING PURPOSE** **What do you think is the writer's main intention in this article? Who do you think is the target audience? Why?**

D **GROUP WORK** **THINK CRITICALLY** **How often do you read product labels on food packaging or health and beauty products? Do you think the labels are misleading and dangerous or helpful and informative? Why? What advice would you give consumers about understanding labels?**

2 WRITING

A **Look at the graphs. Match each graph to the information it displays. Read the report and check your answers.**

1 most popular "free-from" products

2 popularity of "free-from" products in the U.K.

3 reasons why people buy "free-from" products

4 reasons why people don't buy "free-from" products

THE "FREE-FROM" PHENOMENON

In the U.K., "free-from" products now represent the fastest-growing food and drink category and are currently worth £122.9 million.

As can be seen from graph A, 27% of U.K. residents regularly shop in the "free-from" aisle. This figure increased by 8% in one year. This would indicate that there is a strong consumer trend towards buying foods that are perceived as healthy.

Graph B presents the reasons for this trend. It indicates that most "free-from" consumers (39%) choose these products in order to feel healthier, while only 19% cite an actual allergy or intolerance. This would seem to be a valuable insight for food product marketers.

....

The data in these graphs leads us to conclude that "free-from" products are here to stay on our supermarket shelves, and their popularity will continue to rise.

A 2

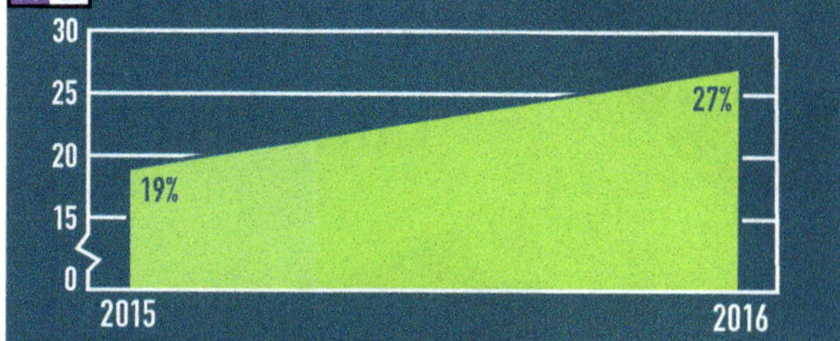

Source: *brandbank.com*

B

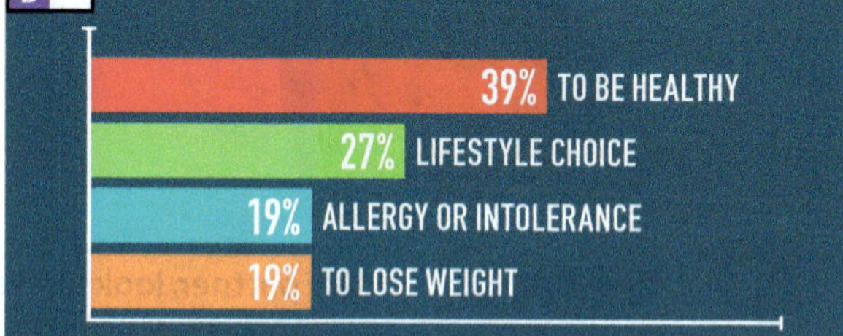

Source: *brandbank.com; mintel.com*

C

Source: *mintel.com*

D

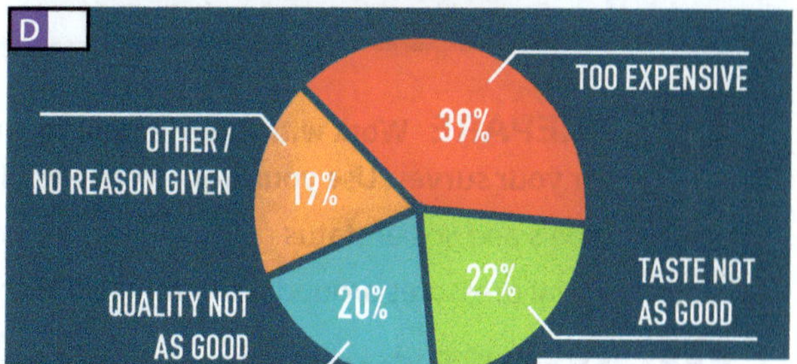

Source: *mintel.com*

B EXPLAIN DATA **Look at the expressions for referring to data. Read the report again and complete them.**

1 As can be *inferred / observed /* ____________ from X, …

2 X *shows / points out / highlights / depicts /* ____________ the reasons for / causes of …

3 X *implies / reveals / suggests /* ____________ that …

4 The data *would suggest / confirms / indicates /* ____________ that …

WRITE IT

C PLAN **You're going to complete the report in exercise 2A by writing the two missing paragraphs. With a partner, analyze the paragraphs on graphs A and B.**

- What information comes first?
- How does each paragraph end?

Discuss how this style can be used to present the information in graph C and graph D.

D **Write the two missing paragraphs on your own.**

E PAIR WORK THINK CRITICALLY **Exchange papers with your partner. Did you both reference all the data from the graphs? Did you draw similar conclusions?**

2.5 TIME TO SPEAK
Labeled out

LESSON OBJECTIVE
- conduct a survey about consumerism and labels

A **RESEARCH** **With a partner, look at the pictures and think about some popular designer labels for each product. What information do shoppers usually assume based on the label (quality, stylishness, fit, etc.)? Are labels an important factor in your own shopping decisions? What else influences you?**

B **Look at the responses on a shopping blog. What questions do you think were asked? Which answer do you most relate to? Why?**

I shop for brand-name clothes online or at outlet stores. It's much cheaper than buying the same thing at the mall. 2 12

I wouldn't buy something just because of the label. I only care about how it looks on me. 1 11 3

If you buy a recognized label, you know that the product is well made and in style. It's worth paying extra for that. 9 48

The people in my office all dress very nicely. If I wore an off-brand suit, they wouldn't say anything, but they would be thinking that I don't look professional enough. 5 20 9

C **PREPARE** **Work with another pair to write ten survey questions on brands and labels. Decide on five to use for your survey. Use your work from exercise B for ideas and consider the topics below.**

labels and social status
personal attitudes on famous labels
social pressures around fashion
the importance of advertising

D **DISCUSS** **Conduct your survey individually. Each person in your group should survey at least three people, for a total of at least 12 responses per question. Then collate your data and highlight the most interesting results. Responses won't be uniform, so draw conclusions and note patterns.**

E **PRESENT** **Form new groups of four. Take turns presenting the results from your surveys. Discuss the most interesting results from the four different surveys and create a statement that summarizes each of them.**

F **Share your statements with the class. Discuss them and agree on a few conclusions that can be drawn from the surveys.**

To check your progress, go to page 153.

USEFUL PHRASES

DISCUSS
Of the people I surveyed, 75% said …
Only one in four respondents agreed that …
The majority of our responses seem to point to …

PRESENT
In general, the survey data indicates …
However, it would appear that …
It would be fair to conclude that labels …

3 IN HINDSIGHT

UNIT OBJECTIVES

- discuss past actions and their present results
- react to past situations
- describe a negative experience; offer sympathy and reassurance
- write a short story based on a set of facts
- discuss and present an alternate history

START SPEAKING

FIND IT

A **People often say "Hindsight is 20/20." What does this mean? Use a dictionary or your phone to help you. Do you agree with the expression? Why or why not?**

B **Now look at the picture. What is happening? Why do you think the man chose to do this? In hindsight, do you think he would make the same choice again? Why or why not?**

C **Think of a time when you did something that didn't end well. What were the consequences? Do you regret it? For ideas, watch Andrea's video.**

EXPERT SPEAKER

Would you say hindsight has helped Andrea learn from this experience?

3.1 I TOLD YOU SO!

LESSON OBJECTIVE
- discuss past actions and their present results

1 LANGUAGE IN CONTEXT

A PAIR WORK **Look at the meme. Do you think it's funny? In what kinds of situations are you likely to hear "I told you so"? When was the last time someone said it to you?**

GLOSSARY
bleach (*n*) a chemical whitener used for laundry

B 1.21 **Listen to part of a podcast about "hindsight bias." What is it? What are the dangers of it?**

1.21 Audio script

"I told you so."

"Well, if you'd mentioned all this road work, I would've gone a different way."

"Well, if you'd been listening, you'd have heard me say that the highway is always better, and we wouldn't be sitting in this traffic jam right now!"

"I told you so" – one of the most annoying phrases in the English language, especially when it isn't true! Did she really **foresee** what was going to happen? No, she just got lucky. This is a classic example of "hindsight bias."

Humans have the ability to **review** and **reconsider** past experiences and **analyze** the decisions we made. This is how we learn from our mistakes. Hindsight bias interferes with this process, making it difficult to accurately **evaluate** past situations. If you're convinced you knew how something would eventually turn out, then you **dismiss** any doubts you might have had beforehand, you **reject** alternative scenarios that might have led to the same outcome, and you **fixate** on a single explanation.

Hindsight bias also makes it easy to **presume** you know what's going to happen in the future. If you're convinced there was only one way to **interpret** a past situation, you're less likely to **envision** creative solutions for new problems. You just go with the first idea that comes to you and **disregard** the advice of others. And soon, *you're* the one hearing "I told you so."

2 VOCABULARY: Thought processes

A 1.22 **Look at the bold verbs in the script. How are they used in context? Match them to the categories. Listen and check.**

1 thinking about the future: ____________, ____________
2 examining something: ____________, ____________, ____________
3 re-examining something: ____________, ____________
4 not accepting something: ____________, ____________, ____________
5 an unproductive way to think: ____________, ____________

B **Now go to page 143. Do the vocabulary exercises for 3.1.**

C PAIR WORK THINK CRITICALLY **Which thought processes would you use to write a summary of a long text? To choose a vacation destination? To examine a friend's unusually bad behavior?**

First, you need to **analyze** the text for main ideas and then **evaluate** which points support them.

3 GRAMMAR: Variations on past unreal conditionals

A Read the sentences in the grammar box. Complete the rules.

Variations on past unreal conditionals

Well, if you**'d mentioned** all this road work, I **would've gone** a different way.
Well, if you**'d been listening**, you**'d have heard** me, …
… and we **wouldn't be sitting** in this traffic jam right now.

1 To refer to an unreal action in the past, use *if* + ____________ + past participle. To describe an unreal action in progress in the past, use *if* + ____________ + *been* + verb + *-ing*.
2 To describe the imagined reaction in the past, use ____________ + *have* + past participle.
3 To describe the imagined reaction in the present, use ____________ + verb OR + *be* + verb + *-ing*.
4 In these sentences, *'d* could be a contraction of *would* or ____________ .

B Now go to page 131. Look at the grammar chart and do the grammar exercise for 3.1.

C 1.23 PAIR WORK **Listen to the story of someone who suffered as a result of hindsight bias. How could he have acted differently to change the outcome? Write three sentences using *if* to talk about possible alternative scenarios.**

4 SPEAKING

A GROUP WORK **What do you think is happening in each situation? Choose one of them and imagine the back story (the events that led up to it). Write three or four sentences to tell the story. Then give your paper to another group.**

A

B

B **Read the story from the other group. Discuss how things could have turned out differently. Write five sentences with *if*. Share them with the class. How many different scenarios did your group come up with?**

If the woman **hadn't left** her purse in her car, …

C THINK CRITICALLY **Why is it important to consider multiple possible back stories? What are some different ways that doing so can be helpful?**

3.2 GO WITH THE FLOW

LESSON OBJECTIVE
- react to past situations

1 LANGUAGE IN CONTEXT

A PAIR WORK **Would you describe yourself as a relaxed or a nervous person? How would your closest friends describe you? Do the quiz. Do your answers support your self-description?**

MELLOW OR MELODRAMATIC?

How good are you at handling awkward situations? When you've done something foolish, do you stay **composed** or do you get **flustered**? When someone offends you, are you **gracious** and **forgiving**, or are you **spiteful** and determined to get even? Take the quiz to find out your true temperament.

QUESTION 1: You arrive home and realize you left your house keys at work. What do you do?

- **A** You get **hysterical** and start to cry. You should have checked that you had your keys before you left! This is a complete disaster!
- **B** Ugh! You should have given an extra key to a neighbor. You call friends until one of them invites you to stay at their place.
- **C** You're **resourceful**; you can solve this problem. Ah-ha! You call a coworker who is working late and lives nearby. She drops off your keys an hour later. You feel **victorious**!

QUESTION 2: Over lunch, you tell some friends an embarrassing story about your new boss. As you're leaving, you see her sitting at the table right behind you.

- **A** You just want to crawl under a rock. You knew she could have been having lunch then, too! Why didn't you look around first?
- **B** You smile and say hello. It was just a **harmless** little story. She might not have been offended by it. She may have even liked that you were talking about her.
- **C** You walk away as if nothing happened. There's no reason to feel **defensive** or guilty. She may not have heard you.

B **Compare your answers as a class. Would you say that you generally go with the flow or blow things out of proportion? What are some other possible reactions to the situations in the quiz? For ideas, watch Andrea's video.**

EXPERT SPEAKER

How are Andrea's answers different from the options in the quiz?

2 VOCABULARY: Describing emotional reactions

FIND IT

A 1.24 PAIR WORK **Look at the bold words in the quiz. Write them in the correct category in the chart below. Look up any words that you're not sure about. Then listen and check.**

Positive reaction	Negative reaction	Context dependent
mellow	melodramatic	

B **Now go to page 143. Do the vocabulary exercises for 3.2.**

C PAIR WORK **Read the situations in the box. Choose one and prepare a short conversation to act out for another pair. Can they guess what emotional reactions you're expressing?**

an accident that is your fault	an argument with your parent(s)
a surprise party for you	winning a prize

3 GRAMMAR: Commenting on the past

A **Read the sentences in the grammar box. Complete the rules with words from the sentences.**

Commenting on the past

You **should have checked** that you had your keys before you left.
You **should have given** an extra key to a neighbor.
You knew she **could have been having** lunch then, too.
She **might not have been offended** by it.
She **may not have heard** you.

1 You can use ___________, ___________, and ___________ to discuss possible alternative scenarios in the past.
2 You can use ___________ and ___________ *not* to criticize a past action or lack of action.
3 To describe actions in progress, use *could/may/might/should* + ___________ + ___________ + verb + *-ing*.
4 You can also use the passive voice: *could/may/might/should* + ___________ + ___________ + past participle.

B **Now go to page 131. Look at the grammar chart and do the grammar exercise for 3.2.**

ACCURACY CHECK

Remember to use the past participle after *have* when talking about the past.
You should have ~~tell~~ her. ✗
You should have told her. ✓

C **Read question 3 from the quiz on page 24. Write three answer choices using *could have, may have, might have,* or *should have.* Check your accuracy. Share your answer choices with the class. Who came up with the best ones?**

QUESTION 3: You are about to go into an important meeting where several people are waiting for you. Your office phone rings, and you answer it without thinking. It's your mother. She doesn't sound upset, but she says she wants to talk to you about something important.

4 SPEAKING

A PAIR WORK **Think of another situation with different possible reactions and create QUESTION 4 for the quiz along with three answer choices.**

How about, you're walking your dog and it scares a little boy and makes him cry?

That's a good one. The mellow answer could be "You're not flustered by it. The little boy **could have been crying** about something else."

B GROUP WORK **Share your quiz question with two other pairs of students. Do they like your answer choices? What other reactions might they have had?**

3.3 A COMPLETE DISASTER!

LESSON OBJECTIVE
- describe a negative experience; offer sympathy and reassurance

1 LISTENING

A PAIR WORK **Look at the picture at the bottom of the page. What has just happened? How do you think the person feels? What problems do you think this might cause?**

B 1.25 LISTEN FOR ATTITUDE **Listen to two conversations in which Ruben tells two different coworkers a story. Answer the questions.**

1 What exactly happened with the coffee?
2 What else went wrong?
3 How does Ruben feel about the situation?
4 Do you think he might be exaggerating?

C 1.25 THINK CRITICALLY **Listen again. In what ways are the two versions of the story different? Why do you think that is? Who is more supportive, Claire or Amelia?**

D PAIR WORK **Have you ever found yourself in a similar situation? Were your friends supportive? What did they say?**

2 PRONUNCIATION: Listening for weak forms in complex verb phrases

You can use *literally* to exaggerate a description.
***I literally** froze!*

A 1.26 **Listen and underline the complex verb phrases.**

1 Don't you think you could be overreacting?
2 I must have brought the wrong one.
3 I'd emailed it to myself.

B 1.27 PAIR WORK **Unscramble the sentences. Circle any words in the complex verb phrases that should be stressed. Listen and check.**

1 day / been / it / had / a / terrible ______
2 could / been / worse / have / things ______
3 me / had / wish / listened / I / you / to ______
4 have / hurt / could / someone / been ______
5 sense / made / that / more / would / have ______

C **Circle the correct words to complete the sentences.**

In a complex verb phrase, auxiliaries are usually [1]*stressed / unstressed*. Modals can be stressed or unstressed, but if they are not being used for deduction, they are usually [2]*stressed / unstressed*.

3 SPEAKING SKILLS

A **Read the expressions in the chart from the conversations in exercise 1B. Match each heading from the box to the correct column and write them in.**

Describing a bad experience   Offering sympathy and reassurance

______________	______________
It can't have been that bad. I'm sure it just felt that way. I'll bet no one even noticed. We've all been there. Everybody (goes blank) now and then. I think you're blowing it out of proportion. Things are never as bad as you think they are. You'll see – everything'll be just fine.	It was a total/unmitigated disaster! I wish I'd just stayed in bed today. I just couldn't believe this was happening! It was the worst presentation ever! You haven't heard the worst part yet. Everything that could possibly go wrong did go wrong.

B PAIR WORK **Imagine that Claire and Amelia just told you about Ruben's "disaster." You go and talk to him and reassure him. Act out the conversation two times, taking turns as Ruben.**

4 PRONUNCIATION: Using intonation to show emphasis

A 1.28 **Listen to the sentences and notice intonation. Does it fall or rise at the end?**

1 I just couldn't believe this was happening!

2 It was the worst presentation ever!

B 1.29 PAIR WORK **Listen. Which reading has more emphasis? Check (✓) A or B. Practice the ones you checked with a partner.**

1 It was such a mess! ☐ A ☐ B

2 Nice try! ☐ A ☐ B

3 I can't believe it! ☐ A ☐ B

4 I wish I'd never bought it! ☐ A ☐ B

5 We got there two hours late! ☐ A ☐ B

6 It was broken, I'm telling you, totally broken! ☐ A ☐ B

C PAIR WORK **Take turns giving details of what went wrong in the situations below. Be creative and use intonation to show emphasis.**

- You forgot your best friend's birthday.
- You borrowed your roommate's sweater and got ink on it.
- You stayed in a terrible hotel.

5 SPEAKING

A PAIR WORK **Read the situations. Choose one to act out. Take turns explaining what happened (add as many details as you want) and reassuring your partner. Then act out the other one.**

- You just damaged your father's car. (Think about how and where it happened and the extent of the damage.)
- You just forwarded a personal email to the whole office by mistake. (Think about what was in the email.)

B GROUP WORK THINK CRITICALLY **Tell the class about the situations and your partner's response. Whose situation was the most awful? Who gave the best advice? In a situation like this, what's more important, sympathy or honesty? Why do you think so?**

3.4 TOO GOOD TO BE TRUE

LESSON OBJECTIVE

- write a short story based on a set of facts

1 READING

A **PREDICT CONTENT** **Read the headlines of the two "clickbait" news stories. What do you think happened in each one? Read the stories to check your ideas.**

MAN SAVES BABY – AGAIN!

One day in the 1930s, in Detroit, Michigan, Joseph Figlock was walking down the street when a baby fell from a window in the building he was passing. He caught the baby and saved his life. One year later, on the exact same street, the exact same baby again fell out of the exact same window. And yes, you guessed it – our hero, Joseph Figlock, just happened to be there! Figlock again caught the baby and saved his life for a second time.

TWO GIRLS, ONE BALLOON, DOUBLE LIVES!

Ten-year-old Laura Buxton released a balloon with her name and address on it. More than 220 kilometers away, another 10-year-old girl found the balloon in her backyard. Her name was Laura Buxton, too! When the girls met, they realized they didn't just share a name. They looked exactly alike – tall and thin with long brown hair – and were even dressed the same in blue jeans and pink sweaters. They even had the same pets: a gray rabbit, a black Labrador, and a guinea pig!

B **EVALUATE CONTENT** **Do you believe the stories are true? Why or why not? Read the report on the two stories from a fact-checking site. Did the stories happen exactly as they were reported?**

FACT CHECKER What's new | Top 50 | Videos | Archive

November 8

We've had a lot of requests today to investigate two clickbait stories that just seem too good to be true. In both cases, the reports may not have been 100% faithful to the facts, but there's enough truth in them to make them incredible coincidences!

Man saves baby – again!

The story claims that the same man saved the life of the same baby twice in the same place. Let's look at the facts:

- Joseph Figlock was a street cleaner, so he was not on that street by chance. He worked there regularly.
- The baby did fall from a window, but it was not caught by the street cleaner. It landed on Figlock and then fell to the ground. It was injured but not killed.
- A little over a year later (not exactly one year), Figlock was cleaning another street when a different baby fell from a different window. Again, both were injured, but they survived.

So, in hindsight, not quite the incredible coincidence that was reported, but if Mr. Figlock hadn't been working on those two days on those two streets, those two babies probably would have died!

Two girls, one balloon, double lives

The second story is about one girl who released a balloon and found her "twin." But let's take a closer look:

- "Laura" was a very common name for girls of that age. And "Buxton" is a fairly common family name where the girls lived.
- The balloon was found by a farmer who knew the second Laura's family, and he gave it to the second Laura.
- The second Laura was nine, almost ten, and it's not unusual for girls of the same age to have similar hairstyles and clothes.
- Black Labradors were one of the most common family dogs in the area, and lots of children have pet rabbits and guinea pigs.

Of course, these stories carefully leave out the non-coincidental details. For example, the two Lauras didn't have the same favorite color or the same number of brothers and sisters. But it's true that if the farmer hadn't found the balloon in the field and recognized Laura's name, the two girls wouldn't be friends today.

C **THINK CRITICALLY** **Do you think it's important to fact-check stories like these? Why or why not? In what other situations do you think it is or isn't important to fact-check details and sources? How can you do that?**

2 WRITING

A **Read the story about another strange coincidence. Compare it with the notes on the right. Which pieces of information from the notes did the writer leave out of the story? Why?**

New World Science Technology Entertainment

One Christmas, twin sisters Lorraine and Levinia, who lived about ten minutes apart by car, **each** suddenly decided, on the spur of the moment, to deliver the other her Christmas present. It was cold and snowy, and the country roads between their **two** houses were dangerously icy. **Neither** of the sisters had snow chains on their tires, and **both** ended up sliding on the ice and crashing head-on into another car. And guess who was in the other car? Yes, that's right. They crashed into each other! They were **both** taken to the hospital, where they were **both** found to have broken their left leg. And of course, they ended up spending Christmas **together** in the **same** hospital!

- Twin sisters, Christmas
- Heading to each other's house to deliver presents
- One in large SUV, other in small sports car
- One coming from work, the other from shopping
- One on her own, other with her kids
- Snow/ice; both no chains on tires
- Crash happened about 8 p.m.
- One broke left arm and leg, other just left leg
- One stayed overnight, other had surgery, stayed two weeks

B CREATE COHESION **Look at the bold words and phrases in the story in exercise 2A. Notice how they are used to highlight the coincidences. Use them to complete the story below.**

1 ________ nine-year-old twin brothers, Mitch and Toby, were playing 2 ________ in their backyard. They were racing each other down the slide. Suddenly, they 3 ________ fell, Mitch from the top of the slide and Toby at the base. The 4 ________ of them were taken to the hospital. They were 5 ________ very brave, and 6 ________ of them cried. However, the doctors found that 7 ________ of them had broken their left arm in exactly the 8 ________ place. The brothers went home with their arms in casts, and 9 ________ of them was allowed to play on the slide again until they'd 10 ________ gotten better!

WRITE IT

C PAIR WORK **Student A: Go to page 157. Student B: Go to page 159. Read about a strange coincidence.**

D PLAN **You're going to write a short story of about 100 words based on the set of facts you read in exercise 2C. Look again at the stories in exercises 2A and 2B.**

- How does each story begin?
- In what order are the events of the story presented?
- How are the coincidences emphasized?

Think about how to organize the facts of your story and emphasize the coincidences similarly. Then write your short story.

E PAIR WORK THINK CRITICALLY **Read each other's stories. Which story is more believable? Why? What improvements can you suggest for your partner's story?**

3.5

TIME TO SPEAK
The ripple effect

LESSON OBJECTIVE

- discuss and present an alternate history

A **DISCUSS** **With a partner, look at the picture of ripples on water. What do you think "the ripple effect" means when talking about our lives? Think of something that has caused ripples in your life recently. What was it and how did it affect you? What could you have done differently? How would that have changed things?**

B **Think about the ripple effect on a larger scale. Read the "what if" scenarios. Choose one of them and discuss possible ripples that would have or might have resulted. Take notes as you go.**

- What if the internet had never been invented? How would your childhood have been different?
- What if you had lived 100 years ago? How would your life have been different? What choices would you have had? What options wouldn't you have had?
- What if you had been born in a different country (choose one)? What would your childhood have been like there? Would you have made the same choices? *Could* you have made the same choices?

No internet – would have played outside more, probably would have become interested in science, might have chosen to study biology instead of math, …

C **DECIDE** **Join two other pairs to form a group of six. Present your ideas and decide which scenario is the most interesting in terms of the changes it might have caused in life today. Choose one scenario to tell the class about.**

D **PRESENT** **Share your scenario and at least three ripple effects with the class. Listen to the other groups. Ask questions to explore more possible ripple effects.**

E **AGREE** **Discuss the scenarios presented and decide which one would have the greatest ripple effect – on your own lives and on society as a whole.**

To check your progress, go to page 153.

USEFUL PHRASES

DISCUSS

If that were the case, I probably wouldn't have …

My whole world would have been different.

DECIDE

We explored the second scenario, and we figured …

We should present your scenario because …

PRESENT

It would have been a disaster because …

We might have stopped … before it happened.

REVIEW 1 (UNITS 1–3)

1 VOCABULARY

A **Complete the paragraph using the correct form of the words in parentheses ( ).**

Most recent developments in technology have [1] unquestionably (question) come about thanks to artificial [2] ____________ (intelligent). Advances in facial [3] ____________ (recognize) mean computers can lip read more efficiently than humans. They are also getting [4] ____________ (progress) better at reading human emotions. They can already detect anger, sadness, and joy. Voice-[5] ____________ (active) is proving helpful in many ways, from being able to ask your phone for directions to ordering groceries through your virtual [6] ____________ (assist). And our computers are getting more [7] ____________ (talk), too! They don't only answer your questions; they also initiate conversations. It seems they're not the cold, [8] ____________ (sensitive) machines of yesterday. Who knows – your computer could [9] ____________ (potential) become your new best friend!

B **What new AI developments would you like to see? Complete the thoughts with at least one of the words in parentheses ( ) and your own ideas.**

1 In the future, robots … (undoubtedly / ultimately)

____

2 Computer-generated speech has the potential to … (radically / drastically)

____

3 Health care and medicine will/won't benefit … (progressively / increasingly)

____

4 Image recognition could … (feasibly / markedly)

____

5 (Open-minded / Narrow-minded) people might just …

____

6 AI could even help (aloof / antisocial / rigid / self-centered) people …

____

2 GRAMMAR

A **Circle the correct options to complete the article about life in the future.**

Want to know what the future holds? Ask a sci-fi fan! They [1]*will / do* always give you the most imaginative answers. Here are five of their craziest predictions:

- You'll [2]*be checking / have checked* your email on your contact lenses.
- Scientists will [3]*be finding / have found* a way to clone dinosaurs.
- Movies will [4]*be using / have used* only computer-generated images instead of actors – and these fake actors will [5]*be winning / have won* all the awards at the Oscars!
- Doctors will [6]*be using / have used* bathroom mirrors to diagnose medical conditions using high-definition cameras and special operating systems.
- We [7]*probably won't / won't probably* have robot butlers, but AI [8]*will eventually replace / will replace eventually* most of the gadgets we use now.

Which of these predictions do you think [9]*are definitely going to / are going to definitely* come true, and which are only for the movies?

B PAIR WORK **Look at the question at the end of the article in exercise 2A. How would you answer it? Think of three more crazy predictions for the future. Use the topics in the box to help you.**

education	food	houses	pets	sports	transportation	vacations

3 VOCABULARY

A **Complete the survey results with the correct form of the words in the box.**

defensive dismiss flustered harmless look mess presume put

What ruins your day?

We asked readers to share their thoughts. Here's what they said …

1. People who act all superior and ______________ down on you for no reason.
2. When you make a suggestion and your boss just ______________ it without even considering it.
3. When you try to make a ______________ joke but someone gets offended by it. Then you feel ______________ and try to explain, but that just makes it worse.
4. When you're in a quiet place and drop something and everybody turns to look at what made that noise, and they realize it was you, and you get ______________ and drop something else, and all you want to do is crawl under a rock!
5. When people ______________ you don't know what you're talking about just because you're young, but actually you know more than they do!
6. Roommates who ______________ around with my stuff. They should keep their hands to themselves!
7. Noisy neighbors – they're the worst! Why should I have to ______________ up with their loud music all night!

B PAIR WORK **Do you identify with any of the complaints above? Think of more things that can ruin your day and explain them. Use vocabulary from Units 1 to 3 if you can.**

4 GRAMMAR

A **Complete the sentences with *had, could, might, should,* or *would.* Use contractions where possible.**

I knew there was something wrong when my boss started staying late at the office. He [1] __________ normally be the first to leave, and sometimes he [2] __________ not even come in at all. One night, I stayed late, too. I told him I [3] __________ help him finish our paperwork. At eight o'clock, a man showed up and went into my boss's office and closed the door. I know I [4] __________n't have done it, but I pressed my ear to the door and listened to their conversation. They were arguing. I guess it [5] __________ have been about something totally innocent, but it didn't sound like it. Then I heard the man pick up a chair and let out an angry growl! I [6] __________ have knocked, but I rejected that idea and just ran into the room and pushed the man down. You [7] __________ have done the same if it [8] __________ been you! But I soon learned that I [9] __________n't interpreted things correctly. My boss and his friend were rehearsing for a play. If only I [10] __________ minded my own business!

B **What would you have done in the same situation? How do you think the situation could have been avoided? Use modals to write three sentences about alternate scenarios in the past.**

4 CLOSE UP

UNIT OBJECTIVES

- discuss the value of changing perspective
- talk about how eyes function in humans and animals
- discuss problems caused by staring at screens
- write a personal profile statement for a résumé
- create and present an action plan for a project

START SPEAKING

A **How would you describe this picture? Which adjectives from the box would you use? What other words can you think of? Do you like it? Why or why not? Can you guess what it shows? (Answer is at the bottom of the page.)**

elegant	impressive	modern	striking	stunning	unusual	weird

B **When you're too concerned with the details of something, people say, "You can't see the forest for the trees." Do you have a similar expression in your language? Can you think of an example of a time when you couldn't see the forest because there were too many trees? For ideas, watch Audrey's video.**

EXPERT SPEAKER

What kinds of things might Audrey call "trees," and what's her "forest"?

Answer: The inside of a guitar.

4.1 UNDER THE MICROSCOPE

LESSON OBJECTIVE

- discuss the value of changing perspective

1 LANGUAGE IN CONTEXT

TAKING A CLOSER LOOK

Microphotography is the perfect blend of art and science. It shows us everyday objects, most of which we ignore at normal size, in all their magnified beauty.

A ____________

B ____________

C ____________

A 1.30 **Read the introduction to a podcast. What is microphotography? Look at the pictures. What do you think they show? Listen to the podcast and label the pictures. Were you right?**

1.30 Audio script

Have you ever let a handful of sand run through your fingers and wondered what each tiny grain might look like close up? Gary Greenberg did. Greenberg is a medical scientist and microphotographer. He collected sand from all over the world, magnified each sample to 250 times its usual size, and revealed a **miniature**, **multicolored** wonderland. The images show grains of sand, each of which is totally unique, to be **circular**, **spiral**, and **cylindrical** particles with textures from silky smooth to **ridged** and rough.

Microphotographers, many of whom are primarily scientists, remake the tiniest pieces of the world around us in **mammoth** size. Pollen, which we usually only notice when it makes us sneeze, looks like a handful of fruity candy. Household dust becomes an **elaborate** assortment of **stringy** fibers, **flaky** discs of dried skin, and micro-drops of cosmetics.

But it isn't all abstract art from the **filthy** floor. Microphotography has practical applications for many branches of science. In medicine, it allows doctors to study the **delicate** structures of viruses that previously they knew very little about. In marine biology, researchers use the technique to track the growth and spread of microplastics in our oceans. Microphotography offers a fresh outlook on the world we live in, helping us appreciate all that we cannot see.

B 1.30 PAIR WORK THINK CRITICALLY **Listen again. What two practical uses of microphotography are mentioned? What other practical uses can you think of?**

GLOSSARY

fibers (*n, pl*) long pieces that combine to make fabric

particle (*n*) a very small piece of something

2 VOCABULARY: Describing things

FIND IT

A 1.31 **Look at the bold words in the audio script. Can you figure out their meaning from context and the pictures? Write them in the correct category in the chart below. You can use a dictionary or your phone to help you. Listen and check.**

Describing size	Describing shape	Describing qualities
miniature	circular	multicolored

B **Now go to page 144. Do the vocabulary exercises for 4.1.**

C PAIR WORK THINK CRITICALLY Find a small object in the classroom, your pockets, your clothing or jewelry, or your bag. Look at it closely and note its size, shape, and particular qualities. Describe it to your partner. Can they guess what it is, based on your description?

It's **cylindrical** and very thin. It's kind of **delicate** but not very **elaborate**.

Oh, I know! It's your earring.

3 GRAMMAR: Quantifiers and prepositions in relative clauses

A **Read the sentences in the grammar box. Then complete the rules with words from the box.**

Quantifiers and prepositions in relative clauses

It shows us everyday objects, **most of which** we ignore at normal size.

The images show grains of sand, **each of which** is totally unique.

Microphotographers, **many of whom** are scientists, remake the tiniest pieces of the world around us.

Pollen, **which we usually only notice** when it makes us sneeze, looks like a handful of fruit candy.

It allows doctors to study the structures of viruses **that previously they knew very little about**.

after | each | many | things | whom

We can use quantifiers such as *all of*, [1] ________ *of*, [2] ________ *of*, *most of*, *much of*, *none of*, and *some of* with the relative pronouns *which* and [3] ________ at the beginning of a relative clause. Use *which* for [4] ________ and *whom* for people.

Except in very formal written texts, prepositions in relative clauses come [5] ________ the verb.

B **Now go to page 132. Look at the grammar chart and do the grammar exercise for 4.1.**

C PAIR WORK **Read the statements and look at the bold phrases. Correct those that are wrong, and reorder the words in those that are unnecessarily formal. Are any of the sentences true for you? In what way?**

1 I have a lot of good friends, **many of which** I've known since kindergarten.

2 My teachers give us a lot of tests, **most of whom** I pass easily.

3 I subscribe to about 12 different podcasts, **to which I listen** during my commute.

4 I'm working with a new person **about whom I know very little**.

4 SPEAKING

A GROUP WORK **Look at the extreme close-ups. What do you think they show? Why? (Answers are at the bottom of page 42.)**

B **Which picture do you find the most interesting? The most beautiful? The most bizarre? How would you describe each image without saying what it is?**

This one is a microphotograph of different fibers, **some of which** are very **stringy**.

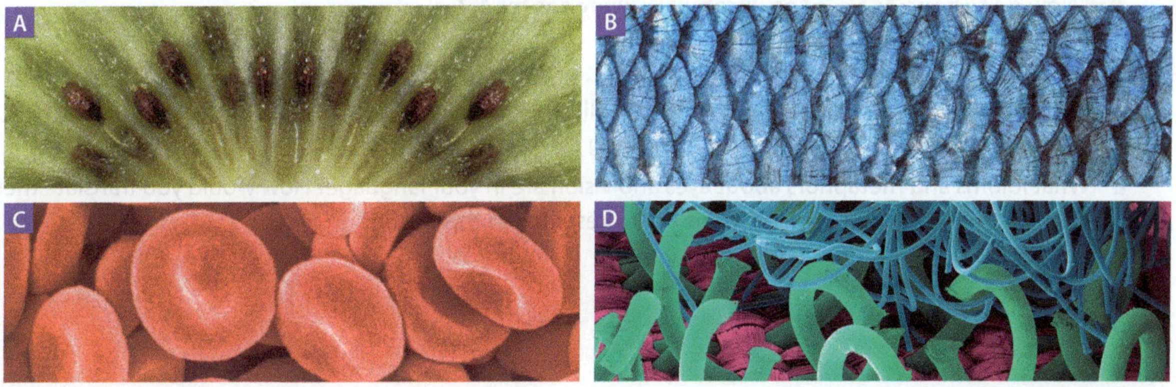

4.2 EYE TO EYE

LESSON OBJECTIVE
- talk about how eyes function in humans and animals

1 LANGUAGE IN CONTEXT

A **Read about the human eye. Check (✓) the information you already knew. Write *!* for information that surprises you and *?* for facts you'd like to learn more about.**

SIX THINGS YOU DIDN'T KNOW ABOUT THE HUMAN EYE

The human eye is an incredible organ, second only to the brain in its complexity. Here are a few amazing facts about what our eyes can do and how they do it.

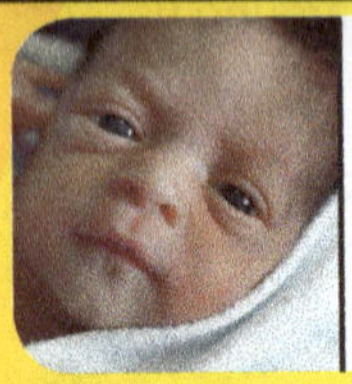

___ 1 Our eyes don't grow. That's why a baby's eyes look so big. Their size is the same as adult eyes, though eyesight won't develop fully until about one year of age.

___ 2 We blink an average of 20 times per minute. That's more than 4 million times a year!

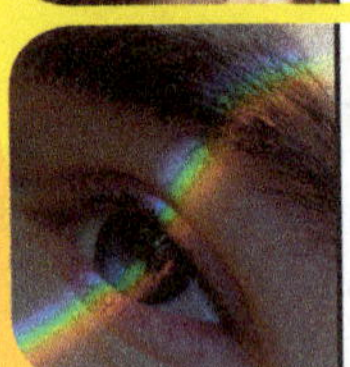

___ 3 Our eyes can process 10 million different colors – but only when there's light! Without light, colors fade, and what we see is a world of grays.

___ 4 We focus and refocus on different objects, details, and distances literally in the blink of an eye. For a camera to equal how well the human eye perceives detail, it would need a resolution of more than 500 megapixels.

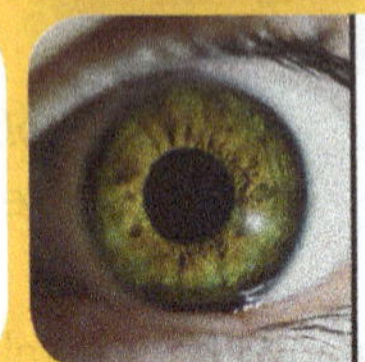

___ 5 Every eye is unique because of the patterns and colors of the iris. Greek physician Hippocrates first noticed this in 390 BCE. Today, security agencies use iris scanning to confirm that we are who we say we are.

___ 6 Blind people who have never had vision dream in colors and images. There's no real way, however, to know if the images in their mind's eye look like things in the real world.

FIND IT

B PAIR WORK **Compare your responses. Did your partner know things that you didn't? Go online to find out more about your "?" items. Share the information with other students.**

2 VOCABULARY: Eye idioms and metaphors

FIND IT

A 1.32 PAIR WORK **Listen to the expressions in the box. Which were used in the article? What do you think each one means? In what situation might you use it? You can use a dictionary or your phone to help you.**

a bird's eye view of	catch your eye	feast your eyes on	in the public eye
in the blink of an eye	in your mind's eye	keep your eyes on the prize	see eye to eye on
turn a blind eye to	without batting an eye	have eyes in the back of your head	

B **Now go to page 144. Do the vocabulary exercises for 4.2.**

C GROUP WORK **Discuss the questions.**

- Share your answers from exercise 2A. Do you all agree on the meaning of the different expressions? What situations did you come up with for using them?
- What idioms and metaphors about eyes and vision are in your language? How would you translate them to English? Are any of them similar to the ones presented in this lesson?

3 GRAMMAR: Noun clauses with question words

A **Read the sentences in the grammar box. Underline the question words in the bold phrases. Then complete the rules below with words from the box.**

Noun clauses with question words

Here are a few amazing facts about **what our eyes can do** and **how they do it**.
Without light, colors fade, and **what we see** is a world of grays.
Today, security agencies use iris scanning to confirm we are **who we say we are**.

how prepositions questions statement subject what who

Question words can be substituted for general nouns. For example, [1] ______________ can be used for *the thing/things*, [2] ______________ for *the person/people*, or [3] ______________ for *the way*.
We can use this type of noun clause as both the [4] ______________ and object of the verb and also with [5] ______________. These clauses use question words, but they are not [6] ______________. The word order is the same as in a [7] ______________.

B **Now go to page 132. Look at the grammar chart and do the grammar exercise for 4.2.**

C **Circle the correct question word for the categories. Add two more categories of your own.**

1 *what / where / how* I can see from the window in my room
2 *which / how / who* I get to work/school every day and *when / which / what* I see on the way
3 *what / which / why* I'm studying English and *what / how / where* I see it affecting my life
4 ______________________________
5 ______________________________

D PAIR WORK **Write example sentences for the categories in exercise 3C and check your accuracy. Then read one of your sentences to a partner. Can your partner guess the category? Read another.**

ACCURACY CHECK

Don't add the auxiliary verbs *do* or *did* in noun clauses with question words.
What ~~do~~ we see is a world of grays. ✗
What we see is a world of grays. ✓

4 SPEAKING

A GROUP WORK **Discuss the questions.**

- Do you think it's important to see eye to eye on everything with your friends? With your family?
- Are you easily distracted or discouraged, or do you always keep your eyes on the prize?
- When you were little, what were your parents strict about, and what did they turn a blind eye to? Did your parents seem to have eyes in the back of their heads? For ideas, watch Audrey's video.

Seeing eye to eye with your family is nice, but it isn't necessary.

EXPERT SPEAKER

In what ways were your parents like Audrey's?

B **Look at the picture to the right. Which animal does this eye belong to? How are the eyes of this animal different from human eyes?**

4.3 LOOK AWAY!

LESSON OBJECTIVE
- discuss problems caused by staring at screens

1 LISTENING

A PAIR WORK **What types of screens do you look at for work or For pleasure? About how many hours a day do you spend a screen? What effect might this be having on your eyes?**

B 1.33 LISTEN FOR MAIN IDEA **Listen to an ophthalmologist (eye doctor) discussing the effect of screens on our eyes. Which statement best summarizes her position?**

a Screen viewing causes serious and lasting damage to our eyes.

b There is no need to cut back on the amount of time we spend looking at screens.

c We can take a number of practical steps to help protect our eyesight.

C 1.33 LISTEN FOR DETAILS **Listen again and pay attention to the structure of the presentation. Use the chart to take notes.**

	How and why this affects eyesight	Proposed solution(s)
Blinking		
Glare and reflections		
Blue light		

D PAIR WORK **Compare your notes. Did you capture all the same information? Was it presented in an organized way? Do you think the ophthalmologist offers good advice? Do you do any of these things? Will you do any of them now?**

INSIDER ENGLISH

Easier said than done. **= It's not as easy as it seems.**

2 PRONUNCIATION: Listening for /t/ between vowels

A 1.34 **Listen to the two sets of phrases. In which set are the underlined /t/ sounds pronounced more like /d/?**

a But the truth of the matter is …
It's a vital function for healthy eyes …

b … there are lots of practical things …
… special yellow-tinted glasses …

B 1.35 PAIR WORK **Underline the /t/ sounds that might sound more like /d/ sounds. Listen and check. Then practice saying the sentences with a partner.**

1 We've invited ophthalmologist Kit Bradley to the studio today …

2 This constant fatigue leads to eyestrain with all its related problems.

3 Blue light is emitted by digital screens.

C **Circle the correct words to complete the sentence.**

The /t/ sound is often pronounced more like /d/ when it comes after [1]*a stressed / an unstressed* vowel and before [2]*a stressed / an unstressed* vowel.

3 SPEAKING SKILLS

A 1.33 PAIR WORK **Complete the sentences from the interview. Listen to the interview again to check your answers. Do any of the bold words have a /t/ sound that is more like a /d/ sound? Underline them.**

Clarifying a problem

1 It's not quite that **straightforward** when you look at it more ______ .

2 That's the **key to** finding a ______ .

3 That has a **major impact** on …

4 **There's** ______ **more to it** than just blinking.

5 The **truth of the matter** is, …

6 This **gets to the** ______ **of** the problem.

7 Blue light isn't a ______ thing **in itself**.

8 It all **comes down to** how much blue light our eyes are exposed to.

9 ______ at it **objectively**, …

B PAIR WORK **Look at the expressions in the chart again. What do the bold words and phrases mean? Which word or phrase from the box below could replace each one?**

big effect	depends on	highlights the basis of
necessarily	realistically	it's much more complicated
reality	simple	most important information for

C PAIR WORK **Using your notes from exercise 1C on page 38 and expressions from the chart in exercise 3A, write an organized summary of the problems that can result from spending too much time looking at screens. Read your summary to another pair of students and listen to their feedback. Revise your summary.**

4 PRONUNCIATION: Saying the stressed syllable in related words

A 1.36 **Listen to the difference in stress in the related words.**

1 objectively an object to object
2 photography photograph photographic
3 complicated complication

B 1.37 **Listen and underline the stressed syllables. Then repeat all the words.**

1 microscope microphotography
2 to magnify magnificent
3 primary primarily
4 technique technical
5 to substitute substitution
6 impact to impact

C PAIR WORK **Choose a set of words from exercise 4B and point to it for your partner. Hum the syllable stress of one of the two words in the set. Can your partner tell which word it is? Reverse roles and do it again.**

HMM-hmm-hmm.

TECH-ni-cal.

5 SPEAKING

A PAIR WORK **Discuss the connections that might exist between screen time and the topics in the box. Can you think of any other areas that might be affected?**

back pain general health poor posture screen addiction sleep problems

B PAIR WORK **Choose two or three of the topics you talked about and discuss possible solutions. Organize your ideas into a short presentation. Look again at the chart in exercise 1C to help you.**

C **Share your solutions with the class. Describe the main factors you took into consideration.**

4.4 ATTENTION TO DETAIL

LESSON OBJECTIVE

- write a personal profile statement for a résumé

1 READING

A PAIR WORK **How would you answer the question in the quiz? Which answer options reflect big-picture thinking? Which focus on details? Read the article to check your answers. Are you a big-picture thinker or more detail oriented?**

DETAILS OR THE BIG PICTURE – WHERE IS YOUR FOCUS?

Question 1 When you meet a person for the first time, which of the following are you likely to notice?

- Their mood
- Whether they make eye contact
- Their shoes
- The fact that they have a coffee stain on their shirt

BIG-PICTURE VS. DETAIL-ORIENTED: HOW DO YOU THINK?

Are you a big-picture thinker who focuses on the main issues but misses some of the important details? Or are you detail oriented, able to see all the parts but not quite able to see the whole? Find out more about the two mindsets.

Big-picture thinkers

Big-picture thinkers look at things from a global perspective. They grasp a situation in the blink of an eye, identify the main problem, and see what needs to be done to resolve it. They are great motivators and often make inspirational leaders. Their coworkers, friends, and family know that they can trust their judgement.

In the business world, big-picture people spot opportunities that others might miss. They are strategic planners, leading their companies from the front, providing the momentum for change and innovation. In fields of science, they push beyond current knowledge and make huge breakthroughs. In an academic context, they are the students who make connections, who see patterns in the shifts and turns of history or economics, who understand the wider significance of phenomena in biology or chemistry.

Awareness of the big picture, the desire to capture and share it, and an ability to communicate it is what has led to mankind's greatest inventions.

Detail-oriented people

Detail-oriented people have a different mindset. They do not lack imagination or inspiration, but they are observant and analytical. They notice everything and foresee difficulties before they become problems. When a problem arises, they break it down into its component parts, resolving each issue to form a complete solution. Nothing escapes their meticulous attention and their eye for detail.

Detail-oriented people are the backbone of any successful business. They make sure the grand plans can be achieved. They dedicate time and energy to checking and rechecking each step and making sure that nothing endangers success. Their support and diligence provide the team with a sense of security and confidence.

In science, they are the tireless researchers whose painstaking work makes sure the big theories have a sound, practical basis. In an academic context, they are the students who know their subject matter inside and out.

The best of both worlds

It's tempting to value one mindset over the other, but the truth is that both big-picture and detail-oriented mindsets are necessary to the success of any enterprise. Fortunately, hardly anybody is exclusively one or the other. We all tend to show qualities of both mindsets, though we also usually lean towards just one. Knowing which way you lean is key to choosing coworkers, friends, and life partners whose strengths will complement yours.

B READ FOR MAIN IDEA **Which single sentence best summarizes the whole article? Underline it.**

C PAIR WORK READ FOR DETAILS **Write *B* for words associated with big-picture thinkers or *D* for qualities of detail-oriented people. Find the expressions in the article and check your answers.**

1 diligence D
2 inspirational leaders ___
3 meticulous attention ___
4 painstaking work ___
5 strategic planners ___
6 tireless researchers ___

D PAIR WORK THINK CRITICALLY **Discuss the questions.**

- The article focuses on advantages. What are some possible disadvantages of each perspective?
- What kinds of careers would be better suited to big-picture thinkers and detail-oriented people? Why?

2 WRITING

A Read the profile statements. What kind of job is each person looking for? Which people seem to be more detailed oriented, and which seem to be more focused on the big picture?

A

I have a clear, logical mind **with a practical approach to problem-solving** and a strong drive to see things through to completion. **As a graduate with a double major in marketing and business,** I am eager to put my degree to good use and apply the principles I have learned to actual business ventures.

B

A seasoned professional **with a successful track record** and strong technical skills, I approach each project **with a keen eye for detail.** I am eager to be challenged in order to improve my IT skills and grow professionally.

REGISTER CHECK

When writing about yourself in formal contexts, be careful not to start every sentence with the personal pronoun *I*.

C

From the corporate world to dot com startups, my abilities at team management have been tested and proven. **With resourceful problem-solving techniques and an optimistic outlook on life,** I excel at motivating others to do their best work.

B CREATE COHESION Look at the **bold** phrases in the profile statements in exercise 2A. They all start with a preposition. Rewrite them as full sentences, making all other changes necessary.

I have a clear, logical mind. I like to follow a practical approach to solving problems. I have a strong drive to see things through to completion as a result.

C PAIR WORK Combine the sentences to make the profile statement below more concise. Compare statements with a partner. Did you make the same changes?

I am an experienced construction foreman. I have had experience with everything from houses to skyscrapers. My greatest strengths are scheduling, budgeting, and anticipating problems. I have proven that I can bring projects to completion on time and on budget. Some of the largest construction firms in the area have entrusted me with their projects. Some of them were their most sensitive projects.

WRITE IT

D PLAN You're going to write a personal profile statement for job candidate new to their career. First, with a partner, discuss the jobs in the box below. What qualities are needed for each job? How might a candidate address them?

elementary school teacher | project manager | research assistant

E Choose one of the jobs and write the candidate's statement on your own. Be sure to combine related ideas to make it concise.

F PAIR WORK Read your statements to each other. Offer feedback for improvement.

G PAIR WORK After a few years in the job, your candidates are now looking for a change. Choose a new career and rewrite the previous statement to incorporate the candidate's experience and how that would address the qualities that the new job would require.

elementary school teacher
medical lab technician
research assistant
hotel manager
project manager
youth club coordinator

4.5 TIME TO SPEAK
Every last detail

LESSON OBJECTIVE
- create and present an action plan for a project

A **PREPARE** **With a partner, look at the poster. What kind of convention or event do you think it might be? Make a list of possibilities. Which of them would you be most interested in attending? Choose one of your ideas and brainstorm activities that would probably take place. Use the prompts to help you.**

demonstrations	exhibitions	film screenings
performances	presentations	social events

B **DISCUSS** **You are the organizers. Think about the things you need to do to prepare for the convention or event. Start with the big-picture categories like those below. What other categories can you think of?**

brochure
catering / food service
guest speakers / performers
promotion / advertising
social events
target audience
venue
____
____
____

C **DECIDE** **Work with another pair of students to create an action plan. Follow the steps.**

Step 1 Make a list of what needs to be done in each category.
Step 2 Prioritize the lists.
Step 3 Decide when each action needs to be completed and how much time it will require.
Step 4 Choose who in your group is responsible for which lists and/or actions.
Step 5 Make a detailed plan of action. Consider which tasks or lists can be done independently and which ones affect other people's work.

D **PRESENT** **Present an overview of your convention or event to the class and then break it down into your action plan. Listen to the other groups. Ask and answer questions.**

E **AGREE** **What did you learn from this experience? Discuss the questions.**

- Which people are better at big-picture tasks? Who is more detail oriented? What about your own strengths?
- Did your group have a good mix of people in it, or were your strengths unbalanced? Do you think this affected your plan positively or negatively? Why? If you did this project again, would you assign tasks differently?
- Considering all the plans presented, which convention or event would you most want to attend? Why?

To check your progress, go to page 154.

USEFUL PHRASES

DISCUSS
For the venue, we'll need to consider … in our decision.
Before we choose … , let's decide …
Figuring out … will help us determine …

DECIDE
For … , it all comes down to …
In this category, the highest priorities are …
Once you've done … , I can start …

Answers to exercise 4A, page 35: A a slice of kiwi, B salmon scales, C human red blood cells, D Velcro fastener

UNIT OBJECTIVES

- discuss traveling to remote places
- comment on loneliness and working in remote places
- discuss cause and effect
- write a company profile
- prepare and present a case for working remotely

REMOTE

5

START SPEAKING

A Look at the picture. Where do you think this is? Do you think the building is a home? Why or why not? How does the idea of being in this place make you feel?

B What would be the challenges of living in a place like this? Think of the type of person who would choose to live here. What physical or mental characteristics do you think they might have?

C What movies, books, shows, or real-life stories do you know in which people live in some type of isolation? How do they handle it? Is isolation a choice or an accident? For ideas, watch Susanne's video.

EXPERT SPEAKER

Do you agree with Susanne's conclusions?

5.1 THE END OF THE ROAD

LESSON OBJECTIVE
- discuss traveling to remote places

1 LANGUAGE IN CONTEXT

A **Look at the pictures and the title of the article. What do you think "Project Remote" is? Read and check your prediction.**

DISCOVERING

PROJECT REMOTE

Walking down a crowded, noisy beach one day in Florida, Ryan and Rebecca Means suddenly looked at each other and had the same thought: Let's find a place that is just the opposite of this. They didn't want just a **deserted** or unpopulated area, they wanted to find a place that nobody had ever visited!

And so Project Remote was born. Their first mission was to find the most remote place in their state. But having explored all the spots close to home, they soon found themselves itching for more. Analyzing satellite imagery, Rebecca identified the places in the U.S. that are farthest away from human structures. Now addicted to the beauty of **unspoiled** landscapes, they drove from state to state, visiting the most isolated places imaginable, and they brought their toddler, Skyla, along.

Searching out the most remote spots sometimes ended in disappointment. They would arrive and find other people had beaten them there or a new road had just been built nearby!

The Means family's favorite places are the **immense**, **nameless** expanses of the West. The most remote spot they have found so far is deep in Yellowstone National Park in Wyoming.

Described in great detail on their blog Project Remote, the family's routes form a **scenic** memoir of their adventures, and their photos bring it all to life: from the **lush** green swamplands of Florida to the **bare**, **hostile** deserts of Arizona. Log on and enjoy the remoteness!

B PAIR WORK | THINK CRITICALLY **What is Project Remote's mission? Would you like to go on one of their trips? Why or why not? In what ways do you think Project Remote's work could be beneficial to society?**

2 VOCABULARY: Describing remote places

A 1.38 **Look at the bold adjectives in the article in exercise 1A. Match them to the synonyms below. More than one match is possible. Then listen to check your work.**

1 isolated ______
2 barren ______
3 vast ______
4 abundant ______
5 anonymous ______
6 picturesque ______
7 abandoned ______
8 harsh ______

FIND IT

B **Which adjectives are usually used to describe places in a positive way? In a negative way? Which are neutral? Use a dictionary or your phone to help you. Then use your phone to find more examples of these words in context.**

C **Now go to page 145. Do the vocabulary exercises for 5.1.**

D PAIR WORK | THINK CRITICALLY **Think of a landscape near you. Which adjectives would apply to it? Describe it in detail.**

The beaches are really unspoiled and scenic, but they are not deserted. They're really popular with families in the summer.

3 GRAMMAR: Participle phrases in initial position

A Read the sentences in the grammar box. Circle the correct options to complete the rules.

Participle phrases in initial position

Walking down a crowded, noisy beach, they looked at each other and had the same thought.
Having explored all the spots close to home, they found themselves itching for more.
Now addicted to the beauty of unspoiled landscapes, they drove from state to state.

1 Participle phrases at the beginning of a sentence **contain** / **don't contain** a subject.
2 The subject of the verb in the participle phrase **is the same as** / **is different from** the subject of the verb in the main clause.
3 There **is only one type** / **are different types** of participles. A participle phrase can start with **only one** / **any** of them.

B Now go to page 133. Look at the grammar chart and do the grammar exercise for 5.1.

C PAIR WORK **Using participle phrases and the prompts below, write sentences that are true for you. Read them to your partner. Then check your accuracy.**

1 look at social media / feel connected
2 study English / understand movies and TV shows
3 strict parents / be strict to own children
4 travel to unfamiliar places / chance to explore / people and cultures

Looking at my family's posts on social media, I feel connected to them, even though they're far away.

ACCURACY CHECK

Don't use *to* + verb in participle clauses.

Finally having ~~to find~~ the right path, we reached the lake in no time. ✗
Finally having found the right path, we reached the lake in no time. ✓

4 SPEAKING

A PAIR WORK THINK CRITICALLY **If you wanted to get away and be by yourself for a week, which type of place would appeal to you more? Why?**

- a bare environment, like a vast expanse of hostile, barren desert
- a lush, scenic jungle, with picturesque views and abundant life, but no people
- a boat floating along in some immense, anonymous part of the ocean

Having lived my whole life in a lush, green area, I think I'd choose the ocean. The weather can be harsh at times, but the vast emptiness of it appeals to me.

5.2 HOW TO BE ALONE

LESSON OBJECTIVE
- comment on loneliness and working in remote places

1 LANGUAGE IN CONTEXT

A 1.39 **Look at the picture on page 47. What is the man doing? Listen to a podcast about two people's jobs and check your answers. Which job is related to the picture?**

1.39 Audio script

Host	Today, we'll learn about two people who live and work alone in remote locations. What **impact** has constant solitude had on them? What **implications** might it have for their futures? Susan, who lives and works on an island, is our first guest.
Susan	My job is to guard the archeological sites here. A few researchers come sometimes, but no tourists. I can see how someone freaked out by solitude would find this job impossible, but people have always been a **source** of anxiety for me, so I'm fine. The quiet helps me think. I've even started writing again. I see solitude as a positive **force** in my life. As a **consequence**, I'm kind of addicted to it.
Host	Next we hear from Austin, who is a fire officer in an area of the Rocky Mountains known to be extremely difficult to reach. Solitude has **influenced** him very differently.
Austin	Wildfires, common during the summer season, can happen really anytime, so five times a day I climb the lookout tower. When I see smoke, I send a signal that **triggers** firefighters to investigate. A few friends have visited me, but I couldn't really talk to them, which probably **stems from** the fact that I hardly talk at all anymore. But that **resulted in** even fewer visitors and more solitude. I want to be around people again. This experience has even **motivated** me to apply to grad school, to study communications!

B THINK CRITICALLY **Is either of the people in the podcast lonely? What would you say is the difference between loneliness and solitude? Does one always trigger the other? Is it possible to feel lonely when you're not alone? Why or why not?**

2 VOCABULARY: Talking about influences

A 1.40 PAIR WORK **Look at the bold words in the audio script. Try to work out what they mean from context. Then make a chart like the one below and write them in the correct category according to how they're used in the text. Listen and check.**

Nouns	Verbs
impact	influence

B **Now go to page 145. Do the vocabulary exercises for 5.2.**

C PAIR WORK THINK CRITICALLY **Think of a problem that you have personal experience with. Discuss your ideas about its source(s), how it influences your life, and what implications it might have for your future.**

I'm always late, and it has a really negative **impact** on my life. My friends get mad because we always miss the beginning of the movie. As a **consequence**, they don't invite me to things anymore.

What do you think this habit **stems from**?

3 GRAMMAR: Reduced relative clauses

A **Read the sentences in the grammar box. Complete the rules.**

Reduced relative clauses

I can see how **someone (who is)** freaked out by solitude would find this job impossible.
Wildfires, (which are) common during the summer season, can happen anytime.
It is an area (that is) known to be extremely difficult to reach.

1 A relative clause consists of a relative pronoun (*which*, ____________, or *that*) and a verb phrase.
2 When the verb phrase starts with the verb *be*, we can drop both the ____________ ____________ and *be*.

B **Now go to page 133. Look at the grammar chart and do the grammar exercise for 5.2.**

C PAIR WORK **Combine the two sentences using a complete relative clause. Then ~~cross out~~ two words to form a reduced relative clause. Compare your work with a partner. What is your opinion about each statement?**

1 Some people are not used to being alone. They probably shouldn't work as freelancers.
People ~~who are~~ not used to being alone probably shouldn't work as freelancers.
2 Some students enroll in distance learning programs. They attend class via a conferencing app.
____
3 Some people are willing to work in solitude for long periods. They are hard to find.
____
4 Language learning is known to be easier for children. It is a common retirement goal for adults.
____

4 SPEAKING

A GROUP WORK THINK CRITICALLY **Discuss the questions.**

- What's the difference between solitude and loneliness?
- What are some consequences of having too much or too little solitude as a child?
- What impact does solitude have on you? Is it a positive, creative force in your life, or is it a source of anxiety?

I'm not **someone afraid of being alone**. Solitude is a **source** of relaxation for me.

B PAIR WORK **Can you think of jobs in which people work alone? Is it by choice or by necessity? What might motivate someone to choose these jobs? Would you like to do any of them? Why or why not? For ideas, watch Susanne's video.**

EXPERT SPEAKER

How similar are you and Susanne?

5.3 WORKING FROM HOME

LESSON OBJECTIVE

- discuss cause and effect

1 LISTENING

A 1.41 PAIR WORK **Look at the pictures. In which context would you prefer to work? Why? What are some pros and cons for each context? Listen to a presentation about working remotely. Does the speaker mention any of your points?**

B 1.41 DIFFERENTIATE FACTS AND OPINIONS **Read the excerpts from the presentation and write *O* (opinion) or *F* (fact). Listen to the presentation again. What difference in tone do you hear?**

1 … we all know that's due to the digital revolution. ___
2 … the productivity of remote workers was ranked as 7.7 out of 10, compared with 6.5 out of 10 for office workers. ___
3 This must be thanks to the reduction in distractions that people have at home … ___
4 … another study found that those who spent 60 to 80 percent of their time away from the office had the highest rates of engagement with their coworkers. ___
5 … remote workers are more likely to report that their coworkers care about them as a person and as a professional. ___
6 What's important is the autonomy of working where I like, instead of where someone else puts me. ___

INSIDER ENGLISH

Say *As it turns out* to indicate an unexpected result or circumstance.

I thought I'd hate working in a big office, but ***as it turns out****, I find it really energizing.*

C 1.41 LISTEN FOR ORGANIZATION **Listen to the presentation again. How does the speaker start? How does she introduce the topic? How does she wrap up her talk?**

D PAIR WORK THINK CRITICALLY **Do you share the presenter's opinion about remote work? Why or why not? Which specific points do you disagree with? Would you say the presentation accurately reflects the experience of working remotely?**

2 PRONUNCIATION: Listening for linking between words

A 1.42 **Listen to the phrases and notice how some words are linked. What sounds are they?**

a … according to a survey of …
b Commuting is a major source of stress.
c … as readily as others.
d For all the reasons I've presented, …

B 1.43 PAIR WORK **Underline where linking sounds will occur between the words below. Listen and check.**

When a word ends with a consonant sound and the next word starts with a vowel sound, the two words are usually linked together if they are in the same word group. When a word ends with a vowel sound and the next word begins with a vowel sound, there is usually also a linking sound.

C **Circle the correct words to complete the sentences.**

If the first word ends in a vowel where the lips are [1]*rounded / spread*, for example /i/, there is a linking sound like /j/.
If the first word ends in a vowel where the lips are [2]*rounded / spread*, for example /u/, there is a linking sound like /w/.
But if the first word ends in /r/, /a/, or /ɜ/, then /j/, /w/, and /r/ link to the next word.

3 SPEAKING SKILLS

A 1.44 **Listen again and complete the phrases from the presentation. What linking sounds do you hear?**

Signaling cause and effect	
1 More and more people are working from home, and we all know that's ___due to___ the digital revolution.	C
2 ___________ studies found lower stress levels among remote workers, ___________ a reduction in their chance of suffering heart attacks and strokes.	___
3 This must be ___________ the reduction in distractions that people have at home.	___
4 ___________ the added flexibility that remote working allows, the gender gap is reduced.	___
5 A common ___________ of working from home is loneliness.	___
6 ___________ I've presented, remote work should no longer be just regarded as a job "perk."	___
7 As an employee, ___________ I have more power over the way I do my work, I'm happier, and I get more done.	___

B PAIR WORK **Look at the sentences in the chart again. Write *C* for expressions that signal a cause and *E* for those that signal an effect. Compare with a partner.**

C PAIR WORK **Student A reads the statement below. Student B responds using a cause-and-effect expression. Take turns and continue with statements of your own.**

Statement: I don't like the idea of working from home.

REGISTER CHECK

The most formal cause-and-effect expressions are usually only found in written contexts:

as a result of *thus* *owing to*
consequently *the consequences of*

That's because you're very sociable. But I find that I get so much more done when I'm working from home.

Thanks to the peace and quiet, I suppose.

4 PRONUNCIATION: Saying tense and lax vowels

A 1.45 **Listen and repeat. Are the underlined vowels tense or lax? Write *T* or *L*.**

1 digital L
3 people ___
5 reduce ___
7 regarded ___
2 employee ___
4 perk ___
6 reduction ___
8 gap ___

B 1.46 PAIR WORK **Read the words aloud and circle all the lax vowels you hear. Listen and check.**

1 architect
3 employee
5 perk
7 remote
2 digital
4 manager
6 real estate
8 stress

C PAIR WORK **Make your own list of words containing tense and lax vowels. Quiz your partner.**

5 SPEAKING

A PAIR WORK THINK CRITICALLY **Choose one of the topics in the box or another topic that you both know something about. Prepare a mini-presentation (2–5 minutes) about the pros and cons associated with it. Look at exercise 1C to help you. Be sure to use phrases for cause and effect. Ask and answer questions to improve your work.**

social media tech devices vegetarianism video games

B **Give your mini-presentation to the class. How many different topics were presented?**

Our topic is tech devices. People have a lot more options for working today thanks to the internet and Wi-Fi, but mostly because of great tech devices.

But in some ways, technology also limits our choices. As a result of the internet, some industries are dying. . . .

5.4 REMOTE SUCCESS STORY

LESSON OBJECTIVE
- write a company profile

1 READING

A **PREDICT CONTENT** **Look at the title of the article and the picture. What do you think the story is about?**

B **READ FOR MAIN IDEA** **Read the article and choose the best summary of it.**

a A company that people have never heard of can be very important to modern life.
b One company has managed to embrace new ways of working successfully.
c A remote company can best compete with its more traditional business rivals.

BUSINESS Home Fortune 100 News Search

Automattic goes fully remote

Automattic – the company behind thousands of blogs and open-source platforms – has closed its gorgeous San Francisco office because their employees never show up. And that's a sign of the times!

Best known for giving the world the free blogging platform WordPress, Automattic powers 20 percent of all websites on the internet today – a staggering figure.

As a result of their success, you might imagine them overseeing their empire from a huge, multi-million-dollar building in a trendy but expensive neighborhood, but you'd be wrong. While they do have an office, it's small, cozy, inexpensive, and now nearly empty.

Thanks to the wonders of modern technology, Automattic's vast web empire is managed completely online. This enables their team of 400 employees distributed across 40 countries to work seamlessly without sharing an office, or perhaps even more amazingly, without using email.

How can they work this way? The secret, ironically, is total transparency. Everybody knows exactly what's going on. All meetings, even those that happen with people in the same location, take place online. Consequently, everyone has equal status and stays in the loop. Day-to-day communication is done through internal blogs hosted on WordPress, the business communication app Slack, and the occasional video chat.

The company provides and maintains all the tools and software an employee needs to work remotely; thus, all employees have access to the same platforms and work in compatible programs. If a home office is the preferred location, the company pays for an ergonomic consultation to ensure a healthy work environment, even remotely. For those who choose to seek out a coworking space, Automattic pays the costs associated with it, including their cappuccino at a coffee shop if that's where employees choose to set up camp.

Automattic has found that remote working helps them attract top talent: not just locals, but also people who don't live in San Francisco or can't live there, owing to that city's famously high rents. But the company saves money, too. They declined to say how much of the savings was due to the office closure, but ditching a 15,000-square-foot office space in San Francisco would have to make a difference to any company's bottom line.

Regardless of where the increased profits come from, Automattic shares the bounty with their employees. Consider "hack week": Automattic will pay for any team to meet in person and work for one week in any location in the world. Now, that can't be bad!

GLOSSARY
in the loop (*phr*) in possession of all current and relevant information needed

C **READ FOR DETAILS** **Find six examples of cause-and-effect expressions in the article. What alternatives might you use if you were telling a friend the same information?**

D **PAIR WORK** **THINK CRITICALLY** **Discuss the questions.**

1 What would you say is the writer's attitude toward Automattic and their decision to go remote? Find examples to defend your opinion.
2 What do you think Automattic's main motivation is – cutting costs, helping their workers, or something else? Why do you think so?

2 WRITING

A Read this profile about another remote firm called "The Company." What are the five main factors they point to for their success?

100% VIRTUAL?

The Company, interested for years in remote business models, has gone 100% virtual. Here, we explain the strategies behind their distributed workforce.

First, The Company hired the right employees. Millennials, already accustomed to working remotely, are the key. Location and time spent on work have always been flexible for them, so they adapt well to working virtually.

Another strategy is to be proactive about communication. Meetings held via video chats are replacing traditional messaging methods. They have found this practice also makes it easier to keep everybody in the loop.

Then there's flexibility around working hours. Employees, happy with their own customized schedules, work far more efficiently. Flexible hours also reduce employee stress.

The next challenge was learning how to manage effectively via technology. Thanks to virtual office software now available, managers at The Company don't have to worry about not being able to monitor what employees are doing. Managers and coworkers can always see when team members are working or available to chat, giving everyone a sense of teamwork.

Finally, The Company never forgets the value of face time. Even if it's only once a year, they look for opportunities for teams to meet in person and work side by side.

B **CREATE COHESION Use participial phrases to connect the ideas and reduce the information to one sentence. Check your work by referring to the text above, but there is more than one correct answer.**

1 The Company had been interested in remote business models for a long time. Now they are 100% virtual.

2 Millennials are the key to a good staff. This is because they are already accustomed to working remotely.

3 Meetings are now held via video chats. This method is in the process of replacing more traditional types of messaging.

4 Employees tend to work far more efficiently now. A big reason for this is their happiness with their own customized schedules.

WRITE IT

C **PAIR WORK Student A: Go to page 157. Student B: Go to page 159. Follow the instructions.**

D **PLAN You're going to work together to write a profile for one of the companies in exercise 2C. Choose the company and decide what points to include and how to structure your profile. Look at the model in exercise 2A to help you. What points should go in which paragraph?**

E **PAIR WORK Write a profile for the company you chose.**

F **GROUP WORK Join another pair of students who profiled a different company. Read your profiles aloud and evaluate each other's work. Then discuss which company you think has the greatest chance of success as a virtual company and why.**

5.5

TIME TO SPEAK
Make the case

LESSON OBJECTIVE

- prepare and present a case for working remotely

A **RESEARCH** **In small groups, look at the key responsibilities of three jobs at Cerben Enterprises, a marketing company with multiple offices in North and South America. Salary and work experience are similar for all jobs.**

A

E-marketing manager

- designs email advertising campaigns
- represents Cerben at industry conferences
- manages team of 6–8 employees

B

UX design manager

- responsible for UX on website and internal company site
- tests and improves functionality and features
- leads training sessions for clients and employees

C

Social media manager

- responsible for social media identity
- monitors trends 24/7 and creates content to connect to them
- manages and assigns projects to large freelancer pool

FIND IT

B **For each job, brainstorm a list of daily tasks the person in the role is likely to do. You can use your phone to research typical job responsibilities. Discuss which tasks can be done remotely and which can be done better in the office.**

e-marketing mgr: write emails – remote *performance reviews – face to face*

C **PREPARE** **The executives at Cerben have decided to allow one of the three jobs above to be based remotely, but which one? Follow the instructions to prepare a case for one of the jobs.**

1 Choose one of the jobs. Using your notes from exercise B, consider travel, personnel management, type of work, etc., to build a case for why your job should be based remotely (the pro side).

2 Anticipate counterarguments (the con side) and prepare responses. Prepare at least two good reasons why the other jobs should <u>not</u> be remote.

3 Decide how to structure your points and who will present each part.

D **PRESENT** **Present your argument to the Cerben executive team (the class or another small group). Respond to their questions and objections. When you are an executive, refer to the points you prepared against the other roles to pose questions or objections.**

E **AGREE** **As a class, discuss the arguments and decide which job can go remote. Is there a clear consensus? Is it necessary to vote? How close is the vote? Did any of the jobs get no votes? Why?**

To check your progress, go to page 154.

USEFUL LANGUAGE

PREPARE

Due to the fact that this role is … ,

Anyone working in an office all day knows … , so …

Having read the description for … , I think it's fair to say …

PRESENT

You might think … , but actually …

Thanks to … , the challenges of … are no longer a problem.

The other jobs … . Consequently, ours is the best candidate.

UNIT OBJECTIVES

- discuss shocks and surprises
- talk about great upsets in sports and other contexts
- discuss the differences between local and global brands
- write a paragraph drawing from multiple sources
- prepare a surprise for somebody

SURPRISE, SURPRISE

6

START SPEAKING

A **Look at the picture. What emotions is the person expressing? What thoughts might be running through her mind? Through the other person's mind? What would you be thinking?**

B **Are you a fan of surprises? Why or why not? What kinds of surprises do you really <u>not</u> like?**

C **Would you say that you are a spontaneous person who is open to the unexpected, or do you usually have everything planned? Can you give an example? For ideas, watch João's video.**

EXPERT SPEAKER

How similar are you to João?

6.1 THE SURPRISE BUSINESS

LESSON OBJECTIVE
- discuss shocks and surprises

1 LANGUAGE IN CONTEXT

A PAIR WORK **Look at the title of the article and the picture. What do you think *Surprise Me!* is? Read the article and check your answers.**

SURPRISE ME!
IS A SURPRISING SUCCESS

Marielle expected a Valentine's Day gift from her fiancé, Drake, but what she never expected was to spend the day falling through the air.

A tandem skydive would be a highly unusual gift for most people, but it was just another fantastic experience arranged by *Surprise Me!*, a Dallas-based company that offers a menu of unexpected adventures to give as gifts and also incredibly helpful tips on how to create your own surprises for that special someone.

Surprises can be tricky, though, and employees of *Surprise Me!* have learned to be careful. The thing that they try hardest to avoid, ironically, is shock – some people have been visibly shaken by (and not at all happy with) their surprises. To guard against this, surprise recipients must fill out a questionnaire about phobias and past surprises, good and bad. This ensures the new surprise is a pleasure.

But it isn't just the clients who love their experiences. "What I love most is being there when the client finds out what they're getting," one worker said. "The reason why is that I get to share in that feeling of being genuinely surprised. There's nothing better."

Marielle agrees. "It wasn't until it was all over that I realized what a great experience it had been," she said, noticeably thrilled by it all. "It was just amazing. I loved it!"

GLOSSARY
tandem (*adv*) two or more things/people acting as one

B PAIR WORK THINK CRITICALLY **Do you think *Surprise Me!* is a good business idea? Why or why not? Would you pay for such a service? How much would you pay?**

2 VOCABULARY: Using adverbs to add attitude

A 1.47 PAIR WORK **Read the adverb–adjective phrases in the box. Find five more in the article and write them below. Listen and check. Which adverbs communicate a positive attitude about the adjective? A negative attitude?**

deeply (anxious)	immensely (popular)	remarkably (calm)
understandably (upset)	utterly (shocked)	

1 highly unusual
2 ______
3 ______
4 ______
5 ______

B Now go to page 146. Do the vocabulary exercises for 6.1.

C PAIR WORK **Think about something that shocked or surprised you recently. Describe how it felt or your attitude toward it. Combine adverbs and adjectives differently and tell your story.**

My sister and I now go to the same school. She just started here last month, but she is already remarkably popular!

3 GRAMMAR: Clefts

A Read the sentences in the grammar box. Then complete the rules below with words from the box.

Clefts

What she never expected was to spend the day falling through the air.

What I love most is being there when the client finds out.

It wasn't until it was all over that I realized what a great experience it had been.

The thing that they try hardest to avoid, ironically, is shock.

The reason why is that I get to share in that feeling.

be emphasis it surprising thing what

1 We use cleft sentences for __________ . The cleft is an introductory clause that focuses attention on particularly interesting, relevant, or __________ information.

2 A cleft often starts with the word __________ or the phrase *The* __________ *that* ..., but we can also use expressions like *The reason* (*why*) ... or __________ *wasn't until* ...

3 Most clefts end with a form of the verb __________ .

B Now go to page 134. Look at the grammar chart and do the grammar exercise for 6.1.

C PAIR WORK Use the prompts to make sentences that are true for you, and check your accuracy. Share your sentences with a partner and explain your ideas.

1 The reason [name] loves surprises is ...

2 The thing [name] doesn't like about surprises is ...

3 How I like to celebrate my birthday is ...

4 The surprises that I've enjoyed most were the ones that ...

ACCURACY CHECK

Don't use *it* between the cleft and the verb *be*.

What I love most about my office ~~it~~ is the location. ✗

What I love most about my office is the location. ✓

4 SPEAKING

A PAIR WORK Student A: Go to page 157. Student B: Go to page 159. Follow the directions.

B PAIR WORK Read the surprises and discuss whether or not each one would be a good choice for the person you read about (Hannah). How might she react?

a hands-on visit to a reptile zoo
an international cooking workshop
a yoga class on the beach
an introductory surfing course
a weekend of whitewater rafting and hiking
a beginner's photography course

C Think of a person from your own life who definitely would or would not like each of the surprises above. How do you think they would react?

My mother would be immensely upset if I took her to a reptile zoo. The thing she hates most in the world is snakes!

6.2 THE MIRACLE ON ICE

LESSON OBJECTIVE

- talk about great upsets in sports and other contexts

1 LANGUAGE IN CONTEXT

DO YOU BELIEVE IN MIRACLES?

A 1.48 PAIR WORK **Look at the picture. What sport is this related to? What "miracle" is it talking about? Listen to the radio program and check your answers.**

1.48 Audio script

Today in History

Friday, February 22, 1980: The "Miracle on Ice"

Host However you look at it, the game still known as the "Miracle on Ice" was one of the greatest sports upsets of all time.

At the Winter Olympics in Lake Placid, New York, Team USA faced the Soviet Union in the ice hockey semifinals. The Soviets had dominated Olympic hockey for decades. By contrast, Team USA was filled with amateurs and college players who had never played together before. In a practice game weeks earlier, the Soviet team's skill and speed utterly overwhelmed the Americans, resulting in a 10 to 3 victory for the Soviets.

Whatever the reason, Team USA was significantly underrated. Fans worried that they might not even score against the Soviet powerhouse. But Team USA shocked the world and beat the Soviet Union 4 to 3.

Sports historian Barry Framm talks about the legacy of this famous upset.

Framm You know, whenever there's a big upset, it's always compared to the Miracle on Ice – like when an unranked underdog, Roberta Vinci, defeated number one-ranked tennis great Serena Williams in the 2015 U.S. Open.

Host To find other comparable upsets, you have to leave sports and go into the political arena. Whoever you ask will surely point to Truman's victory over Dewey in the 1948 U.S. presidential election. Overconfident of Dewey's victory, some newspapers actually published front pages with the wrong result!

2 VOCABULARY: Using the prefixes *under-* and *over-*

FIND IT

A 1.49 PAIR WORK **Look at the words in the box and answer the questions below. Use a dictionary or your phone and the audio script above to help you. Listen and check.**

confident	crowded	developed	estimated	paid
priced	rated	whelmed	worked	

1 Which of the words can have both the prefix *under-* and *over-*? Which ones typically only use *over-*? Underline the ones that were used in the radio program.

2 Which word is never used *without* a prefix?

3 Find a noun in the audio script that includes one of the prefixes. What do you think it means?

! For prefixes that are words on their own, like *over* and *under*, there are no definite rules about hyphenation. Choose one dictionary as your reference for consistency in your writing.

overwhelmed (no hyphen)
over-confident OR
overconfident (sources differ)

B **Now go to page 146. Do the vocabulary exercises for 6.2.**

C PAIR WORK **Replace the underlined expressions with a word that uses *under-* or *over-*, making any changes necessary to the sentence. Which of the statements do you agree with? Why?**

1 Some people think professional athletes make too much money. But people don't calculate correctly how difficult an athlete's job is and how unsure their future is.

2 Athletes usually have months off, but during training and the season, they often do more than they should. They sometimes feel unable to handle the stress, physically and psychologically.

3 Of course, some athletes have an ego that is larger than it should be. They would say that they don't get a high enough salary.

3 GRAMMAR: Question words with *-ever*

A **Read the sentences in the grammar box. Then circle the correct options to complete the rules.**

Question words with *-ever*

However you look at it, the "Miracle on Ice" was one of the greatest sports upsets of all time.

Whatever the reason, Team USA was significantly underrated.

Whenever there's a big upset, it's always compared to the Miracle on Ice.

Whoever you ask will point to the 1948 U.S. presidential election.

INSIDER ENGLISH

Whatever. **= I don't care.**

But be careful of your tone of voice!

1 Adding the suffix *-ever* to the question words *who*, *where*, *what*, *which*, *how*, and *when* indicates that the exact person, place, thing, manner, or time **matters a lot** / **doesn't matter.**

2 Question words with the suffix *-ever* can also be used to indicate that you **know** / **don't know** the exact details.

3 Although question words with *-ever* can be found in questions, they **are** / **are not** used to form questions.

B **Now go to page 134. Look at the grammar chart and do the grammar exercise for 6.2.**

C PAIR WORK **Use the questions words in the box with *-ever* to make general statements about upsets in sports or politics. Share your statements with a partner. Do you agree with each other?**

however whatever whenever wherever whichever whoever

Whichever team you follow, it is probably going to suffer an overwhelming upset at some point.

4 SPEAKING

A PAIR WORK **Think about the Miracle on Ice. What other upsets do you know about from different contexts (sports, politics, awards, etc.)?**

B PAIR WORK **Student A: Go to page 158. Student B: Go to page 160. Follow the instructions.**

C THINK CRITICALLY **Why do people cheer for the underdog? Think of examples to support your opinion. Why might people not cheer for the underdog in a particular situation? For ideas, watch João's video.**

EXPERT SPEAKER

In João's example, what would you do?

6.3 A SURPRISING COMEBACK

LESSON OBJECTIVE

- discuss the differences between local and global brands

A

B

C

1 LISTENING

A **What do the pictures on this page show? Why might these businesses be seen as surprising?**

B 1.50 LISTEN FOR MAIN POINTS **Listen to a news feature about the revival of local stores. Circle the two main points the speakers want to make.**

- **a** Global companies are winning out against local competition.
- **b** Local stores are making a surprising comeback against big chains.
- **c** Global business predicted this rise in local independent stores but can do nothing about it.
- **d** There is a relationship between nostalgia for the past and local independent businesses.
- **e** Having a store of your own can be surprisingly profitable if you choose the right location.

C 1.50 PAIR WORK LISTEN FOR DETAILS **Listen again and take notes in the chart. Compare with a partner. Did you capture the same information?**

Reasons why local businesses succeed	Reasons why certain things are coming back
People are tired of big chains.	

D PAIR WORK **Think of a small business that recently opened where you live. What kind of business is it? Would you say it's part of the trend described in the news feature? Why or why not?**

INSIDER ENGLISH

the good old days = a simpler time in the past

2 PRONUNCIATION: Listening for the pronunciation of foreign words and phrases

A 1.51 **Read the sentence and underline the Spanish word. According to English norms, how would you pronounce it? Listen. How does the speaker pronounce it?**

I'm here with Josh Stephens, a longtime resident and a coffee aficionado.

FIND IT

B 1.52 PAIR WORK **Look at some foreign words and phrases commonly used in English. What language do you think they originally come from? Are any of them also in your language? What do they mean? Use your phone to help you. How do you say them in English? Listen and check.**

avatar	bona fide	cappuccino	carte blanche	chaos	glasnost
hoi polloi	hurricane	ketchup	maelstrom	schadenfreude	tsunami

C **Circle the correct word to complete the sentence.**

When foreign words and phrases are taken into English, they usually *change / keep* their original pronunciation.

3 SPEAKING SKILLS

A 1.50 **Complete the phrases for adding emphasis. Listen to the news feature from exercise 1 again to check your answers. Find at least four additional words or phrases for adding emphasis as you listen.**

Adding emphasis

1 Since then, Seattleites have been ________ ________ with the drink.
2 But the ________ that's most surprising is, despite the hundreds …
3 ________ local businesses they want to support now.
4 Vinyl is really making a comeback. ________ new music is coming out on vinyl.
5 Not long ago people really ________ ________ that we'd stop buying books altogether.
6 So, ________ , we're talking about two trends here …
7 ________ they have in common is that desire for interaction.
8 I ________ ________ whether this trend … is having an effect on the corporate world.

B PAIR WORK **What are some ways to help a local business be successful? Discuss your ideas with a partner. Add emphasis to the points you feel strongly about.**

> What you need is something surprising to make your place memorable. For a record store, you could hire a DJ to play music as people shop.

4 PRONUNCIATION: Saying clefts

A 1.53 **Listen to the cleft sentences. Do you hear one or two thought groups? Mark where the intonation goes up and goes down in each sentence.**

1 What the digital revolution has taught us is physical things have value.
2 What they have in common is that desire for interaction.
3 The thing that's most surprising is … small local coffee shops are actually coming back.
4 It is local businesses they want to support now.

B 1.54 PAIR WORK **Unscramble the words to make cleft sentences. Mark the intonation, and then listen and check. Practice saying the cleft sentences with a partner. Is your intonation appropriate?**

1 really / it / low / costs / was / made / difference / having / the / all / that
2 still / mystery / why / is / the / business / a / failed
3 good / is / the / thing / plan / you / business / a / need

C PAIR WORK THINK CRITICALLY **Complete the cleft sentences about running a business with your own ideas. Read your sentences to each other. Do you agree?**

1 What I have noticed is …
2 It is your customers that …
3 The reason why most businesses fail is …
4 The thing that separates successful from unsuccessful businesses is …

5 SPEAKING

A PAIR WORK **Which types of stores are more successful where you live: multinational chains or local businesses? Why do you think so? Have there been any surprising trends where you live?**

> When McDonald's came to my city, everybody ate there. But that didn't last. People went back to the local sandwich places.

B GROUP WORK THINK CRITICALLY **What are some advantages that global companies and chain stores have over local businesses? Do you find any of these advantages surprising in any way? If the people in your area had to choose one type or another exclusively, which would they pick? Why?**

6.4 JUMP SCARE

LESSON OBJECTIVE

- write a paragraph drawing from multiple sources

1 READING

A **Look at the picture on page 61. It's a toy called a Jack-in-the-box. Did you have one as a kid? How does it work? What reaction do people usually have to it? Why do you think kids like it so much?**

B PAIR WORK PREDICT CONTENT **Look at the headlines from the collection of texts below. What's the theme of the collection? Explain your ideas.**

C PAIR WORK READ FOR MAIN IDEAS **Read the stories and write in the correct headline for each one. Compare your answers with a partner. Discuss any differences in your choices.**

An instinct to startle | Sharing the fear | Startled and viral | The simplest "jump scare" ever

A ________________________

It takes very little to get Brian Fletcher to jump, and his grandson Mikey loves it! Mikey has quite a following from sharing his "jump scare" videos on YouTube. Watch how Brian leaps out of his seat when a plastic spider falls on his dinner plate or how he jumps halfway across the room when Mikey sneaks up behind his grandfather, peacefully snoozing in his favorite armchair, and blows a whistle. Absolutely everything startles Brian, from a gentle tap on the shoulder to a slamming door. Luckily, he's got a good sense of humor. After each scare, he soon calms down and laughs along with the rest of us!

B ________________________

The startle reflex is one of the few instinctual behaviors humans have. Notice what happens when you lay a baby down. They throw out their arms and legs as if to save themselves from falling, but when they feel safe again, they relax. Though it's particularly noticeable in babies, the startle reflex remains part of our biological makeup our whole lives. When we sense danger, it puts the body on full physical alert. For some people, this translates into jumping to their feet. For others, it's a simple tensing of the muscles. Basically, the startle reflex is the first step in the "fight or flight" response of all mammals – that split-second decision of whether to defend yourself or run away.

C ________________________

When was the last time you watched a scary movie in a dark theater full of people all on the edge of their seats? With the rise of digital options, movie theaters everywhere are getting smaller or closing completely. Now, most of us just grab the hand of the person next to us on the couch when things get suspenseful. This might be comforting, but it isn't as much fun. Experiencing fear in large groups is enjoyable because reactions are highly contagious. Everybody jumps and screams together. Surprisingly, another very common group response to scary movies is laughter. It's the nervousness that provokes the laughter, then relief when the suspense breaks. Or maybe we just don't want people to know we totally fell for it.

D ________________________

On the face of it, it looks like a very simple toy – just a box and a spring and a handle to turn. But this little machine is one of the oldest tricks in the book. No matter how many times you turn the crank, no matter how long it takes for the box to spring open, that moment when the clown pops out still makes your heart skip a beat. You know it's coming, but it still gets you every time! Watch the face of a small child at that fateful moment. Notice how the expression of fear melts almost immediately into a smile of delight. That's the real magic of this toy, not the scare in itself, but the delicious relief of knowing that the danger has passed.

D TAKE NOTES **Read the texts again. Take notes in your notebook on what the different stories say about each topic below.**

the funny side of fear | the exploitation of fear | how humans react to fear

E THINK CRITICALLY **What fears or phobias do you have? How serious are they? Why do you think we are so fascinated by fear? Why do some people enjoy being scared more than others?**

2 WRITING

A Read this paragraph about one of the topics in exercise 1D. Which topic is it? Which stories in exercise 1C does it draw information from? Does it cover all the information given in the stories?

> Fear is a basic human emotion. We feel it at all ages. Even though our reactions can vary in intensity and different events can trigger the reaction, the basic physical response is always the same. Fear can be prompted by relatively simple events. A sudden noise or movement can startle us and set off a chain of physical reactions, even when there is no actual danger. Once the fear has passed, the body relaxes, and we can even laugh at our reaction.

B **PARAPHRASE** Compare the language used in the stories with the language used in the paragraph above. Underline the paraphrases – information from the original text that is stated in different words. Highlight the information in the original texts.

WRITE IT

C **PLAN** You're going to write two short paragraphs – one on each of the other topics in exercise 1D. With a partner, follow the steps to prepare:

- Review your notes on the topics in exercise 1D.
- Highlight information in the stories in exercise 1C that relates to each topic.
- Discuss how you could paraphrase the information.
- Review the model paragraph in exercise 2A. How does it start? How does it end? How does the writer paraphrase the information from the stories in the paragraph?

D Write your two paragraphs. Be sure to include paraphrased information from the stories in exercise 1C.

E **PAIR WORK** Read your first paragraph to your partner. How many of the stories did your partner refer to? Did they paraphrase the information well? Then read your second paragraphs to each other and evaluate them also. Which topic did you each find more difficult to write about? Why?

6.5

TIME TO SPEAK
Planning a surprise

LESSON OBJECTIVE
- prepare a surprise for somebody

A **Look at the picture with a partner. If this was a surprise present for you, what would you hope was inside? What pleasant surprises have you experienced in your life?**

B **RESEARCH** **You are going to plan a pleasant surprise for another pair of students. It doesn't have to be realistic, but it should be something you truly think both of the people would like. Use the topics below and your own ideas to come up with interview questions.**

experience of past surprises
fears / phobias / allergies
interests / hobbies / abilities
response to being startled or scared
"wish list" ideas (places they want to go to, etc.)

C **DECIDE** **Interview the other pair. Discuss their responses and come up with a plan. Write notes for yourself about the key elements and why you chose them. Use the example to help you.**

<u>Surprise for Pavel and Manny:</u> A diving vacation in Madeira
<u>Madeira:</u> P loves scuba, M wants to learn
famous for diving; lots of diving schools
M spks Portuguese
Nice weather all year
<u>2-BR apt:</u> P likes to cook (can't in hotel)
M can bring wife (also wants to learn to scuba)
<u>5 days:</u> both have busy jobs

D **PRESENT** **Tell the class about the surprise you planned. Be sure to reference the other pair's responses to explain your choices. Let the intended recipients ask questions to clarify points. Then ask them to give your plan a rating from 1 (not a good plan) to 10 (excellent plan).**

E **AGREE** **As a class, review which pairs got the highest ratings on their surprise plans from the intended recipients. What did they do that the lower-rated pairs didn't do? If you could pick whatever surprise you wanted for yourself, which one would you choose? Why?**

To check your progress, go to page 154.

USEFUL PHRASES

RESEARCH
We should ask if they prefer …
A good question would be, "How do you feel about … ?"
Let's be sure to ask about …

PRESENT
The reason why we chose X is because …
The best thing about this surprise is …
They can … whenever they want.

REVIEW 2 (UNITS 4–6)

1 VOCABULARY

A **Complete the paragraph with the correct words.**

abandoned impact anonymous elaborate source filthy motivated mammoth eye to eye blind

I've worked as a freelancer for years. Like everything, there are pros and cons, but working from home has had a positive [1] ________________ on my health. I used to work in an open office with hundreds of people in it. The atmosphere felt so [2] ________________, like nobody even knew who you were or what you did. It didn't help that I never saw [3] ________________ with my boss, either. I didn't like him, and he didn't like me. My coworkers came in late and left early all the time, and he just turned a [4] ________________ eye to it. But if I was five minutes late, he yelled at me.

Now, I'm my own boss. No more [5] ________________, complicated management structure. Just me. No more [6] ________________ room full of unhappy people. Just a comfortable little office next to the living room. And it's clean, too – the bathrooms at my old office were [7] ________________. At first, I worried that I might feel lonely, [8] ________________, isolated. But then I realized that a big [9] ________________ of stress at my old job was other people. Working alone is great, and it has [10] ________________ me to do more things socially, which is also great. I should have quit that awful job years earlier!

B PAIR WORK **Discuss other advantages of working from home. What disadvantages can you think of?**

2 GRAMMAR

A **Use the words in parentheses ( ) to combine the sentences into one.**

1 I have a lot of nice coworkers. I've known many of them for quite a while. (whom)

2 I do lots of different tasks at work. Different skills are required for every task. (each)

3 I receive a lot of emails. I don't even read most of them. (the majority)

4 I used to work in restaurants. As a result, I know what goes on in those kitchens! (Having)

5 I live alone. The last thing I want to do is work alone, too. (Living)

6 I was excited to see my name in the paper. I didn't even notice that it was misspelled. (So excited)

B PAIR WORK **Look at the sentences in exercise 2A again. Which are true for you or somebody you know? Share your stories.**

3 VOCABULARY

A **Circle the correct words to complete the story.**

I have to tell you this story about the day I got lost. We were in a remote place in the Amazon. I was [1]*genuinely surprised / visibly shaken* when the guides told me our route because it didn't seem to be the usual path. But I was an experienced hiker, though perhaps a little [2]*overworked / overconfident*. The landscape was beautiful and [3]*barren / lush*, but it was hard to see under the trees. These two factors [4]*resulted in / motivated* me getting separated from the group. Also, I had [5]*overestimated / underestimated* how quickly it gets dark in the jungle. But I have to say I stayed [6]*utterly upset / remarkably calm*. I was sure the group would soon realize I wasn't with them and come find me.

One day later, I was still alone. By then I had become [7]*understandably anxious / noticeably shocked*: I was lost in this [8]*vast / picturesque* jungle, and I was starting to believe that nobody would ever find me. Just as the sun was starting to go down, I heard voices. It was the search party! The feeling of relief was [9]*overwhelming / overrated*, and I was so happy to see them I couldn't speak. My rescuers were so nice and [10]*visibly unusual / immensely helpful*. They gave me a blanket and food and water, and they made me feel safe and secure immediately.

B PAIR WORK **Has anyone you know ever gotten lost in a remote place? How did they feel? How did it all turn out?**

4 GRAMMAR

A **Complete the sentences with an appropriate word or phrase from the box. More than one answer may be possible.**

however	the reason	the thing	what	whatever	wherever

1 ______ I never expected was to speak English so well.
2 ______ you live, English is an important language.
3 ______ I like about my hometown is people are so friendly.
4 Say ______ you want about politicians, but I just don't trust them.
5 ______ I'd like to live abroad is that it would widen my horizons.
6 ______ expensive it is, traveling is worth it.

B PAIR WORK **Do you agree with the statements above? Why or why not? Change the underlined parts and make new statements with your own ideas.**

UNIT OBJECTIVES

- discuss the growing interest in DNA testing and genealogy
- talk about celebrations in your family and community
- share a story about visiting a place with special significance
- summarize information about a topic
- present a plan to promote a cultural celebration

ROOTS

7

START SPEAKING

A **Look at the picture. How are the people probably related? Which of your relatives are you most similar to physically? Are you similar in other ways, too (style, personality, gestures, etc.)?**

B **How many generations of your family have you met? How much family history do you know? What or who would you like to know more about? Why?**

C **Does everyone in your family come from the same area? If not, where do (or did) they come from? Where do they live now? For ideas, watch Andrea's video.**

EXPERT SPEAKER

How is your family similar to Andrea's?

7.1 IT'S IN THE BLOOD

LESSON OBJECTIVE

- discuss the growing interest in DNA testing and genealogy

1 LANGUAGE IN CONTEXT

A **What does the graphic show? Why do you think people want to know information like this? Would you like to have your DNA tested? Why or why not?**

B **Read the article. Whose results are shown in the pie chart above? Why did the two people decide to take the test? How do they each feel about their results? What do you think your reaction would be?**

DNA Results

- **52%** Southern Europe
- **21%** Southeast Asia
- **15%** Native American
- **2%** Neanderthal
- **10%** Other regions

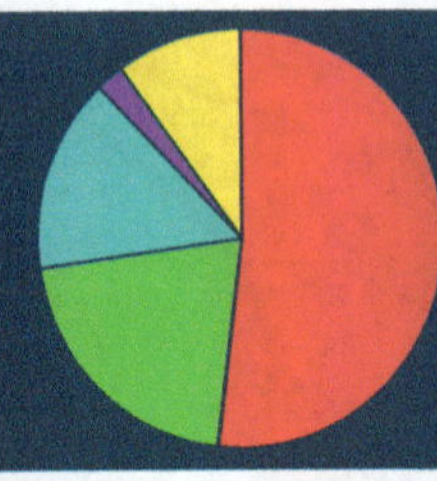

! *DNA* = deoxyribonucleic acid, a chemical in the cells of living things that contains genetic information

What's so great about your DNA?

DNA **ancestry** kits are all the rage these days, with companies in fierce competition to provide the cheapest, most accurate, most detailed information about a person's **genetic** history. But what do people really gain from this information?

CRISTIANO | 40, Texas

My wife gave me the kit as a birthday present. No way would I have done it otherwise. I already knew a lot about my family's **heritage**, so I sent off my sample for testing and forgot about it. Little did I know how fascinating my results would be! My father's family goes back to Italy, and my mother's family has Native American roots, but never had I imagined that I had **ancestors** from Asia, nor that I'm 2% Neanderthal! Now I'm hooked on **genealogy** – and my wife wishes she'd bought me a tie.

SABINE | 22, Quebec

I was adopted as a baby, and we only have a little information about my birth mother. I thought the DNA test might help answer some questions. My dark skin comes from my mother, but who did I **inherit** these green eyes from? I was excited to learn more, but only when the results arrived did I realize how little my **ethnic** background really matters. Not until then did I fully appreciate my wonderful **adoptive** parents. I can now say that my background is mainly Afro-Caribbean with a touch of French, but so what? I am who I am because of my upbringing. That's far more important than genes.

INSIDER ENGLISH

a touch of = a small amount of

2 VOCABULARY: Talking about ancestry

A 2.02 **Use the bold words in the article to complete the word families. Then listen to check your work.**

Abstract nouns	Nouns	Verbs	Adjectives
adoption		adopt	adoptive / adopted
________	________		ancestral
ethnicity			________
________	genes		________
________		________	hereditary

B **Now go to page 147. Do the vocabulary exercises for 7.1.**

C PAIR WORK THINK CRITICALLY **Which do you think has a greater influence on who a person is, upbringing or genes? Why? What examples can you think of to support your ideas?**

3 GRAMMAR: Negative and limiting adverbials

A **Read the sentences in the grammar box. Complete the rules.**

Negative and limiting adverbials

No way would I have done it otherwise.

Little did I know how fascinating my results would be!

Never had I imagined that I had ancestors from Asia.

Only when the results arrived did I realize how little my ethnic background matters.

Not until then did I fully appreciate my wonderful adoptive parents.

To add emphasis, you can start a sentence with a negative or limiting adverbial phrase.

1 Examples of negative adverbials include *No way*, *Never*, and ______________ .

2 Examples of limiting adverbials include __________ *did* … and *Only when* ….

3 When a sentence starts with a negative or limiting adverbial phrase, the word order in the verb phrase changes so that the auxiliary verb for that tense comes before the __________ .

4 When the verb is simple present or simple past, it expands to include the auxiliary verb *do*/*does* or __________ .

B **Now go to page 134. Look at the grammar chart and do the grammar exercise for 7.1.**

C PAIR WORK **Find and correct the mistakes in the sentences. Check your accuracy. What additional uses of the information from DNA tests does each sentence describe? Discuss with a partner.**

1 Not only you can find out about your ancestors, you can also learn about possible hereditary health influences.

2 Only when you subscribe you get a full report about possible previously unknown relatives.

3 Little realize people that they're giving away their full genetic code, which might be shared with other organizations.

✓ ACCURACY CHECK

When the verb is in the simple present, remember to include *do*/*does*.

Little ~~they know~~ what awaits them. ✗

Little do they know what awaits them. ✓

4 SPEAKING

A GROUP WORK THINK CRITICALLY **What might be some of the disadvantages of having your DNA tested? Make a list of questions to ask a DNA testing service.**

B **Share your questions with the class and discuss them.**

We wondered about privacy. Can anybody see my genetic information? I mean, no way would I want total strangers to have detailed information about my ethnic heritage!

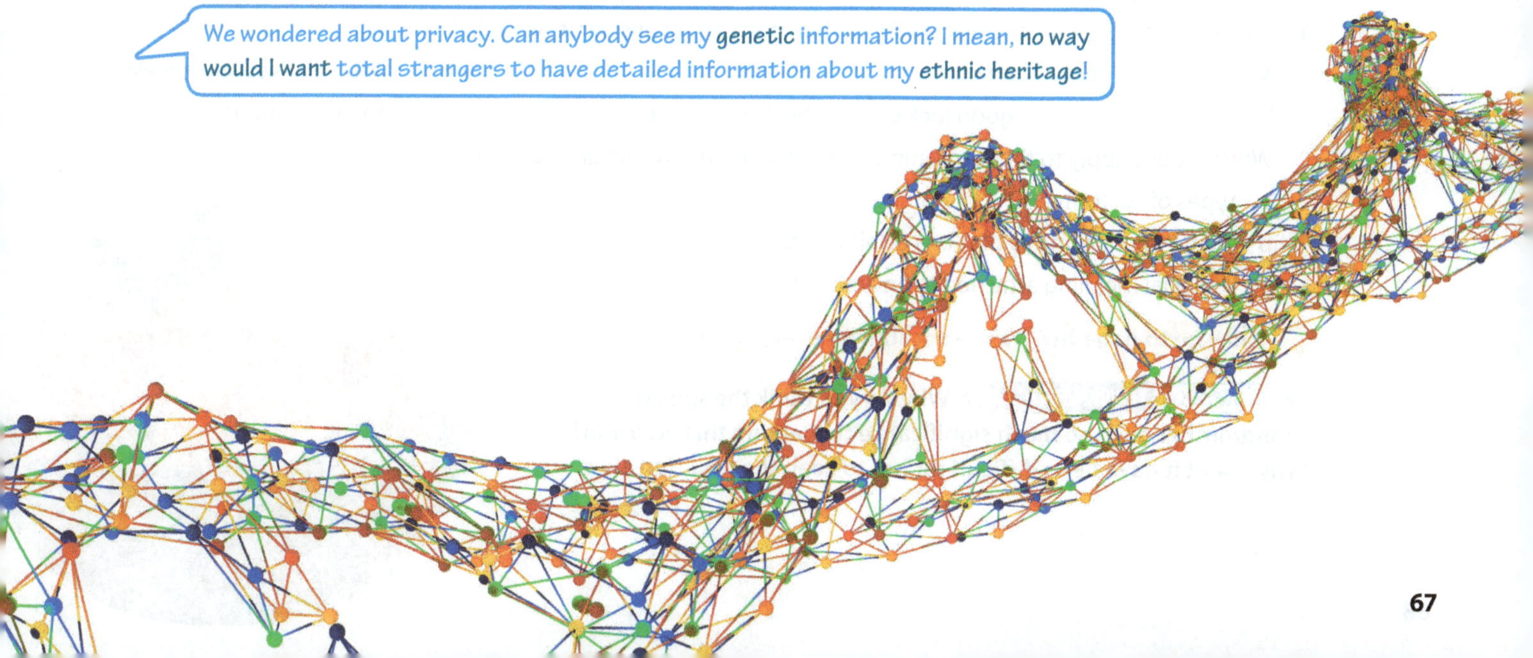

7.2 A VERY SPECIAL OCCASION

LESSON OBJECTIVE

- talk about celebrations in your family and community

1 LANGUAGE IN CONTEXT

A 2.03 **Look at the pictures. What celebration do these things relate to? What culture uses them? Listen to part of a podcast to check your answers. Does the speaker enjoy this occasion?**

2.03 Audio script

On the table sits an enormous bowl of oranges and tangerines – they **symbolize** wealth. Around the walls hang red and gold decorations – they **signify** good luck. And through the kitchen door wafts the delicious smell of fresh dumplings. It's Chinese New Year, and we're all at my grandmother's house to **mark** the occasion and take part in the **festivities.**

My grandmother's been preparing for this moment for days. First, she cleaned the house from top to bottom. This **ritual** sweeps away past bad luck. Then she decorated with lanterns and banners that wish everyone good fortune and good health!

Everywhere I look I see red – the main color for any Chinese celebration because it's supposed to bring good luck. On the red tablecloth in the dining room lies a stack of red envelopes. In the envelopes are crisp new dollar bills. The older generations give these to the younger members of the family. This **practice** has a special **significance**, reminding the younger generation of the debt they owe their elders.

My grandmother came to the United States as a child, but she works hard to **keep** our traditions **alive**. That's why it's so important that we're all here today to **observe** the ancient **rites**, to **honor** our grandmother and heritage, and to **pay tribute to** all our ancestors.

B 2.03 PAIR WORK **Listen again and read. In the speaker's culture, what's the significance of cleaning the house? The color red? The envelopes of money? What are some things associated with a celebration that you enjoy?**

INSIDER ENGLISH

***from top to bottom* = very thoroughly**

2 VOCABULARY: Talking about customs and traditions

A 2.04 PAIR WORK **Look at the bold words in the script and use them to answer the questions below. Listen and check. Can you think of an example from your life or family for each answer?**

1 Which verbs match these objects? (More than one correct answer is possible.)

a *mark, observe* an occasion

b ______ good luck or good health

c ______ older relatives and ancestors

d ______ family traditions

2 Which nouns apply to these meanings? (More than one correct answer is possible.)

a types of customs: ______

b all the things done as part of a celebration: ______

c a special meaning attached to an action or object: ______

B Now go to page 147. Do the vocabulary exercises for 7.2.

C PAIR WORK THINK CRITICALLY **Why do you think the speaker's grandmother gives so much significance to marking this occasion? Why might it have been difficult for her to keep the tradition alive?**

3 GRAMMAR: Fronting adverbials

A Read the sentences in the grammar box. Then complete the rules below.

Fronting adverbials

Through the kitchen door wafts the delicious smell of fresh dumplings.

On the red tablecloth lies a stack of red envelopes.

In the envelopes are crisp new dollar bills.

1 To add dramatic effect, you can bring adverbials of place or movement to **the front** / **the end** of a sentence.

2 The subject and verb of the main clause change position when …

- the verb is *be*.
- the verb indicates placement, like *sit* or ___________ .
- the verb indicates movement, like *fly* or ___________ .

B Now go to page 135. Look at the grammar chart and do the grammar exercise for 7.2.

C PAIR WORK **Add dramatic effect by bringing the adverbials in bold to the front of the sentence. Make any changes to word order that are needed, and check your accuracy. What occasion do you think is being described?**

1 Sounds of laughter and scents of cooking come **from the kitchen.**

2 A huge turkey sits **in the oven** slowly roasting.

3 Three generations of the family wait **in the dining room**, ready to eat!

4 We hear the distant sounds of a football game **from the TV in the living room.**

ACCURACY CHECK

In a sentence with a <u>direct object</u>, such as *We found <u>family portraits</u> in the library*, the word order does NOT change when there is a fronting adverbial.

In the library ~~found we~~ family portraits. ✗

In the library we found family portraits. ✓

4 SPEAKING

A GROUP WORK THINK CRITICALLY **Discuss the questions.**

- What rites usually bring your family members together, even those who live far away?
- Why do people make so much effort to observe rites, rituals, and customs? What significance do they hold?
- What rituals does your family observe around specific occasions? Do you have any rituals that are unique to your family? What are they?

*In my family, we **mark** every birthday with a party. My mom decorates the whole house, and it's beautiful!*

B **Do you enjoy big family get-togethers? Why or why not? For ideas, watch Andrea's video.**

EXPERT SPEAKER

Why do you think Andrea mentions her children?

7.3 THE STORY OF A RETURNEE

LESSON OBJECTIVE
- share a story about visiting a place with special significance

1 LISTENING

A 2.05 **Look at the pictures from Katerina's trip. Where do you think she went? Why do you think she went there? Listen to Katerina being interviewed about the trip. Were you right?**

B 2.05 PAIR WORK LISTEN FOR ATTITUDE **How did the following things affect Katerina? How does she feel looking back on the experience? How do you know? Discuss your ideas with a partner. Listen again to check your answers.**

- the way it looked
- meeting her relatives
- the food

FIND IT

C 2.05 PAIR WORK DEDUCE MEANING **What do you think these words and phrases from the interview mean? Listen again and use the context to help you figure them out. Write your definitions. Then use a dictionary or your phone to check your answers.**

1 You can say that again! ______________________
2 idyllic: ______________________
3 harbor: ______________________
4 exhausting: ______________________
5 frantically: ______________________
6 a stone's throw: ______________________

D GROUP WORK THINK CRITICALLY **Join another pair of students and discuss the questions.**

- Do you know anyone like Katerina, who has roots in more than one culture? How did they end up where they are? Do they still have relatives in the other culture(s)? Do they ever visit them there?
- What are some of the advantages and disadvantages of coming from a bicultural background?

2 PRONUNCIATION: Listening for missing /t/ and /d/ sounds

A 2.06 PAIR WORK **Listen to the sentences. Which of the underlined /t/ and /d/ sounds are pronounced? Circle them. Compare with a partner.**

1 I have to admit, it's a little weird, as well. It's difficult to put into words.
2 Especially visiting my grandparents' village. I mean, they told me so many stories about this village that I'd built this kind of idyllic picture of it in my mind.

B 2.07 PAIR WORK **Listen to the sentences. Which of the underlined /t/ and /d/ sounds are not pronounced? ~~Cross~~ them out. Compare with a partner.**

1 Sounds intriguing. Tell us about seeing the place for the first time, your first impressions.
2 I think I can understand that. And did you meet your cousins that day?
3 That was the best part! It was like being back in my grandmother's kitchen.
4 The food and the setting just went together.

C **Circle the correct words to complete the sentence.**

When /t/ and /d/ sounds come [1]*in the middle / at the end* of three consonants, [2]*except for / including* between words, they are often left out.

3 SPEAKING SKILLS

A **PAIR WORK** **Read the expressions in the chart aloud. How do the expressions within each set relate to each other? Match each set to a heading in the box and write it in.**

Commenting on your own story | Expressing an opinion | Responding to someone else's story

______________	______________	______________
I have to admit, ….	I can see how it would be strange.	It's difficult to put into words.
To tell you the truth, …	I think I can understand that.	It's hard to describe.
To be (perfectly) honest, …	How did you handle that?	It's difficult to say why exactly.
Don't get me wrong, …	It must have been pretty overwhelming.	That was the best part!
	It can't have been easy.	… if you know what I mean.

B **PAIR WORK** **Think of a personal story about one of the topics below. Use phrases from the chart above as you tell your partner the story. Respond to your partner's story as you listen.**

The first time you were the center of attention at an event

The first time you met someone in person that you had heard or read a lot about

4 PRONUNCIATION: Saying diphthongs

A 2.08 **Listen for the diphthongs in each word. How many sounds do you hear for each one?**

/eɪ/ str<u>a</u>nge /aɪ/ descr<u>i</u>be /ɔɪ/ disapp<u>oi</u>ntment /oʊ/ <u>o</u>verwhelming /aʊ/ backgr<u>ou</u>nd

B 2.09 **PAIR WORK** **Unscramble the sounds into words and circle the diphthongs. Listen and check. Then work with a partner and use the sounds to make at least one other word with the same diphthong.**

1 en / ʃən / dʒ / ə / r / eɪ ___dʒenəreɪʃən – *generation*___ ___/reɪdʒ/ – *rage*___

2 tɪn / aʊ / n / m ______________ ______________

3 aɪ / s / ə / t̬ / iː / s / ə ______________ ______________

4 m / ɪ / əʳ / p / l / ɔɪ / r ______________ ______________

5 p / n / v / g / r / eɪ / aɪ ______________ ______________

6 g / b / æ / d / k / aʊ / n / r ______________ ______________

7 eɪ / f / ɪ / æ / ŋ / sɪn / t ______________ ______________

8 r / b / əʳ / ɑː / k / oʊ / t ______________ ______________

C **PAIR WORK** **Write the new words you made above on a separate piece of paper, but scramble the sounds. Give your list to another pair of students. Can they figure out your words?**

5 SPEAKING

A **Think about a time when you visited a place that holds significance for your family or met relatives for the first time.**

- What things felt familiar? What things felt strange?
- Were you disappointed, or did reality exceed your expectations? Why?

B **GROUP WORK** **Tell your stories and comment as you listen.**

They kept asking me if I remembered all these people and places. I didn't want to be rude, but to be honest, I didn't remember anything!

I can see how that would be awkward.

7.4 WHEN A LANGUAGE DIES

LESSON OBJECTIVE
- summarize information about a topic

1 READING

A **Look at the graph. What does it tell us about world languages? What information do you find the most interesting or surprising?**

B READ FOR MAIN IDEAS **Read the three texts below. Match them to the correct main ideas.**

a Minority languages should be saved. ___
b Minority languages should be allowed to die out. ___
c The story of a minority language ___

Write an appropriate title for each text based on its main idea.

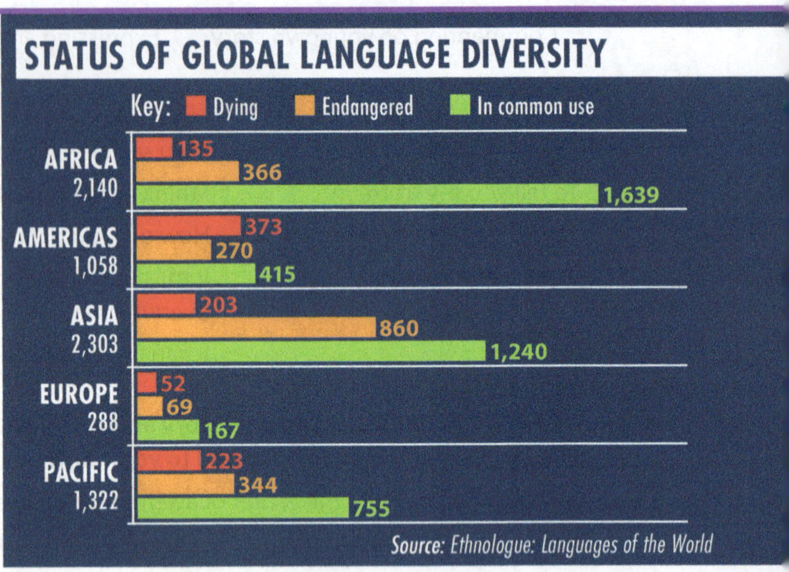

1 ___

A few years ago a compelling story was circulating on the internet. The last two speakers of the language Ayapaneco didn't like each other and had refused to talk to each other for decades. This ancient language was destined to die out, all because of the stubbornness of two old men!

Social media fanned the flames of the story, and it went viral – even taken up as part of an advertising campaign for a phone company. But of course, the story was too good to be true. Yes, their language was in danger, but they were not the only people who spoke it. And though the two men weren't the best of friends, neither were they giving each other the silent treatment.

Though the story may be false, the true tale is still worth telling. The two old men, along with other members of their family and community, were giving language lessons to the children in the village. The number of speakers had more than doubled in a few years. Far from losing their linguistic heritage, they had actually managed to save it!

Source: Schwa Fire

2 ___

There are about 7,000 living languages spoken around the world today. That might seem like a lot, but the number is diminishing. Experts estimate that we now lose a language every two weeks. Many scholars predict that by the end of the 21st century, we will have lost 50–90 percent of all languages spoken today. And each time we lose a language, our collective knowledge of the human experience is reduced.

A language is so much more than a channel for communication. It is the reflection of a unique interpretation of the world. This is especially true of oral languages. Of the 2,400 languages that researchers estimate are in immediate danger of extinction, many have no written form. All the wisdom and knowledge conveyed by those languages is passed from generation to generation through speaking. When the last speakers die, that wisdom dies with them.

Sources: Ethnologue, Day Translations, Pendleton Translations

3 ___

Linguistic landscapes are like ecosystems: They grow and adapt based on need and usage. Some languages blossom and grow; others wither away and die. It's nature's way. As much as I sympathize with speakers of minority languages who are fighting to keep their languages alive, sometimes extinction is inevitable. And when a language ceases to serve the needs of the community, hanging on only in the nostalgic conversations of village elders, then its time has come. The most gracious thing to do at that point is let it die, gently and peacefully.

Rather than desperately striving to breathe life back into dying languages, let us instead honor them by collecting written records, compiling dictionaries, forming academic societies to preserve their history. These are all valid linguistic pursuits that pay tribute to a lost culture but also let it die with dignity.

C PAIR WORK READ FOR ATTITUDE **Read the three texts again. Which writer is the most emotionally engaged? Why do you think so?**

D GROUP WORK THINK CRITICALLY **What are some possible advantages of speaking a minority language? What actions could people take to try to save a language from extinction? Do you think these efforts should be made? Why or why not?**

2 WRITING

A Read the summary of the three texts from exercise 1B. Has the writer fairly captured the main ideas and arguments of all three? Is any key information missing? Does the summary draw on one of the stories more than the others?

> Human-interest stories like the one about the two feuding old men who refused to speak to each other in their dying language draw attention to the issue of minority languages around the world, but they tend to oversimplify the situation. The question of how to save these languages, and whether it's actually worth reviving them, is a complex one. **On one side**, linguists argue that each language embodies a unique view of the world, thus should be saved, **while on the other**, pragmatists point out that when a language dies, it may well be because it is no longer relevant in the world, so its death is natural and should be accepted as such.

REGISTER CHECK

When you're writing a formal summary and synthesizing other people's work, it is not appropriate to let your own opinion or personal bias show. Summaries are only meant to inform the reader.

Human-interest stories like these draw attention to the issue of minority languages.

Opinion pieces are usually intended to inform and persuade.

Human-interest stories like these draw attention to the issue of minority languages, but they tend to oversimplify the situation.

B SUMMARIZE ARGUMENTS Look at the **bold** phrases in the essay above. How do they relate to each other? Rewrite the end of the essay using one of the other parallel structures below.

Some argue that … but others disagree, saying …

While some say … , others feel …

Many claim that … However, others maintain that …

WRITE IT

C GROUP WORK Student A: Go to page 157. Student B: Go to page 160. Student C: Go to page 158. Follow the instructions.

D PLAN You're going to write a paragraph summarizing the main arguments around the value of writing by hand in 100–120 words. Use your notes from exercise 2C and share the key points with your partners. Take notes on the information they share. Review the model paragraph above for structure.

E Write your paragraph, drawing on information in all three texts. Present different perspectives by using parallel structures.

F GROUP WORK With the same two partners, read your paragraphs. Did you all include the same key points? Do you detect any bias or personal opinion in their paragraphs?

7.5 TIME TO SPEAK
Preserving a custom

LESSON OBJECTIVE
- present a plan to promote a cultural celebration

FIND IT

A **DISCUSS** Look at the pictures of Songkran festivities. In small groups, talk about what the people are doing. Where do you think these festivities take place? What might this practice symbolize? Use your phone to go online and learn about it.

B Think of a special occasion or cultural celebration that you know well. Share your personal experiences of it. Recall as many details as possible about its traditions and origins.

FIND IT

C **PREPARE** As a group, choose one of the events you discussed. Put together a plan to promote it on social media and in your community. Try to appeal to people who may not know about it. Choose one or more of the promotional tools from the box. What other tools should you consider? Why? You can look online to get ideas.

competitions	flyers and posters	local celebrity endorsements
local TV and radio spots	social media posts	

D **PRESENT** Divide your plan into sections, one per person in your group, and decide which person will present each part. Practice your part of the presentation within your group. Then present your whole plan to the class.

E **AGREE** As a class, discuss which plans were the most interesting. Which do you think will be most effective? Which event would you personally most like to attend? Why?

To check your progress, go to page 155.

USEFUL PHRASES

DISCUSS

The thing that makes it special for me is …

From every direction come the sounds of …

Not until you take part it in yourself do you fully appreciate the …

PRESENT

In the center of the poster sits a colorful …

It's really important to stress that it's fun for the whole family …

UNIT OBJECTIVES

- discuss distractions and attention spans
- talk about instincts and gut reactions
- describe the best features and selling points of apps
- write presentation slides
- pitch a company, an idea, or a product to investors

8 SHORT

START SPEAKING

A Look at the picture. What do you think is happening? Are all the kids engaged with it? How can you tell? Can you find one child who is not engaged with the activitiy? How can you tell?

B How long can you stay focused on an activity if it's something you want to do? How about if you don't want to do it? Think of some examples for both scenarios.

C What techniques do you use to stay focused on a task? Do you know of any others? For ideas, watch Eric's video.

EXPERT SPEAKER

What do you think of Eric's techniques?

8.1 THE ATTENTION SPAN MYTH

LESSON OBJECTIVE
- discuss distractions and attention spans

1 LANGUAGE IN CONTEXT

> “You now have the attention span of a goldfish.”
>
> TIME magazine (May 2015)

A 2.10 **Look at the picture and the quote. What do you think it means? Listen to an editorial about this idea. Were you right?**

2.10 Audio script

I have something to say, but you'll probably stop listening before I get to it. I know this because we humans have very short attention spans. It's true – well, according to *TIME* magazine. It seems we can't get anything done because we constantly **get interrupted** – by text messages, shopping alerts, that *ding* that says someone just updated their status – and find it impossible to **avoid distractions**.

According to the experts, our ability to **concentrate** is getting eaten away by technology and the tempting **distractions** it offers. It is increasingly difficult for us to **get focused** and **stay focused** for any length of time. In fact, your average person **loses focus** in just eight seconds – about the same as your average goldfish.

A goldfish? Really? I don't buy it. And neither does Dr. Gemma Briggs, a psychology professor who studies attention span and the things that **distract** us. In a television interview, she said, “How much attention we apply to a task will vary depending on what the task demand is,” that is, on how difficult a task is to do.

This got me thinking about all the things demanding my attention these days – my job, the kids, the dog, not to mention my fantasy football team. Frankly, I'm a master of task-demand management. We all are. Our powers of **concentration** are stronger than ever because they have to be!

Take that, goldfish.

INSIDER ENGLISH

I don't buy it. **= I don't believe it's true.**

B 2.10 PAIR WORK THINK CRITICALLY **Listen again and read. Why does the speaker think our powers of concentration have improved? Do you agree with him? Why or why not?**

2 VOCABULARY: Talking about attention and distraction

A 2.11 PAIR WORK **Look at the bold words and phrases in the audio script. What do you think they mean? Use them to complete the chart below. Listen and check.**

Nouns	Verbs	Phrases
concentration	________	
________	________	be / get distracted (by) ________ distractions
________	focus (on)	get / ________ focused (on) lose focus
interruption	interrupt	be / ________ ________ (by)

B **Now go to page 148. Do the vocabulary exercises for 8.1.**

C PAIR WORK **Discuss the questions.**

1 What thing(s) do you find most distracting? Why?
2 What tasks require a lot of concentration for you? What happens when you get interrupted?
3 How do you avoid distraction when you need to concentrate? Does it work?

My phone is my main distraction. I get interrupted by messages and alerts all the time.

3 GRAMMAR: Phrases with *get*

A **Read the sentences in the grammar box and notice the bold phrases. Then circle the correct options to complete the rules. Match each rule to a sentence.**

Phrases with *get*

A We can't **get anything done** because we constantly get interrupted.

B Our ability to concentrate **is getting eaten away** by technology.

C It is increasingly difficult for us to **get focused** and stay focused.

D This **got me thinking** about all the things demanding my attention.

The verb *get* is often used with other verbs. It can express different things depending on form and context.

1 To describe the completion of a task, use *get* + noun/pronoun + … Sentence ___
   a past participle b verb + *-ing*

2 To describe the changing state of something/somebody, use *get* + … Sentence ___
   a past participle b verb + *-ing*

3 To explain that something/somebody is prompting action, use *get* + noun/pronoun + … Sentence ___
   a past participle b verb + *-ing*

4 To describe a process in the passive, use *get* instead of *be*: *get* + noun/pronoun + … (+ *by* …) Sentence ___
   a past participle b verb + *-ing*

B **Now go to page 135. Look at the grammar chart and do the grammar exercise for 8.1.**

C PAIR WORK **Rephrase the sentences using a *get* phrase. Which ones could you restate using *have* instead of *get*? Check your accuracy.**

1 I promise to answer your questions by the end of the day.
2 He has hired a professional designer to redecorate our new offices.
3 The interview made me wonder if I was the right person for the job.
4 I am becoming very frustrated with this computer program!

✓ ACCURACY CHECK

To show that someone else will do a task, you can use *get* or *have*. If the subject is doing the action, however, use *get* only.

He can't ~~have~~ the printer to work. ✗
He can't get the printer to work. ✓
He's going to get / have it repaired. ✓

4 SPEAKING

A PAIR WORK **When you have a long to-do list, how do you prioritize the tasks? Do you stay focused and finish them all at once? What distractions or interruptions do you usually have to deal with? For ideas, watch Eric's video.**

EXPERT SPEAKER

How could Eric avoid his biggest distraction?

B **Share your experiences with the class. What gets done first on your to-do list? What, if you're honest, never gets done? Why?**

I like to **get the laundry done** on Sunday so I have clean clothes for the week. All the other jobs can **get pushed** to Monday or Tuesday.

8.2 GUT REACTION

LESSON OBJECTIVE
- talk about instincts and gut reactions

1 LANGUAGE IN CONTEXT

A **Look at the title of the article and read the quote. What do you think the article is about? Read the article and check your answer.**

HOME NEWS BLOG CONTACT US

SPLIT-SECOND THINKING

In his best-selling book, *Blink: The Power of Thinking Without Thinking*, Malcolm Gladwell tells the story of a museum that wanted to buy an ancient Greek statue. The price was almost $10 million, so the museum got the statue checked out carefully. After more than a year of investigation, everyone agreed that the statue was genuine, and the museum got the go-ahead for the purchase.

Before they bought it, however, another art historian took one look at the statue and immediately declared that it was fake. And he was right! As Gladwell points out, sometimes all it takes is one person's intuition to get it right. And as can be seen from this example, there really is something to be said for "split-second thinking."

Gladwell refers to this idea as "thin-slicing" – making a big judgment based on a first impression. What he is getting at is the idea that initial instincts – *hunches* – have value. As we can all attest, split-second decisions are often more accurate than those we spend hours debating and getting frustrated over. People are often suspicious of this idea at first, but when they see the research, they get blown away by just how reliable a hunch can be.

But let's get one thing straight: Gladwell is not saying that *all* first impressions prove to be right, just that we shouldn't dismiss them. We should get accustomed to listening to ourselves and taking our gut reactions seriously.

> "There can be as much value in the blink of an eye as in months of rational analysis."
> *Malcolm Gladwell*

FIND IT

B PAIR WORK **Read the article again. How many different expressions does the writer use to refer to "thinking without thinking"? List them. Use a dictionary or your phone to look up any terms you don't know.**

2 VOCABULARY: Expressions with *get*

A 2.12 PAIR WORK **Listen to the expressions in the box. Then answer the questions.**

get accustomed to	get at	get attached to	get blown away by
get complicated	get frustrated	get lost	get rid of
get something right	get something straight	get the go-ahead	

1 Which expressions are used in the article? Underline them.

2 Can you guess the meaning of the ones you don't know from the individual words?

3 In which expressions does *get* mean "become"? Circle them.

B **Now go to page 148. Do the vocabulary exercises for 8.2.**

C PAIR WORK THINK CRITICALLY **What do you think about Gladwell's "thin-slicing" idea? Do you agree that it's a good thing? Give examples to support your ideas.**

*I think it's good to **get accustomed** to trusting your instincts, even if you don't **get things right** all the time.*

3 GRAMMAR: Phrases with *as*

A **Read the sentences in the grammar box and notice the bold phrases. Then complete the rules with the words in the box.**

> **Phrases with *as***
>
> **As Gladwell points out**, sometimes all it takes is one person's intuition.
>
> **As can be seen from this example**, there really is something to be said for "split-second thinking."
>
> **As we can all attest**, split-second decisions are often more accurate.

evidence | illustrate | imagine | passive | statement

1. Phrases with *as* are used to support a ________________ by referring to statistics, ________________, or shared experience or knowledge.
2. We often use phrases with *as* in the ________________ to simplify and reduce introductory information, especially in formal writing or presentations.
3. When a phrase with *as* refers to the reader/listener, we often use these verbs: *attest, guess,* ________________, *infer, see.*
4. When a phrase with *as* refers to some type of support, we often use these verbs: *explain,* ________________, *indicate, point out, present, show, underline.*

B **Now go to page 136. Do the grammar exercise for 8.2.**

C PAIR WORK **Look back at the audio script on page 76. Summarize the main points using phrases with *as*.**

As presented in the article in TIME magazine, research suggests that a human's attention span is now shorter than that of a goldfish.

4 SPEAKING

A PAIR WORK **Think about different decisions: ordering food, choosing a vacation destination, shopping for clothes, etc. Do you usually go with your gut reaction? Why or why not?**

B PAIR WORK THINK CRITICALLY **How do you make big decisions? Explain your process. Does it always result in the best choice?**

Whenever I need new sneakers, I line up my options on the bench in the store. Then I get rid of the ones that are too expensive. Next, I . . .

8.3 IT'S THE APP YOU NEED

LESSON OBJECTIVE

- describe the best features and selling points of apps

1 LISTENING

A PAIR WORK **Look at the app on the computer screen. It's designed to control other apps. How and why do you think it might do this?**

B 2.13 LISTEN FOR MAIN POINTS **Listen to a conversation between Andrea, an app designer, and her friend Will. Were you right about the Focus app? How does it work?**

C 2.13 LISTEN FOR DETAILS **Listen again and write specific information about the topics in the chart.**

Topic	Details
A website blacklist	
The purpose of "locked mode"	
Target market	
The latest update	

D PAIR WORK **Compare your charts. Did you both note the same details? Think about the app as Andrea describes it. Do you think it would work for you? Would you like to try it? Why or why not?**

INSIDER ENGLISH

go off the rails **= not go as planned**

stay on track **= go according to plan**

2 PRONUNCIATION: Listening for long word groups

A 2.14 **A *word group* has one main stress, and it is separated from the next word group by a slight pause. How many word groups are in the extracts?**

1 Is that the think tank you were telling me about?

2 Then you create a "blacklist" of sites or tools that distract you the most.

3 No other app on the market offers a feature like this.

B 2.15 PAIR WORK **Listen and write down the number of words in each word group. Then listen again and write down all the words.**

1 ___ ______________

2 ___ ______________

3 ___ ______________

4 ___ ______________

5 ___ ______________

6 ___ ______________

C **Check (✓) the correct sentence.**

☐ **a** Long word groups contain both stressed and unstressed words, and there is one tone movement.

☐ **b** All the words in long word groups are unstressed, and there are several tone movements.

3 SPEAKING SKILLS

A 2.13 PAIR WORK **Listen to Andrea and Will's conversation again and complete the phrases for speaking persuasively.**

Speak persuasively about a product

1 **It** ________ **users to** block distractions.
2 **That's the** ________ ________ **of** this new app.
3 **The** ________ ________ **is**, with this app, you can …
4 **What the app also** ________ **is** a way to …
5 **Our** ________ **is to** make this as customizable as possible.
6 **We're** ________ **to give users** all the flexibility they could possibly want.
7 ________ ________ ________ **on the market offers** a feature like this.
8 This **is a great** ________ **to** remove that temptation …
9 **You won't want to** ________ ________ **on** this great product.
10 **We're** ________ ________ keeping you on track …

B PAIR WORK **Think of an app that you really like and use regularly. Explain its best features and main selling points to your partner. Ask questions to learn more.**

I use an app called Skyscanner to find flights. Its main aim is to make searching for the right flight really easy.

What's its best selling point?

I'd say the route finder tool …

4 PRONUNCIATION: Saying primary and secondary word stress

A 2.16 **Listen to the words. Circle the primary stress and underline the secondary stress.**

1 opportunity
2 application
3 customizable
4 flexibility
5 automatically
6 notification

B 2.17 **Choose the correct primary and secondary stress pattern. Listen and check.**

1 a destination b destination
2 a technological b technological
3 a responsibility b responsibility
4 a interruption b interruption
5 a concentration b concentration
6 a intuition b intuition

C PAIR WORK **Complete the sentences with one of the words from exercise 4A or 4B. Read the sentences out loud and discuss them.**

1 People in the past had better ________ because there were fewer distractions.
2 Parents have a ________ to make sure their children don't become too dependent on digital devices.
3 The ________ of electronic books makes them more appealing than print books to many customers.
4 Technology means that anyone with internet access has the ________ to get a great education.

5 SPEAKING

A GROUP WORK THINK CRITICALLY **How much time, energy, or money do you think apps really save? If you could only download three apps, what would they be? What purpose(s) would they serve?**

My commuter app doesn't save me time, but it prevents me from getting frustrated because of a late train.

8.4 THE PERFECT PITCH

LESSON OBJECTIVE

- write presentation slides

1 READING

FIND IT

A **PAIR WORK** **Make a list of all the different ways people and companies sell things today. Go online to find even more. Which have you experienced?**

B **Read the title and introduction to the article. What is an "elevator pitch"? Why is it called that? Why is it so important? How is a pitch different from a presentation? Read the rest of the article to check your answers.**

SIX TIPS FOR THE PERFECT PITCH

When you meet a potential investor, it is crucial to be able to get your message across in no more time than it would take to ride up an elevator together. To get your "elevator pitch" just right, take some tips from entrepreneurs who have mastered the art of the perfect pitch.

TIP 1 Keep it short and sweet.

Keep in mind that investors typically watch hundreds of presentations. To stand out from the competition, think of an intriguing mission statement that features your product and states why it is unique. A good example of a catchy mission statement is Google's "to organize the world's information and make it universally accessible." You can't argue with that!

TIP 2 Solve a problem.

Know your potential investor and focus your pitch on their interests. Highlight why *your* company provides a unique solution to a problem they might have. Here, it's important to focus on positive aspects, such as growth and risk protection. This way, you'll anticipate your investor's concerns and give them the answer before they have to ask you.

TIP 3 Practice, practice, practice.

When you speak in public, you need to be confident and sure of your facts. Have everything crystal clear in your mind and anticipate difficult questions or surprising reactions. The best way to do this? Practice as much as you can. The good thing about practicing an elevator pitch is that it's short – you can do it again and again. If you're succinct and get to the point fast, you'll do fine!

TIP 4 Use an analogy.

Pitches often include abstract concepts that can be difficult for people to grasp. An image or an analogy can help explain your idea. A good example comes from Trello, a web-based app that helps organize projects into different boards, like "sticky notes on a wall." This conjures up a familiar image and makes the idea clearer and more accessible.

TIP 5 Read the crowd.

Although you only have a minute or so, it's important to read your audience and react accordingly. There's no point in following your script, however brilliant it might be, if it isn't going well. If things are going off the rails, reshape your pitch based on the signals your audience is giving you. Be spontaneous and respond to the here and now.

TIP 6 Make it personal.

To be truly convincing, you need to talk from the heart. If you don't bring personality and passion into your pitch, your potential investor will lose interest. People don't just invest in an idea or a product, they invest in the people behind it. If you are truly excited about your big new idea, your enthusiasm will get them excited, too.

Follow these tips, and potential investors will know you mean business – in more ways than one!

C **EVALUATE INFORMATION** **Read the article again. Indicate which tips address the different aspects of an elevator pitch below.**

Aspects of an elevator pitch	Tip 1	Tip 2	Tip 3	Tip 4	Tip 5	Tip 6
1 your knowledge of the product or idea	✓	✓	✓			
2 listener interaction						
3 your delivery						
4 content						

D **PAIR WORK** **THINK CRITICALLY** **Which tips do you think apply to any type of public speaking? Which tip(s) do you find most useful for yourself? Why?**

I think practice is important to overcome nerves. If you speak smoothly, it will help your confidence. That's important whenever you speak in public.

2 WRITING

A **PAIR WORK** **Look at two slides from a presentation about the article "Six Tips for the Perfect Pitch." Compare the language used in the original article with the language used in the presentation slides. What are the main differences?**

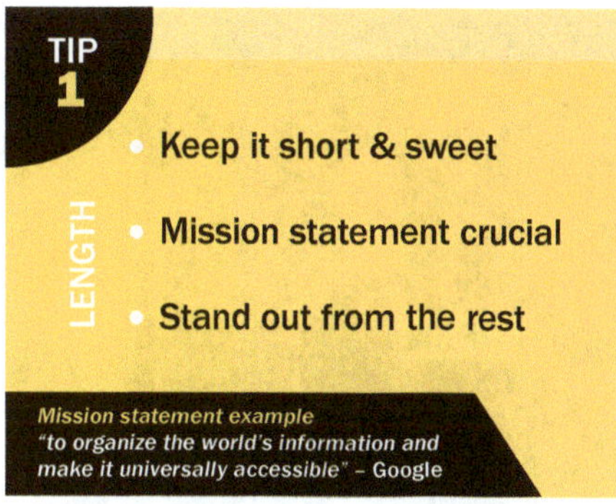

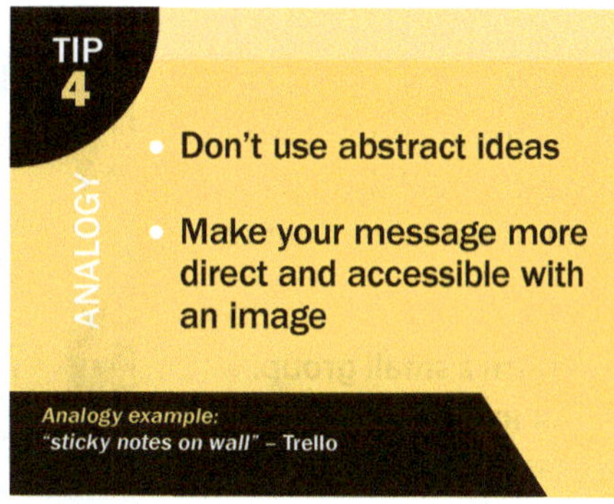

REGISTER CHECK

Written documents tend to use the most formal language.

Think of an intriguing mission statement that features your product and states why it is unique.

Oral presentations are usually more succinct and less formal.

An intriguing mission statement should highlight the product's unique features.

Presentation slides are even more succinct.

- *Mission statement crucial*

B **PAIR WORK** **Think about the different elements of a presentation slide and answer the questions.**

1. Why use bullet points?
2. What is the relationship between the text on the slide and what the presenter says?
3. What are some ways to enliven presentation slides without distracting the viewer from what the speaker is saying?

C **ADAPT CONTENT** **Look at your chart in exercise 1C again, and then complete this slide about the first aspect of a good elevator pitch. Be as succinct as possible. Compare slides with a partner. Which of you was more succinct?**

KNOW YOUR PRODUCT

- Practice!
- Keep it [1] ____________
- Create a [2] ____________
- Anticipate [3] ____________
- Be [4] ____________ of your facts

"To organize the world's information and make it universally accessible" – Google

WRITE IT

FIND IT

D **PLAN** **You're going to create a presentation about the most important aspects of a good elevator pitch. With a partner, compare charts from exercise 1C and resolve any disagreements about how the information in the article relates to the categories in the chart.**

E **Follow the steps to create your presentation. Your slides should contain no more than 120 words total.**

- Make one introduction slide.
- Make four content slides, one for each aspect presented in the chart. (You can use the slide in exercise 2C as your first content slide.) Go online and do some research of your own, if you can.
- Make one ending slide.
- Add images, quotes, and statistics to make your slides more interesting.
- Review the slides from exercise 2A and compare your slides to them. Are your points presented succinctly? Are your slides graphically interesting?

F **GROUP WORK** **Join another pair of students and share your slide presentations. How are your slides similar? How are they different? Whose presentation do you think would be more interesting?**

8.5 TIME TO SPEAK
Make a pitch

LESSON OBJECTIVE
- pitch a company, an idea, or a product to investors

A PREPARE **Look at the picture. With a partner, discuss what had to happen before these entrepreneurs could open their new cafe. Write down all the stages. How much time do you think each stage took? Who did they need to talk to, and why? How much money did it take to get to their big grand opening?**

B **Join another pair of students and form a small group. Compare the stages you thought of in exercise A. Did you both come up with a similar process? Then look at the products below that would likely need investment to get started. Think of more and add them to the list.**

customizable sneakers

a service to help new students set up their dorm rooms

vegan coffee shop near a university

C PLAN **Choose one of the products from exercise B to pitch to investors. Start planning your pitch by identifying key information:**

- the problem(s) that your product/service will solve
- an analogy that will make the idea accessible
- the main selling points of your product/service
- questions people might ask
- a mission statement

Write your pitch in bullet-point format on index cards, and create presentation slides if you can. Remember, however, that these are only cues to help guide your presentation. You will not read them aloud. Decide who will present which parts of your pitch. Practice the transitions from one speaker to the next.

D PRACTICE **Work with another group and present your pitches to each other. Offer and listen to feedback. Then work in your original group again to refine your pitch.**

E PRESENT **Pitch your idea to the "investors" (the class). Use visuals if you can to support your presentation. Ask questions when you're an investor.**

F AGREE **Discuss which pitches were the most interesting. Which products or services were the most original? Which idea would you like to invest in, and why?**

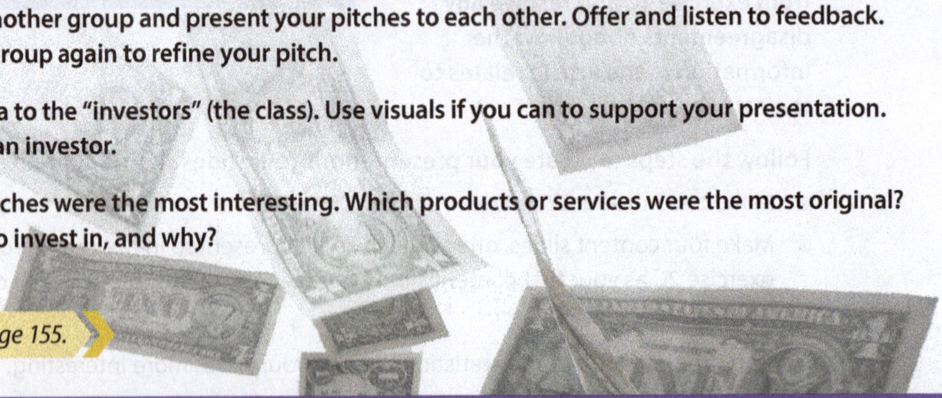

To check your progress, go to page 155.

USEFUL PHRASES

PLAN

What's a unique selling point for our product?

… is something no other product on the market can offer right now.

I think … should present the details because I'll get confused if people ask questions.

AGREE

I love the idea of … – it's simple but exciting.

I don't think there's much of a market for …

UNIT OBJECTIVES

- discuss the effects of a sedentary lifestyle
- suggest ways to establish good sleep habits
- ask and deflect probing questions
- write about a clean-water initiative and how it works
- present and explain choices that you have made for other people

HEALTH VS. MODERN LIFE

9

START SPEAKING

A **Look at the picture. What is this man doing? Why do you think he's doing it in this location and not in the mountains? Is this location just as good? Why or why not?**

B **What does the picture suggest to you about staying fit and healthy in cities? What are some health advantages and disadvantages of life in an urban environment?**

C **What advice would you give for enjoying city life and staying healthy? For ideas, watch Audrey's video.**

EXPERT SPEAKER

How important is Audrey's point for you personally?

9.1 THE SITTING DISEASE

LESSON OBJECTIVE
- discuss the effects of a sedentary lifestyle

1 LANGUAGE IN CONTEXT

A **Look at the pictures and the title of the article. How do they relate to each other? What do you expect to learn about in this article? Read and check your answers.**

Sitting – a growing health risk for all ages

New evidence suggests that 19-year-olds spend as much time sitting as 60-year-olds, and that the "sitting disease" is something that affects all of us, from preschool to retirement.

A **sedentary lifestyle** has well-known medical **side effects**. It increases **blood pressure** and **cholesterol levels** and the risk of **cardiovascular disease**. It has a negative effect on **posture**, putting pressure on **internal organs**, which has a knock-on effect on **digestion**. It causes **chronic pain** in **joints**, negatively affects **circulation**, and even compromises the **immune system**. This doesn't make for a big news story, but the fact that the sitting disease now affects *all ages* does.

It's worrying to think that even young children are not getting enough exercise, but a solution to the problem may lie in creative alternatives to traditional desks and chairs.

Standing desks alleviate the stress on the back, neck, and internal organs. Stand-up meetings give similar results.

By trading standard chairs for exercise balls and installing pedal desks, schools make it easy for students to stay active and be focused at the same time. Adopting treadmill desks allows companies to do the same for their employees.

The balls force users to sit up straight, which keeps them alert, and the action of pedaling or walking not only gets them moving, it also means they stay physically and mentally engaged with their work.

We may not be able to cut the number of hours we spend at work or school, but sitting all day is something we don't have to stand for anymore!

B PAIR WORK **Are you surprised by any of the information in the text? Which type of alternative furniture would you like to try out? Why?**

INSIDER ENGLISH

knock-on effect = indirect consequence of an action

2 VOCABULARY: Discussing health issues

FIND IT

A 2.18 PAIR WORK **Look at the bold words in the article. What do they mean? Use a dictionary or your phone to help you. Write them in the correct categories in the chart below. Then listen and check.**

Features of the body	Factors associated with the "sitting disease"
blood pressure	*sedentary lifestyle*

B **Now go to page 149. Do the vocabulary exercises for 9.1.**

C PAIR WORK THINK CRITICALLY **How can people add physical activity into their daily routines? What could workplaces, schools, and the government do to help? Do you think these measures would be enough to balance out a sedentary lifestyle?**

3 GRAMMAR: Referencing

A **Look at the extracts from the article in the grammar box. Then complete the rules below.**

Referencing

This (*the knowledge of side effects of a sedentary lifestyle*) doesn't make for a big news story, but the fact that the sitting disease now affects all ages **does** (*make this a big news story*).

It's worrying to think that even young children are not getting enough exercise.

Stand-up meetings give **similar results** (*to those of standing desks*).

By installing pedal desks, schools make it easy for students to stay active. Adopting treadmill desks allows companies to **do the same** for their employees. (*make it easy to stay active*)

The action of pedaling or walking not only gets **them** (*users*) moving, **it** also means **they** (*users*) stay physically and mentally engaged with **their** (*the users'*) work.

Referencing techniques make it possible to avoid repetition in your writing.

To avoid repeating a noun or concept mentioned earlier in the same text …

- use possessive adjectives (such as *its* or [1] ____________).
- use pronouns (such as *it*, [2] ____________ , *them*, or *this*).
- use phrases like *the same* or [3] ____________ + noun.

To avoid repeating a verb, use an auxiliary verb such as *be*, *have*, or [4] ____________ in the correct form.

B **Now go to page 136. Look at the grammar chart and do the grammar exercise for 9.1.**

C PAIR WORK **Take turns and talk about one of the topics below for 30 seconds without repeating any of the bold words. Your partner will time you.**

- the **bike-sharing** program in [**name of our city**]
- **walking** up the **stairs** instead of taking the **elevator**
- using a **standing desk** at work
- **sitting on an exercise ball** when you **watch TV**

I think **this** is a great idea. **It** makes a lot of sense. The vehicles people ride are easy to use, and you can find **them** all over Quito. A lot of people use **this program**. I **do**, too.

Oh, no! You said "Quito." Start over!

4 SPEAKING

A GROUP WORK **Choose one of the groups below and think of three ways they could discourage a sedentary lifestyle.**

- teachers of young children
- parents of teenagers
- companies that employ a lot of office staff

B **Share your ideas with the class. Who has the most creative suggestions?**

Companies could provide yoga classes that help you have good **posture** …

9.2 A GOOD NIGHT'S SLEEP

LESSON OBJECTIVE
- suggest ways to establish good sleep habits

1 LANGUAGE IN CONTEXT

A 2.19 **Look at the infographic. What are the main physical benefits of getting a good night's sleep? In what ways do you think modern life interferes with sleep? Listen to part of a podcast. Are any of your ideas mentioned?**

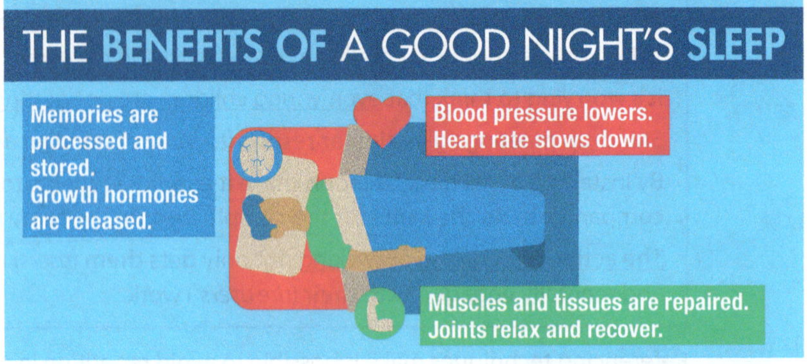

2.19 Audio script

GLOSSARY
flip side (*n*) the opposite result of a good situation

Host Before the break, Dr. Raymond Shaw talked about the benefits of good sleep, but now we're going to be looking at the flip side – the dangers of sleep deprivation. We all know lack of sleep is dangerous, so why do we *still* not get enough of it?

Shaw Well, first off, we seem to be packing way too much into our days. We get up too early and go to bed too late. We know we need to be racking up at least seven hours of sleep a night, but it's hard to fit those seven hours into our busy schedules.

Host So, what might be stopping us? And what can we do about it?

Shaw Well, physical stimulants don't help, so we should try to cut out caffeine and sugar, or at least cut back on them. Also, the pressure of work or school means tension builds up during the day, making it harder to wind down at night. But the main thing keeping us up is FOMO.

Host FOMO? You mean, *Fear Of Missing Out*?

Shaw Uh-huh. That's what drives us to our screens late at night – social media updates, breaking news stories, the latest Tweets. We kid ourselves that we're just taking a quick peek before we drift off to sleep, but time just slips away. Those minutes add up to hours, and soon you're watching cat videos when you should be sleeping!

B PAIR WORK THINK CRITICALLY **Do you agree that FOMO is a big factor in bad sleeping habits? Why or why not? Is it a problem for you? For ideas, watch Audrey's video.**

EXPERT SPEAKER

Are you more like Audrey or the people she describes?

2 VOCABULARY: Discussing (lack of) sleep

A 2.20 PAIR WORK **Listen to the phrasal verbs in the box and then find them in the audio script above. Can you figure out their meaning from context? How would you rephrase them using different words?**

add up	build up	cut back on	cut out
drift off	drive somebody to	fit something into	keep somebody up
pack something into	rack up	slip away	wind down

B **Now go to page 149. Do the vocabulary exercises for 9.2.**

C PAIR WORK **Discuss the questions. Use phrasal verbs from the box above in your answers.**
- How many hours of sleep do you normally get per night? Is it different on weekends?
- Do you ever find it difficult to get to sleep at night? What kinds of things keep you up?
- Would you agree that sleep deprivation is an inevitable consequence of modern life? Why or why not?

3 GRAMMAR: Continuous infinitives

A **Look at the sentences in the grammar box. Complete the rules.**

> **Continuous infinitives**
>
> We're going **to be looking** at the flip side.
> We seem **to be packing** way too much into our days.
> We know we need **to be racking up** at least seven hours of sleep a night.
> You're watching cat videos when you **should be sleeping**!

1 A continuous infinitive is formed with *to* + ______________ + verb + *-ing*. It emphasizes that an action is in progress over a period of time.
2 It is used with the verbs *appear* and ______________ to comment on ongoing actions and situations.
3 It is used with the verbs *want*, *would like*, and ______________ to comment on intentions and plans.
4 It is used with the modals ______________, *could*, and *might* to criticize or speculate about an ongoing action or situation.

B **Now go to page 137. Look at the grammar chart and do the grammar exercise for 9.2**

C PAIR WORK **Complete the sentences with the correct verb in the continuous infinitive, and check your accuracy. Which statements do you agree with? Why?**

ask get worse sacrifice sleep

1 People seem ______________________ sleep in order to binge-watch their favorite shows as soon as a new season is released.
2 Doctors need ______________________ their patients about sleep and other lifestyle issues. This information will alert them to possible health problems.
3 I'd love ______________________ right now. In general, I'd rather sleep fewer hours at night and take naps during the day.
4 Since I started college, the situation with sleep deprivation seems ______________________.

> ✓ **ACCURACY CHECK**
>
> **The linking verbs *need* and *seem* are always followed by an infinitive form of a verb.**
> *Traffic seems ~~moving~~ fairly smoothly.* ✗
> *Traffic seems to be moving fairly smoothly.* ✓

4 SPEAKING

A GROUP WORK **Look at the descriptions of different categories of people. Add another one to the list. What do you think each group needs to be doing to make sure they get enough sleep?**

- high school students who rack up too many hours online
- people who have to fit a lot into a day, like parents with young children and full-time jobs
- doctors and first responders who are on call at all hours and find it difficult to wind down and relax
- ____

B **Tell the class what advice you came up with for each group.**

> *We think parents need* **to be monitoring** *how much time their kids spend online. If it gets too extreme, they should make them* **cut back on** *screen time.*

9.3 CLEARING THE AIR

LESSON OBJECTIVE
- ask and deflect probing questions

1 LISTENING

A 2.21 **Look at the pictures of two major industries in California. What are they? What effect do you think they have on air quality? Listen to an interview with an administrator from Waylons, California, and check your answers.**

B 2.21 LISTEN FOR PURPOSE **Listen again. Is the administrator interested in finding solutions to the air quality issues? How do you know? Is the interviewer satisfied with the administrator's answers? Why do you think that?**

C 2.22 PAIR WORK **Look at some of the questions the interviewer asks. Listen and note what the bold words refer to. Compare your answers with a partner. Listen again if needed.**

1 Isn't it fair to say that **the situation** is critical here at the moment? ____________
2 Wouldn't you agree that this is **an issue** that deserves attention? ____________
3 Are you suggesting that there's nothing that can be done to regulate **those industries**? ____________
4 Is **that** a policy your department supports? ____________
5 What's your reaction to **that**? ____________
6 Is **that story** not true? ____________
7 Is **that** the administration's position? ____________

D PAIR WORK THINK CRITICALLY **How does your hometown compare with Waylons in terms of industrialization, air quality, and the local government response to environmental and health issues?**

2 PRONUNCIATION: Listening for stressed and unstressed grammar words

A 2.23 **Listen. In which sentence is the underlined word stressed?**

1 a … the current administration in Washington is planning to relax those regulations, and that could, in fact, make matters worse …
b I'm sorry, but could you give me some concrete examples?

2 a What do you mean?
b … but I do know that there are a lot of interesting initiatives being explored …

B 2.24 **Complete the sentences. Which word should be stressed? Listen and check.**

1 I'm afraid I ____________ comment on federal legislation. But I ____________ say we're doing everything we can to make sure that industries abide by the state and local regulations currently in place.

2 ____________'s not what activist groups are saying. They claim ____________ your department is pro-industry and anti-community.

C **Circle the correct words to complete the sentence.**

Grammar words are usually [1]*stressed / unstressed*, but they are [2]*stressed / unstressed* to emphasize a point.

3 SPEAKING SKILLS

A 2.21 PAIR WORK **Read and complete the sentences from the interview in the chart. Listen again and write down more examples of each type. Compare the examples you found with a partner and read them aloud to each other. Be sure to stress the main word in complex noun phrases.**

Asking probing questions	Buying time to think / deflecting questions
Surely you can't be suggesting that … ?	I'm glad you brought that up …
Isn't it [1] ________ to say that … ?	Well, that's an interesting point …
Wouldn't you [2] ________ that … ?	[6] ________________ ?
How do you explain the fact that … ?	[7] ________________
[3] ________________ ?	[8] ________________
[4] ________________ ?	[9] ________________
[5] ________________ ?	[10] ________________

B PAIR WORK **Imagine the situations below. Would you be more likely to ask probing questions or deflect questions in each one? Why? Act out one of the situations for another pair of students.**

- a conversation with a friend
- a heated argument with your roommates
- a question-and-answer session after a presentation
- a meeting with your parents about your grades

4 PRONUNCIATION: Saying consonant clusters

A 2.25 **Listen to some common consonant clusters and example words. Repeat them.**

/str/ straightforward /kw/ quality /kr/ concrete /sp/ spokesperson
/pr/ preventable /nts/ pollutants /tr/ control /bl/ blocking

B 2.26 **Listen and write in the missing words you hear. Practice the conversation with a partner. Does your partner pronounce the consonant clusters clearly?**

A Well, there is too much [1] ________ . That's [2] ________ obvious.
B But we can't just ask people to stop driving! That's too extreme.
A We could [3] ________ heavy [4] ________ from the city. That would be a start.
B Interesting idea, but I'm not sure the solution is that [5] ________ .

C GROUP WORK **Add six more lines to the conversation, using consonant clusters from exercise 4A in every line. Join another pair and read your conversations. What consonant clusters did they use? Does everyone pronounce the consonant clusters clearly?**

5 SPEAKING

A PAIR WORK **Choose one of the issues in the box or another that you know something about. Discuss the main problems in relation to your town and take notes.**

noise pollution pollution from industry residential recycling traffic

B PAIR WORK **Act out a discussion between a reporter and a local politician about the issue you chose.**

I'd like to start by asking why your administration is cutting funding for recycling?

Well, I'm not sure that's totally accurate. I mean, the situation isn't quite as simple as that.

But isn't it true that you have slashed the recycling budget by more than 50 percent?

9.4 A THIRSTY WORLD

LESSON OBJECTIVE

- write about a clean-water initiative and how it works

1 READING

A PAIR WORK **Look at the pictures. What do they have in common? What do they tell us about issues with water today?**

B **Read the titles of three short articles. What aspect of the water crisis do you think each one will cover?**

a Big business giving back
b Star power in the fight for clean water
c The water crisis: Facts and figures

C IDENTIFY PURPOSE **Read the stories and write in the correct titles from exercise 1B. From whose point of view is each story being told? Which stories do you think give a balanced account of the situation? Why?**

Home Health Business Politics World More ▾

Water is essential to life, we all know that. But access to water is something most of us take for granted. Around the world, one in nine people do not have access to safe, clean water supplies. In countries where water is scarce, 80 percent of illnesses are linked to poor water quality and lack of proper sanitation. Providing access to clean water could save as many as two million lives every year.

Clean water would also have dramatic effects on the lives of millions of people, especially women and children. In the most badly affected areas, they spend up to six hours a day simply providing water for their families. Their lives are sacrificed to the daily chore of collecting water. Children have no time to go to school, and women can't pursue work outside the home, creating a cycle of poverty in the community.

Help us fight this global crisis. Click here to donate.

Source: businessconnectworld.com

More and more celebrities are using their fame to promote water charities and raise money to solve water issues around the world. But does celebrity appeal really work? We look at two examples.

1 Matt Damon, known for such movie roles as Jason Bourne, was one of the first celebrities to use his fame to bring attention to clean water issues. In 2009 he co-founded a water charity called Water.org that provides microloans to families in developing countries to connect to water and sanitation systems or build their own. The organization has helped more than seven million people around the world.

2 NFL star Chris Long was so struck by the problems he saw when he visited Tanzania to climb Kilimanjaro that he started a charity called Waterboys. Along with fellow football players recruited by Long, the foundation raises money to provide safe, clean water throughout East Africa. In its first two years, the charity raised enough money to build 23 wells and provide water for more than 100,000 people.

Sources: globalcitizen.org; waterboys.org

The Coca-Cola Company is committed to working with communities in need all over the world. It has set up a number of collaborative projects with local and global charities to join the fight in making the world a better place.

In India and Africa, Coca-Cola is currently involved in two major projects to provide clean drinking water for poor communities. The Support My School program in India is building modern bathrooms with access to clean water in hundreds of schools, improving sanitary conditions and school attendance for nearly 100,000 students.

In Africa, the corporation is investing heavily in RAIN (the Replenish Africa Initiative), with the aim of building new wells and providing access to clean water for two million people over the coming years.

Through these and other projects, Coca-Cola is helping fight poverty on the front lines: reducing the incidence of waterborne diseases, keeping children – especially girls – in school, and empowering parents to pursue a better life for their families.

Sources: worldvision.org/corporate/; The Coca-Cola Foundation

D PAIR WORK THINK CRITICALLY **Why do celebrities and big corporations get involved with charitable projects? Are they motivated by the same things?**

2 WRITING

A **Reread the story in exercise 1C about Water.org's initiative. How is it different from the other initiatives? Then read the paragraph below. Does it explain the nature of the organization accurately and completely?**

Water.org does not provide people with clean water, **per se**. It does not drill wells, build sanitation facilities, or provide water pipes. It does something that is, **at its heart**, much more important. It empowers people to solve problems for themselves and take the matter of access to clean water into their own hands. The problem is, **inherently**, a financial one. **More often than not**, people who spend hours every day in search of water do not have time to work and can't make or save the money they need to pay for clean water. It's a vicious cycle, but money, **in and of itself**, won't break it. By offering families microloans to establish a reliable connection to clean water sources, Water.org is, **fundamentally**, investing in communities, giving them the power to invest in themselves.

FIND IT

B **Look at the bold words in the paragraph above. Which terms in the box have a similar meaning and could replace them? More than one option might be possible. Use a dictionary or your phone to help you.**

as a matter of course	as such	by definition	by its very nature	essentially	intrinsically

C EXPLAIN DISTINCTIONS **Complete the sentences with adverbials from exercises 2A and 2B. More than one option may be possible.**

1 Microloans are, ______________________________, a tool for empowerment.

2 Microloans are not enough, ______________________________. People also need to find a way to make money to be able to pay back the loans.

3 Freeing people from the chore of finding water is, ______________________________, giving them a chance to live a better life.

4 Access to clean, safe water is, ______________________________, the basis of a happy and healthy life.

WRITE IT

FIND IT

D PLAN **You're going to write an explanatory paragraph about another solution to the problem of clean water from the LifeStraw organization. With a partner, look at the diagram and discuss how the device works.**

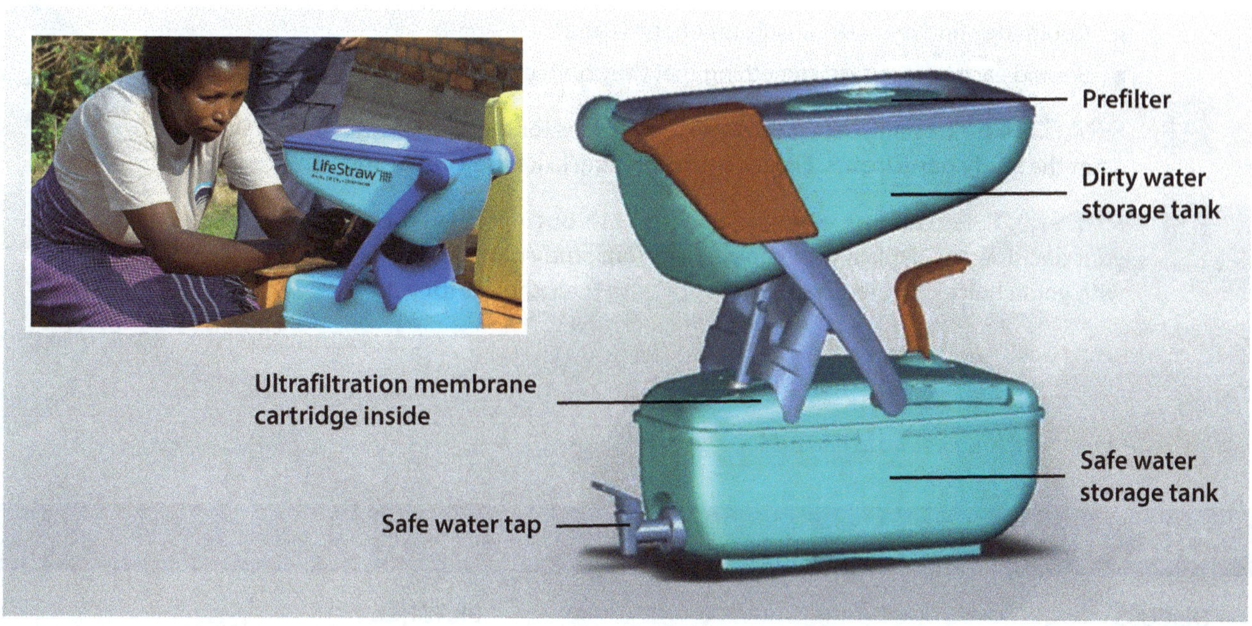

In what ways is this initiative different from the other ones presented in this lesson? You can use your phone to do more research if you want.

E **Write your paragraph in 120–150 words. Use adverbial expressions from exercises 2A and 2B.**

F PAIR WORK **Read each other's paragraphs. Offer and listen to feedback and revise your work.**

9.5 TIME TO SPEAK
Desert island dilemma

LESSON OBJECTIVE

- present and explain choices that you have made for other people

A **RESEARCH** **What are the best things about modern life? With a partner, make a list of your ideas. Look at the pictures to help you. Then write 6–10 survey questions to find out what your classmates think.**

B **Interview another pair of students. Ask your questions and take careful notes.**

C **DISCUSS** **Read the announcement.**

> Two students have been chosen to live on an isolated island for two years as part of an experiment. Only basic food supplies and shelters are provided. Study participants may bring one thing with them.

The students you just interviewed are the study participants, but you will choose the one thing they can take to the island. Consider the following questions and consult your notes to reach a decision.

- What will each person miss most?
- Could they find or make substitutes on the island?
- Should each person take something that they both can use?

D **PRACTICE** **Present your choices and the reasons for them to another pair of students – not the study participants. Listen to their feedback. Revise your proposal.**

E **PRESENT** **Focusing on your study participants but in front of the whole class, share your decision and explain your choices. Are your study participants happy with your choices for them? Are you happy with their choices for you?**

To check your progress, go to page 155.

USEFUL PHRASES

DISCUSS

What will … miss most about … ?

… loves … , but he could use … as a substitute.

If we let her take … , they could both use it.

PRACTICE

… appears to be studying … in her free time, so …

… will be taking … because he'll miss … more than anything else.

People need to be doing something, or they go crazy.

Maybe think about …

REVIEW 3 (UNITS 7–9)

1 VOCABULARY

A **Complete the conversation with the correct words.**

concentrating, mark, keep alive, ethnic, interrupt, rituals, focused, distracted, genealogy, ancestors, inherited, festivities

Marcia Ted, do you have any interest in [1] ______________ ______________?

Ted Funny you should ask that. The other day, my mother was telling me about some family research she's been doing – our [2] ______________ and our [3] ______________ background, etc. It was really interesting, but I couldn't stay [4] ______________. My boss kept texting me, and I'd get [5] ______________ and miss what she was saying.

Marcia I know the feeling! The other day I was with my family – it was my parents' anniversary, and we [6] ______________ the occasion every year with a little party. I really like how we [7] ______________ that tradition ______________, especially now that there are grandkids. Anyway, I noticed that everybody was [8] ______________ on their phones rather than the conversation.

Ted Were your parents upset by that?

Marcia Not really. But it was a special day, and I didn't want beeps and buzzes to [9] ______________ the [10] ______________, so I told everyone to put their phones away. And they did. It was nice.

Ted That's great. Those family [11] ______________ are so important. The kids will realize that one day. Oh, and guess what I learned! My great-great-grandmother had bright red hair, so that must be who I [12] ______________ mine from.

B PAIR WORK **Think about an occasion or practice that your family observes together. Does it have significance for other people, too? When you're all together, does everyone put their phones away? Why or why not? Does anyone get upset about it?**

2 GRAMMAR

A **Rewrite the sentences using the words in parentheses ( ).**

1. I never would have thought that my parents' native language could die out. (*Never …*)
2. After the article was published in the newspaper, then I realized my mistake. (*Only …*)
3. The memories of ancient festivals linger in the town square. (*In …*)
4. The remains of last night's celebration lie on the city streets. (*On the …*)
5. That documentary made me think I should donate money to water charities. (*… got me …*)
6. I haven't been able to do any work this morning. (*… get …*)

B PAIR WORK **Change your sentences from exercise 2A so that they say something true about you and your experience.**

Never would I have guessed that my grandmother likes rock music, but she does! I just learned that she went to concerts all the time in the '60s and '70s!

3 VOCABULARY

A **Circle the correct terms to complete the advice column.**

ASK DR. OLIVIA WATTS

Home | New posts | Forum | Profile

Brian, Chicago, 2:45 p.m.
I'm 42 and starting to notice changes in my [1]*circulation / posture*. Sometimes, I can't stand up straight. Any good advice for me?

Dr. Watts
Do you have a [2]*chronic pain / sedentary lifestyle*? I'll bet you do. You need to get [3]*rid of / attached to* your traditional desk and invest in something better. Physical therapy can help, although many people get [4]*frustrated / complicated* when they don't see immediate results. Be patient. If you haven't had a general physical exam in a while, get one. As we get older, it's important to monitor things like [5]*immune system / cholesterol levels* and weight and adjust our diet accordingly. Take care of yourself!

Celia, Santiago, 6:02 a.m.
I have [6]*high blood pressure / side effects*. It's an inherited condition, but isn't there something I can be doing to reduce it? I'm really scared.

Dr. Watts
Celia, let's get something [7]*straight / right* – you can't cure this condition, but you absolutely can improve it with behavior changes. First, try to [8]*build up / cut back on* fatty foods as much as possible. You also need to reduce stress. Learning how to [9]*wind down / slip away* in the evening so that you fall asleep faster is fundamental. We're all busy, but it's so important to [10]*fit / break* some exercise *into* your daily routine, even just walking. Get a dog! That will force you to walk.

Take control! Talk to your doctor, make a plan, and stick to it.

B **PAIR WORK** **Have you or has anyone you know suffered from these complaints? Which one? Is the doctor's advice good? Why or why not? What advice would you give Brian and Celia?**

4 GRAMMAR

A **Complete the sentences from an essay about medical advice websites with the phrases in the box.**

appear to be	can all attest	points out	should be getting
to be looking at	to be suggesting	you can see	

1 As ________________ from the questions in the "Ask Dr. Olivia Watts" example, people know their health issues, but they don't know how to get help with *these issues*.

2 As the doctor ________________ , diet is very important. In fact, some doctors say *diet* is the most significant factor in maintaining good health.

3 As we ________________ , being constantly mindful of health issues isn't easy or fun, but *thinking about health* is necessary if we want to have a good life.

4 Another important factor is sleep. Based on clinical studies, researchers assert that we ________________ at least seven hours per night, and based on experience, doctors report *identical findings to those of the researchers*.

5 The research seems ________________ that kids need even more. Teenagers function better if they get nine hours of sleep a night, and younger children *function better with nine hours of sleep*, too.

6 Teenagers may believe they can catch up on sleep on the weekend, but many experts *feel this is not true*. Though teens might ________________ well rested, oversleeping actually makes them more tired the next day.

7 We are going ________________ two studies from Canada that back up this assertion and two others from Brazil that produced *not identical but closely correlated* results.

B **PAIR WORK** **Look at the sentences in exercise 4A and replace the *italicized* words with an appropriate referent to avoid repetition.**

UNIT OBJECTIVES

- talk about future food options and how likely they are
- discuss new ways to use natural energy sources
- discuss the advantages of rethinking daily habits
- write a summary of a discussion about the new economy
- present and evaluate an idea for reinventing pet ownership

10 REINVENTION

START SPEAKING

A Look at the picture. What has been reinvented? In what way? How might this change the whole idea and experience of driving? Do you think the design will become a reality? Why or why not?

B What things do you think will be dramatically reimagined in the next 10 to 20 years? What do you expect to stay the same forever? Why?

C Think of something that you've reinvented. What changes did you make to it, and why? How extreme was your reinvention? What do people think of it? For ideas, watch Ryoko's video.

EXPERT SPEAKER

What do you think of Ryoko's reinvention? How extreme is it?

10.1

BUGS NOT BEEF

LESSON OBJECTIVE
- talk about future food options and how likely they are

1 LANGUAGE IN CONTEXT

A 2.27 **Look at the picture. What type of insect is this? Where can you find them? Have you ever eaten one? If not, would you consider it? Listen to the news story. Were your answers correct?**

2.27 Audio script

We all love food, but our **consumption** of it will soon overwhelm both **supply** and production. Take meat, for example. Animal agriculture will increase at least 70 percent by 2050. Already, one-third of the world's **grains** and **cereals** are used to feed **livestock**, and **cattle** farming alone occupies 24 percent of land globally. It takes 15,000 liters of water to produce one kilogram of beef, so greater production means more water **shortages** worldwide.

Imagine if we could reduce our **appetite** for this inefficient protein source. Though some people would rather we gave up meat altogether, most agree that it's time we started exploring alternatives.

This idea is what led Brown University students Gabi Lewis and Greg Sewitz to buy 2,000 live crickets in 2013. Insects are common **foodstuffs** in many parts of the world, but not in the U.S. and Canada. So they wondered, *What if we created a cool new food product to introduce insect protein to people here?* With only a basic recipe for cricket flour, Lewis and Sewitz created a company – Exo. Today, Exo offers many healthy food products, including their popular protein bars made with cricket flour.

Crickets are **wholesome** and **nutritious**, with essential proteins, **fiber**, and twice as much iron as spinach. They're super green, too – making food from crickets uses just one liter of water per kilogram. Crickets might just be the new **superfood**.

B PAIR WORK THINK CRITICALLY **What are the environmental advantages of using insects such as crickets as food? What protein alternatives to beef and other livestock meats can you think of? What environmental advantages might they have?**

2 VOCABULARY: Discussing global food issues

A 2.28 PAIR WORK **Look at the bold words in the article. Write them in the correct category below. Then listen and check.**

1 related to food quantity: ________________ , ________________
2 non-meat foods: ________________ and ________________ , which both contain ________________
3 describing the healthfulness of food: ________________ , ________________
4 collective words for animals we eat: ________________ , ________________
5 other ways to categorize things we eat: ________________ , ________________
6 related to eating: ________________ , ________________

B **Now go to page 150. Do the vocabulary exercises for 10.1.**

FIND IT

C GROUP WORK **How is a superfood different from regular foodstuffs? Use your phone to help you. What other superfoods are there? For ideas, watch Ryoko's video.**

EXPERT SPEAKER

What do you think of Ryoko's alternative to eating superfoods?

3 GRAMMAR: Simple past for unreal situations

A **Look at the sentences in the grammar box. In each sentence, what is the use of the underlined simple past verb? Match the sentences to the use(s) below.**

Simple past for unreal situations

A **Imagine if** we could reduce our appetite for beef?
B Some people **would rather** we gave up meat altogether.
C **It's (high) time** we started exploring alternatives.
D **What if** we created a cool new food product?

! ***It's time (that) we …*** = *We should …*
It's high time (that) we … = *It's urgent that we …*

Use the simple past for unreal situations …

1 to express present wishes and preferences. Sentence(s) ________
2 to speculate about or describe an imaginary situation. Sentence(s) ________
3 to express the need to do something. Sentence(s) ________

B **Now go to page 137. Look at the grammar chart and do the grammar exercise for 10.1.**

C PAIR WORK THINK CRITICALLY **How would you like to see the world change? Write sentences using the expressions for simple past for unreal situations. Use the categories in the box to help you. Share your sentences in small groups. How likely are all your desired changes? Why?**

food social media transportation

Imagine if our school served gourmet meals! But honestly, I'd rather it offered more vegan options.

4 SPEAKING

A **Look at the pictures of protein sources from around the world. Which ones are you familiar with? Do you like them? Would you like to try the others? Does their nutritional value influence your decision?**

A Scorpion snack

B Fried silkworms

C Peanuts and grasshoppers

D Rare steak

E Seitan

F Vegan burrito

10.2 ACCIDENTAL STARTUPS

LESSON OBJECTIVE

- discuss new ways to use natural energy sources

1 LANGUAGE IN CONTEXT

A PAIR WORK **Look at the article title and headings and the pictures. What will the article be about? What other ideas might be presented in the article? Read and check your answers.**

A LIGHTER CARBON FOOTPRINT

The need to find **carbon-neutral** sources of energy is a fact of life these days. The resistance to these efforts, primarily from multinational energy companies based on **fossil fuels,** is a fact of business. Stepping in to fill the gap are "social enterprises." It would appear that these community-minded initiatives, motivated by need rather than profit, are leading the way in our search for innovative, **renewable, low-carbon** solutions and becoming thriving businesses almost by accident. Here are a few of our favorites.

Solarkiosk

This startup has developed a kiosk with built-in **solar panels** that generate enough energy to charge batteries for everything from cell phones to appliances. The panels make it **self-sustainable.** Solarkiosk was designed as an energy resource for remote, **off-grid** locations. Though currently only in Ethiopia, Kenya, and Botswana, it is believed that this technology could be adapted for use almost anywhere.

Bio-Bean

Coffee already **energizes** us to start the day, but bio-bean has found a way to make it **power** more than our morning routines. This U.K.-based green energy company recycles coffee grounds into advanced **biofuels** and biochemicals that are more efficient than traditional ones. It would seem this company has found an affordable, **low-emission** energy source suitable for industrial-scale heating, among other uses.

Makani

This startup has come up with a renewable energy solution for island countries that have limited land. Their "energy kite" is a wind-propelled flying generator that flies in circles, gathering wind energy and turning it into electricity. It is reported that kites like these require 90 percent less construction material than conventional wind farms.

2 VOCABULARY: Discussing global energy issues

A 2.29 **Look at the words and phrases related to energy from the article. Write *N* (noun), *V* (verb), or *A* (adjective) according to how they are used in the article. Listen and check. Which words have a positive or a negative connotation?**

1 biofuel ___
2 carbon footprint ___
3 carbon-neutral ___
4 energize ___
5 fossil fuel ___
6 low-carbon ___
7 low-emission ___
8 off-grid ___
9 power ___
10 renewable ___
11 self-sustainable ___
12 solar panels ___

B **Now go to page 150. Do the vocabulary exercises for 10.2.**

FIND IT

C PAIR WORK THINK CRITICALLY **Which forms of energy are the most common where you live? Why do you think that is? Use your phone to find out more if you can.**

We live in a very sunny place, but there aren't any solar panels anywhere! We still depend on fossil fuels.

3 GRAMMAR: *It* constructions

A **Look at the sentences in the grammar box. Then complete the rules below with the words in the box. Which sentences in the grammar box apply to each rule?**

***It* constructions**

A **It would appear that** these initiatives are leading the way.

B **It is believed that** this technology could be adaptable for use almost anywhere.

C **It would seem** this company has found an affordable energy source.

D **It is reported that** kites like these require 90 percent less construction material.

appear report

1 *It* constructions in the passive are often used to ________ what people say or believe, especially in writing. Sentences ________

2 To speculate about something or indicate that you aren't sure of the truth of the information, use the verbs ________ and *seem*. Sentences ________

B **Now go to page 138. Look at the grammar chart and do the grammar exercise for 10.2.**

C PAIR WORK **Work together to report the information in the sentences using the verb in parentheses ( ). Then comment or speculate on the information. Check your accuracy.**

1 Most people think that wind power is the cleanest energy source. (believe)

2 A lot of people like the idea that primary energy sources like coal will soon disappear. (hope)

3 Estimates indicate that many countries will have only renewable energy sources by 2050. (report)

4 Scientists believe that "waste products" like coffee grounds can continue to be useful. (think)

ACCURACY CHECK

Use linking verbs such as *seem* and *appear* after *It* + *would*. Don't use reporting verbs (*believe, claim, report, say, tell, think*, etc.).

It would ~~think~~ that solar power is a good option there. ✗

It would seem that solar power is a good option there. ✓

Many social enterprises focus on providing solar panels or windmills because **it is believed that** these are the most self-sustainable options.

Yes, **it would seem** wind energy is especially useful in coastal communities.

4 SPEAKING

A PAIR WORK THINK CRITICALLY **Which of the initiatives described in the text in exercise 1A would work well where you live? Why? How might they be modified to work better?**

People drink a lot of coffee around here, so **it would seem** that recycling coffee grounds is a good low-carbon option.

FIND IT

B GROUP WORK **What other nature-based energy sources might work in your area? Use your phone if you can to do some research. Then report back to the class with your ideas.**

There is now a soccer ball that can catch and store energy as it moves. **It has been reported** that it can hold enough energy to power a light bulb for three hours!

10.3 A LIFE WITHOUT PLASTIC

LESSON OBJECTIVE

- discuss the advantages of rethinking daily habits

1 LISTENING

A **Look at the pictures. What are these things? What are they usually made of? What are they usually made of?**

B 2.30 DISTINGUISH MAIN IDEAS FROM DETAILS

Look at the points in the chart. Which do you think are main ideas, and which are details? Listen to Grace and Jake's conversation about adopting a plastic-free lifestyle and check your answers. Circle the ones you predicted correctly.

	Main idea	Detail
1 be mindful of your daily routine		
2 buy a reusable coffee cup		
3 avoid plastic straws		
4 how to live plastic-free		
5 recycle		
6 avoid over-packaging		
7 demand alternative containers		

INSIDER ENGLISH

It's doable = It will take some effort, but it's possible.

C PAIR WORK THINK CRITICALLY **Can you think of other everyday things that could be made of something besides plastic? Would they work as well? Why or why not?**

2 PRONUNCIATION: Listening for sound changes in connected speech

A 2.31 **Listen to the sentences and match the underlined letters to the sound changes you hear.**

1 But that talk really made me want to try it. ___
2 How did you start? ___
3 There are lots of products out there that come in plastic containers. ___

a /d/ /j/ → /dʒ/
b /n/ → /m/
c /d/ → /b/

B 2.32 **Circle the word that would cause a sound change when connected to the sound underlined. Listen and check.**

1 Please don't use that *plastic* / *horrible* cup.
2 A recycling project needs very good *leadership* / *management*.
3 Was the presentation *planned* / *organized* in advance?
4 Could *we* / *you* try a little harder?

C **Circle the correct words to complete the sentences.**

In connected speech, words that end with /t/, /d/, or /n/ [1]*never* / *often* change if the following word starts with /p/, /b/, or /m/. Additionally, when a word [2]*starts* / *ends* with /t/ or /d/ and the following word [3]*starts* / *ends* with /j/, these sounds often combine to make /tʃ/ or /dʒ/.

3 SPEAKING SKILLS

A 2.30 PAIR WORK **Listen to the conversation again and complete the expressions in the chart below.**

Defending an opinion and concluding a turn	
1 The speaker said that **it all** ______ being mindful of your daily routine.	C
2 **You** ______ **, but actually** … they're coated in plastic.	___
3 We can just recycle straws, too. **I mean, it's** ______ .	___
4 No, listen, **it's not as** ______ . I'm talking about …	___
5 It's too much all at once. **That's** ______ .	___
6 Anything that reduces plastic trash is worth doing. ______ **I'm trying to make.**	___
7 Recycling is only skimming the surface. **There's** ______ **that can be done.**	___
8 I hear you, **I just** ______ **anything so radical is necessary.** I think …	___
9 Well, **I guess we're going to have to** ______ on this.	___

B PAIR WORK **Look at the expressions in the chart again. Write *D* for those that indicate the speaker is defending an opinion. Write *C* for those that signal the speaker is concluding a turn. Compare answers with a partner.**

C PAIR WORK **Have a conversation about alternatives to other forms of plastic using the expressions from the chart above.**

If everyone used crumpled paper instead of Styrofoam in shipping boxes, then packaging would be recyclable. I mean, it's not that difficult.

It's not as simple as that. Styrofoam works better for fragile stuff.

4 PRONUNCIATION: Saying the /ŋ/ sound

A 2.33 **Listen to some phrases containing the /ŋ/ sound. Repeat them.**

The first thi<u>ng</u> I did was buy a travel mug.

I'm talki<u>ng</u> about not usi<u>ng</u> plastic at all.

B 2.34 **<u>Underline</u> the /ŋ/ sounds in the following extracts and listen for them. Practice the conversation with a partner. Does your partner pronounce the sound clearly?**

A The speaker said that it all comes down to being "mindful of your daily routine"; that's when you notice things.

B I'm not sure going totally plastic-free is something people will respond to. It's too much all at once. That's all I'm saying.

A For me, anything that reduces plastic trash is worth doing.

B So, what other plastic things should we all give up, besides coffee cups and grocery bags, I mean?

C PAIR WORK **Complete the sentences with your own ideas and discuss them.**

1 You know something, I watched …
2 I'm going to start by recycling …
3 I think it's worth …

5 SPEAKING

A PAIR WORK THINK CRITICALLY **What are some other ways we might rethink the way we live daily life in order to be more eco-friendly? Consider the ideas in the box and come up with three or four more. Defend your opinions.**

appliances	a vegan diet	electric cars
importing food	walking	

B GROUP WORK **Join another pair of students and discuss your ideas. Defend your opinions.**

It's crazy to buy cherries that have to come all the way from Australia when you can buy papayas that are grown right here.

10.4 WHAT'S YOURS IS MINE

LESSON OBJECTIVE
- write a summary of a discussion about the new economy

1 READING

FIND IT

A **Look at the picture of people using a ride-share service. Is this an example of the *gig economy* or the *sharing economy*? What's the difference? You can use your phone to help you. What's your opinion of these new economic models? Why?**

B PREDICT CONTENT **Look at the key words related to the discussion thread below. Which do you think will be used to defend new economic models and which to criticize them? Read the thread and check your answers.**

unfair competition   human-scale commerce   minimum wage

THE NEW ECONOMY: HAVE YOUR SAY!

Who are the real winners and losers in the gig economy? Is a sharing economy model any better? What do you think?

A ✗ **Kevin** 102 posts

When you read about the gig economy, it seems great for everybody, but let me tell you, there are losers in this story. Like taxi drivers. In some countries, it's very expensive to obtain a license – it's an investment. And once you get one, that's your job for life. Then ride-share companies come along, and because of the increased competition, they take away the taxi drivers' livelihood. It's unfair competition because it doesn't cost the other drivers much at all.

B **Amanda** 58 posts

It's time that an economy based on everyone having regular, long-term jobs was challenged. The gig economy is all about on-demand services. Conditions might be more precarious for the worker – job security, insurance, benefits, etc., but we have to get used to that. It's the way the world is going.

C **Abdul** 12 posts

What I like about the sharing economy is that it's a human-scale version of commerce, where you often meet the person who you're doing business with. Take Airbnb. That's a whole lot better than staying in an anonymous hotel somewhere. It's much more personal, and you get better service because of it.

D **Daniel** 642 posts

The sharing economy is nothing new. Just look at libraries. We're just extending that model into the high-tech world. It's inevitable, like economic evolution. There's nothing we can do to stop it, so we might as well go with it.

E **Laura** 21 posts

The "gig economy" business model revolves around tech companies that view legal regulations as outdated or irrelevant. They don't want to follow the rules, so they come up with a way to get around them. They still make money, but the people actually doing the work are NOT better off. In fact, the workers are all independent contractors rather than employees, so they don't get vacations or a minimum wage or sick pay or help saving for retirement. And what's worse, they can be fired without warning or explanation, so they can't even complain!

F **Carolina** 33 posts

At first glance, I really liked the idea of opening up the economy. It's great for us customers, but I think a lot of people actually lose out. I mean, look at streaming music services. We save by not having to download music, but how much money do the musicians make once all the middlemen take their cut? And the food delivery apps! They take such a large cut that many restaurants can't afford to use them, so they lose customers they used to have. People need to understand that these cool new companies could be destroying small neighborhood businesses.

G **Sven** 512 posts

Not so fast! In many places the gig economy has really benefited people, like places where there are no taxis, for example. Now people can use a ride service. How is that a bad thing? People can make extra money and learn new skills. I read that Uber offers English courses to their drivers because they know that it'll help them in their work.

C PAIR WORK EVALUATE INFORMATION **Put a check (✓) for the contributors in favor of the new economic models and an X (✗) for those against them. Highlight the main idea in each comment.**

D GROUP WORK THINK CRITICALLY **Which of the opinions in the discussion thread do you agree with? Why? What could be the long-term effects of these new economic models?**

2 WRITING

A **Read the summary of the discussion thread. Does it focus on arguments for or against new economic models?**

The gig economy and sharing economy raise many different issues and opinions. The topic is **not at all** a simple one, but two clear arguments in favor of new economic models emerge from the discussion thread: freedom of choice and flexibility.

Gig and sharing economy practices liberate people from the rigidity of a traditional working model, **so** it is beneficial to society. **In terms of** customers, they can have whatever they want when they want it – music, a place to stay, food delivery, a ride to the airport. **And for** workers, they are their own bosses, free to set their own hours and determine their income by working as much as they want. **In a nutshell**, the freedom and flexibility offered by these new ways of working make it beneficial to everyone.

Though **probably true** that the gig/sharing economy is here to stay, **even if** we don't like it, the freedom and flexibility it offers has won it many champions.

B USE APPROPRIATE REGISTER **Look at the bold expressions in the summary and their synonyms in the box below. Which set is more formal? Which expressions from the box could substitute for each expression in the summary?**

by no means	in brief	in this respect
it would seem	regarding	regardless of whether
with respect to		

REGISTER CHECK

When writing a summary, establish up front that the opinions you're writing about are not your own and then write from that perspective. This avoids the constant repetition of phrases like *According to …* and *As stated by …* .

WRITE IT

C PLAN **You're going to write a formal summary of the negative viewpoints expressed in the discussion thread. With a partner, look at the main ideas you identified in exercise 1C. What themes could you focus on in your summary?**

D PAIR WORK **Examine the structure of the summary of positive viewpoints in exercise 2A and discuss the questions.**

- What is the role of each paragraph?
- How many points are presented in the body (middle) paragraph?

E PAIR WORK **Work together to write your summary in 150–200 words. Use formal expressions like those in exercise 2B.**

F GROUP WORK **Share your summary with another pair of students and offer feedback. Is the register definitely more formal than the comments in the thread? Did they present all the main points? Did you organize your summaries around the same or different themes?**

10.5 TIME TO SPEAK
Rent-a-Pet

LESSON OBJECTIVE
- present and evaluate an idea for reinventing pet ownership

A **DISCUSS** **With a partner, look at the pictures of people and their pets. How do people usually get their pets? What's the best way?**

B **PLAN** **Form groups of three or four students. Half the groups are Group A, and the others are Group B. Read the instructions.**

Group A: You want to start a business called Rent-a-Pet, a service that allows busy people to have a pet part-time. You must get town council approval. Come up with points in favor of the idea and take notes.

1 Our business provides a home for rescue dogs and cats.

2 Busy people want pets but not all the responsibility of one.

3 …

Group B: You are the town council. You approve or reject new business ideas like Rent-a-Pet, a service that allows busy people to have a pet part-time. Come up with points to explore and challenge this idea and take notes.

1 Some pet renters might abuse or neglect the animal.

2 What if an animal bit or scratched the renter? Who would be responsible?

3 …

C **PREPARE** **Meet with one person from the other group to test your main points. Return to your group and share what you learned. Then prepare your presentation (Group A) or prepare a formal list of issues that must be addressed in order for Rent-a-Pet to get approval (Group B).**

D **PRESENT** **Carry out town council meetings with one Group A and one Group B. Each town council makes its own decision for or against Rent-a-Pet.**

E **DECIDE** **As a class, share the decisions of all the town councils. Did they all come to the same conclusion? What were some of the strongest arguments for Rent-a-Pet? What were the best arguments against it? In what way does this business idea fit the sharing economy model?**

To check your progress, go to page 156.

USEFUL PHRASES

PREPARE

It's a kind and clever way to …

It's not as straightforward as that. …

The supply of animals in shelters … , but the supply of pet owners …

… That's all I'm saying.

PRESENT

We want to rethink the assumptions about pet ownership. First, …

Most people would rather … than …

But just think: What if we could … ?

From our perspective, it all comes down to …

UNIT OBJECTIVES

- discuss the importance of color for businesses
- talk about color expressions and their meaning
- respond to questions in different ways
- write a short opinion essay
- create a flag for a specific group

TRUE COLORS

11

START SPEAKING

A Look at the picture. Why do you think these people have painted their faces in this way? What do the colors represent? Have you ever done (or would you ever do) something like this? Why or why not?

B Think of a group that you belong to. How do the members show their connection to the group (a song, posters, T-shirts, etc.)? What about other groups you belong to? Does the way you show connection change for different groups? Why or why not? For ideas, watch João's video.

EXPERT SPEAKER

What other examples can you think of to illustrate João's point?

11.1 THE COLOR COMPANY

LESSON OBJECTIVE
- discuss the importance of color for businesses

1 LANGUAGE IN CONTEXT

A **What is the thing in the picture, and what is it used for? Have you ever used one? How many colors do you think it contains? Read the article and check your answers.**

Everyone knows the famous Pantone color swatches.

COLORS THAT WORK

Pantone, the world's number one color company, has a library containing 10,000 unique colors – from **bold** reds, **pastel** pinks, and **muted** greens to 71 different shades of white. The company has facilities around the world, and its products are used by 10 million designers and manufacturers every day.

Color has powerful associations. Any company knows that choosing the right combination of shades for logos and branding is crucial to success. For example, it's no surprise that gold and black **imply** luxury, but did you know that yellow **transmits** the idea of low cost? But which yellow exactly? Each shade **evokes** a different feeling. In this case, a **vibrant**, lemon yellow **conjures up** images of childish things (as all **saturated** colors tend to do), suggesting the product is cheaply made. If mixed with a **neutral** tone like gray, however, yellow **conveys** something more sophisticated. If neither of those yellows **resonate with** customers, they can easily choose one of the hundreds of other shades that Pantone has standardized with exact formulas.

Data also shows that Pantone has a big impact on the fashion industry. Every year, Pantone picks one shade that **reflects** current trends and **captures** the collective mood. News of Pantone's "Color of the Year" is anxiously awaited by designers. The next minute, it fills store windows everywhere!

B PAIR WORK THINK CRITICALLY **Do you think that the relationship between color and business success is as strong as the article suggests? Why or why not?**

2 VOCABULARY: Describing color associations

A 2.35 **Match the verbs in the box to the correct definition. Listen and check.**

capture conjure up convey evoke imply reflect resonate with transmit

1 suggest ____________
2 communicate beliefs, ideas, feelings, or knowledge ____________ or ____________
3 accurately represent something that is happening ____________
4 have a particularly pleasing quality for someone ____________
5 cause someone to remember or imagine ____________ or ____________
6 perfectly represent an idea or feeling ____________

FIND IT

B 2.36 PAIR WORK **Listen to the adjectives that describe shades of colors and repeat them. Then find something around you or a picture on your phone that communicates each shade. Does your partner agree?**

bold muted neutral pastel saturated vibrant

C **Now go to page 151. Do the vocabulary exercises for 11.1.**

FIND IT

D PAIR WORK **Find pictures of things in different colors for your partner to describe. What shade is it? What do the colors convey, in your opinion? Do they evoke anything special for you?**

That couch is sort of a neutral tan color. It conveys feelings of calm and comfort to me.

3 GRAMMAR: Subject–verb agreement

A **Look at the sentences in the grammar box, paying particular attention to the bold words. Then read the rules below and match them to a sentence in the grammar box.**

Subject–verb agreement

A **Everyone knows** the famous Pantone color swatches.
B The **company has** facilities around the world.
C **News** of Pantone's "Color of the Year" **is** anxiously awaited.
D If **neither of those yellows resonate with** customers, they can choose another shade.
E **Data** also **shows** that Pantone has a big impact on the fashion industry.

1 Collective nouns (*group*, *company*, *team*) take a singular verb when the sentence is about the organization. When referring back to them, however, use plural pronouns. Sentence ______
2 Singular nouns that end in *-s* (*news*, *politics*, *physics*, *economics*) take a singular verb. Sentence ______
3 Some nouns that come from Latin form the plural with the ending *-a*. Some (*data*, *media*) take a singular verb, and others (*criteria*, *phenomena*) take a plural verb. Sentence ______
4 Words beginning with the prefixes *every-*, *any-*, *some-*, and *no-* take a singular verb. Refer back to them with plural pronouns. Sentence ______
5 Subjects with *either* or *neither* can take a singular or plural verb, depending on context. Refer back to them with plural pronouns. Sentence ______

B **Now go to page 138. Look at the grammar chart and do the grammar exercise for 11.1.**

FIND IT

C PAIR WORK **Rephrase the sentences using the words in parentheses ( ) and check your accuracy. Then discuss the questions. Use your phone to help you find examples.**

1 We all have a favorite color, but is anyone's favorite color brown? What's your favorite color? (everybody / nobody)
2 Generally, the ocean is referred to as blue, but to my mother it looks green, and my father says it's gray. What do you think? (people / neither)
3 If you're going to a party with people you don't know well, you shouldn't wear colors that imply support for a particular political issue. Why do you think that is? Do you agree? (politics)

ACCURACY CHECK

When the subject is *anyone* / *anywhere* / *anything*, don't use a negative form of the verb. Change it to *no one* / *nowhere* / *nothing* + a positive form.

Does anybody like my idea for the new logo? ✓
~~Anybody doesn't like~~ my idea. ✗
Nobody likes my idea. ✓

4 SPEAKING

FIND IT

A PAIR WORK THINK CRITICALLY **Imagine you're talking to a graphic artist. Think of a popular brand and describe their logo and/or signature colors. What do you think of them? Use your phone to find pictures if you want.**

IKEA's colors are the **saturated** blue and yellow of Sweden's flag, **transmitting** their identity as a Swedish company. For me, these colors **imply** bold simplicity, which **reflects** IKEA's style pretty well.

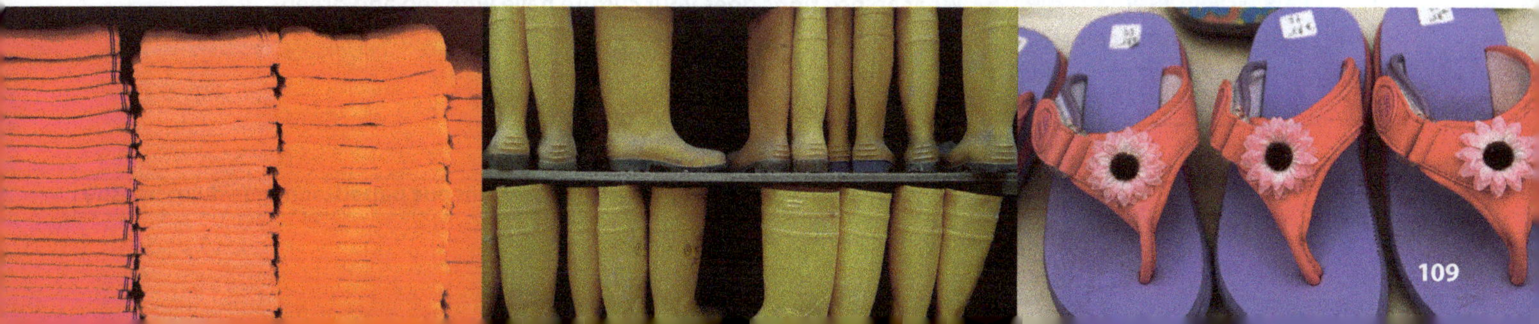

11.2 COLORFUL LANGUAGE

LESSON OBJECTIVE

- talk about color expressions and their meaning

1 LANGUAGE IN CONTEXT

A **Look at the picture and read the quote. What do you think "out of the blue" means? (Answer is at the bottom of the page.) Do you have an expression for this idea in your language?**

B 2.37 **Listen to Hyuk's report on color expressions. Do you have the same ones?**

2.37 Audio script

My report is on the creative use of color in different languages.

Did you know that red is the color with the most common associations across cultures? When you ***see red***, you get angry, and if you're ***in the red***, then you owe money. In many languages you ***turn red*** when you're embarrassed, but only in English do you ***cut through red tape*** when you have to deal with lots of government rules and regulations. But don't cheat because people who get ***caught red-handed*** also get punished. (In Spanish, you *get caught with your hands in the dough*. I love that image!) So, red usually conjures up ideas of danger or negative consequences.

Green, on the other hand, is a positive color that evokes the spring, new life, and nature. In many languages, an ecological political group is called a ***green party***, as in, "He's a green-party candidate for mayor." Someone like a gardener, who's very good with plants, has *einen grünen Daumen* – ***a green thumb*** – in German and English.

All you have to do is look at a traffic light to see that green means "go." And when you ***get the green light***, it means you have permission to go ahead with a plan. So, green is generally positive, but color expressions aren't always black and white. Calling someone ***green*** or ***a greenhorn*** means they're too young and inexperienced to be taken seriously. And if you look ***green around the gills***, then you probably don't feel well at all!

C 2.37 PAIR WORK **Listen again and read. Find a color expression not related to green or red. What does it mean? Which color expression has two different meanings?**

2 VOCABULARY: Color expressions

A 2.38 PAIR WORK **Use the categories in the box to group the color expressions in Hyuk's report. Some could go in more than one category. Listen and check.**

age	approval	bad behavior	emotion	government	health	money	nature

B PAIR WORK **Think about the expressions Hyuk mentions. To express the same idea in your language, would you use a color association or something else? How would you translate it into English?**

C **Now go to page 151. Do the vocabulary exercises for 11.2.**

D PAIR WORK THINK CRITICALLY **What associations does your culture have with red and green? What about other colors?**

For us in China, red doesn't convey anger or danger, but good luck.

Answer: completely unexpected and surprisingly unusual, like a sudden lightning strike

3 GRAMMAR: Articles

A Look at the sentences in the grammar box. Then complete the rules with the words in the box.

Articles

Red is **the** color with **the** most common associations.

People who get *caught red-handed* also get punished.

Someone like **a** gardener, who is good with plants, has ***a*** *green thumb*.

category	generalization	superlatives

1 Don't use an article when you're making a ______________ .

2 Use the definite article (*the*) with ______________ , with unique things, and to identify a specific noun that people share knowledge about.

3 Use an indefinite article (*a/an*) when the noun is first mentioned, not specifically identified, or part of a ______________ .

B **Now go to page 139. Look at the grammar chart and do the grammar exercise for 11.2.**

C PAIR WORK **Complete the sentences about the color blue with *the*, *a*, *an*, or – (no article). Compare with a partner. Did you make the same choices?**

1 Her eyes were ________ same shade of blue as ________ sky and ________ sea.

2 Royal blue is too dark for this room. I prefer ________ lighter shade.

3 My daughter always paints ________ sky ________ purple in her pictures. To her, it just doesn't look ________ blue.

D PAIR WORK **Choose another color and write three sentences about it on any topic. Trade papers and check your partner's work. Did they use articles correctly? Did you? Give each other feedback.**

4 SPEAKING

A PAIR WORK **Look again at the color expressions in the report on page 110. Think of situations in which you might use one of them. Choose one of the situations and create a conversation.**

B GROUP WORK **Act out your conversations with another pair of students. Did you all use articles correctly?**

I'm so angry **I'm seeing red!** *I just bought this plant and it's already almost dead!*

Poor thing. Give it to me. I have **a green thumb.** *Maybe I can bring it back to life.*

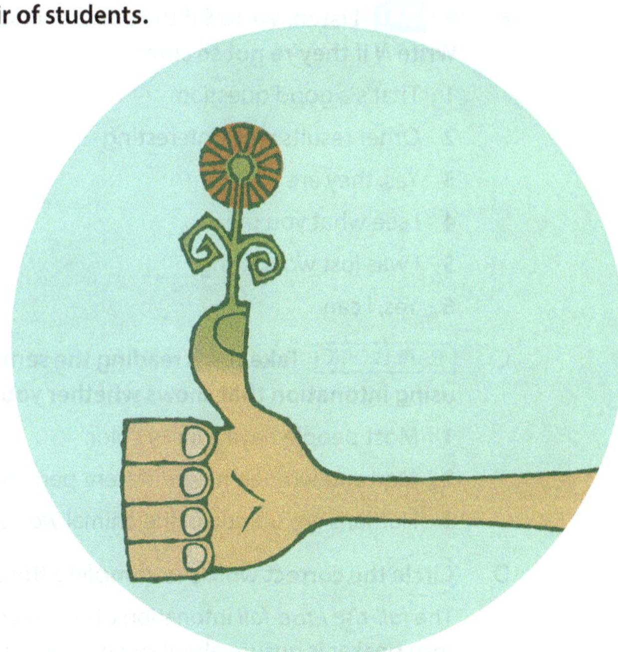

C PAIR WORK **Think of color expressions in your language that use yellow, silver, pink, or orange. What do they mean? When are they used? Are there equivalents in English? For ideas, watch João's video.**

EXPERT SPEAKER

Do you have the same color associations as João?

11.3 IT TASTES LIKE GREEN!

LESSON OBJECTIVE
- respond to questions in different ways

1 LISTENING

INSIDER ENGLISH

***happen to* + verb = coincidence**
"It could be another food that just ***happens to look like*** *a chocolate cookie."*

A PAIR WORK **Look at the different foods in the pictures. What do you think each food will taste like? Do you think they'll be sweet or savory? Why?**

B 2.39 LISTEN FOR MAIN POINTS **Listen to a Q&A (question-and-answer) session after a presentation. Take notes on the main points that each speaker makes about the relationship between food and color.**

Prof. Jenkins People imagine different tastes based on color

C 2.39 PAIR WORK LISTEN FOR DETAILS **Listen again and write specific information about the topics below. Compare your work with a partner. Did you both note the same details?**

- Expectations of taste and specific colors
- Color and the other senses
- Colored foods and marketing
- Cultural associations and food color

2 PRONUNCIATION: Listening for uncertainty

A 2.40 **Listen to the sentences from the Q&A session. Is the intonation of the underlined words the same or different? What does that tell you?**

1 Well, that was fascinating.
2 Well, I'm afraid that's not really my area.

B 2.41 **Listen. Write *S* if the speaker is sure of what they're saying. Write *N* if they're not so sure.**

1 That's a good question ___
2 Other results were interesting ___
3 Yes, they are ___
4 I see what you mean ___
5 I was just wondering ___
6 Yes, I can ___

C PAIR WORK **Take turns reading the sentences to each other. Reply using intonation that shows whether you're sure of your response.**

1 Most people have a lucky color.
2 Men and women have different perceptions of color.
3 Humans are unique in the animal world for appreciating color.

D **Circle the correct words to complete the sentence.**

The *fall-rise / rise-fall* intonation often means that there is something the speaker is unsure about or not fully prepared to state.

3 SPEAKING SKILLS

A 2.39 PAIR WORK **Read the different responses to questions from the Q&A session. Match them to the correct function and write *A*, *B*, or *C*. Consider the context of the conversation to help you. Listen again if needed.**

A Clarifying or asking for repetition **B** Thinking aloud to formulate an answer **C** Redirecting the question

Responding to questions

1	That's a good question …	___	7	I'm afraid that's not really my area.	___
2	Would you like to take this one?	___	8	Perhaps [*name*] can answer that one.	___
3	I guess I would have to say …	___	9	Let me think …	___
4	I'm glad you asked that.	___	10	Sorry, but what do you mean by that exactly?	___
5	Let me just check that I've understood your question.	___	11	I'm not sure I understand. Could you rephrase the question, please?	___
6	Well, the short answer is yes / no. …	___	12	Well, I've never really thought about it like that, but now that you ask, …	___

B PAIR WORK **Think of some difficult questions related to color to ask your partner. Use the responses in the chart in exercise 3A in your answers.**

What colors are in the South African flag?

I'm afraid that's not a country I'm familiar with.

4 PRONUNCIATION: Saying vowels before consonants

A 2.42 **Listen. Circle the word with the longer vowel sound. Are long vowels (like /iː/) longer before voiced consonants (like /d/) or unvoiced consonants (like /t/)?**

1 a white b wide
2 a green b greet
3 a sweeten b Sweden
4 a broad b brought
5 a loose b lose

B 2.43 PAIR WORK **Say the word pairs to each other. Write *S* for the shorter vowel sound and *L* for the longer vowel sound. Listen and check. Correct your pronunciation and practice them again.**

1 a feed ___ b feet ___
2 a leaf ___ b leave ___
3 a suit ___ b sued ___
4 a cause ___ b caught ___
5 a route ___ b rude ___
6 a use (*n*) ___ b use (*v*) ___

C PAIR WORK **Choose four word pairs from exercises 4A and 4B. Write a sentence for each pair but leave out the target word. Then swap papers and read one of the sentences aloud, including your guess for the missing word. Did you pronounce it clearly?**

Hmm. "There is a … *broad* range of colors in my son's toy box." Am I right? Is it *broad*?

5 SPEAKING

A GROUP WORK THINK CRITICALLY **Discuss the questions.**

- Think of a colorful dish or type of drink from your culture. Would a visitor be surprised by the flavor based on the color? Why or why not?
- If you could reinvent the item, how would you do it? Would your changes also change taste expectations? How?

Fried green tomatoes are my grandma's specialty. They look like kiwi slices, but they're hot and salty.

Would they taste good as a sweet dish?

11.4 A SENSE OF IDENTITY

LESSON OBJECTIVE
- write a short opinion essay

1 READING

A **Look at the pictures of fans dressed in their team's colors. Which color scheme do you like most? Why? How important do you think a team's colors are? Why?**

B **Where does each team come from? Which sport does the team play? Read the article and label the pictures with the team's name.**

A

B

C

D

The fans win out

When you're talking sports, the importance of color cannot be overestimated. In 2012, Vincent Tan, the Malaysian chairman of Cardiff City soccer team in the U.K., decided to change the team's jerseys from blue to red because red represented good luck for him. At the same time, a dragon replaced the bluebird as the team's symbol. It turned out to be a huge mistake. Cardiff City had been playing in blue jerseys since 1908, and fans were not happy. After three years of uproar, Tan finally surrendered to tradition and changed it all back.

This story of fans embracing the iconography of their team's colors and symbols to give themselves a sense of identity and belonging is typical but not universal.

The Ecuadorian soccer team Barcelona de Guayaquil was founded in 1925 by Eutimio Pérez, a Spanish immigrant who named the club after his home city. They originally played in the characteristic blue and red striped jersey of Perez's beloved Barça team, but after a series of losses, the team president swore never to wear those colors again. In the 1940s, yellow was introduced and would eventually become the team's principal color, though the team still retains the crest, which is almost identical to that of the Spanish team in color and design. Thus, Barcelona de Guayaquil is a sort of hybrid – based on Barça but with its own colors and traditions.

In the United States and Canada, pro sports teams are privately owned, so it is not unusual for them to move when ownership changes hands. One team, however, is unique. The Green Bay Packers, an American football team from Wisconsin, is actually a non-profit, community-owned enterprise. The team's signature color, bay green, reflects the town's forested landscape and is a point of great pride for residents and Packers fans everywhere. It is unimaginable that the team would ever change its famous green and gold color scheme.

But that is by no means the norm. For a new or transplanted team, the owners usually choose a name and colors to reflect or honor their new home. For example, when the Pittsburgh Penguins ice hockey team was formed, it used the same black and yellow as the other teams in Pittsburgh – colors also on the city's flag. Some years ago, the Penguins changed the yellow to a true gold, but even that very subtle change displeased fans because the other teams in the city had kept yellow. So gold was out, and yellow was back in. As with Cardiff City, in the end, the fans won out!

C EVALUATE INFORMATION **Read the article again. Take notes about the different stories related to the teams and their colors.**

D PAIR WORK THINK CRITICALLY **Think of a sports team that you know something about. What is their nickname? What is their symbol or mascot? What are their colors? What do they represent for the fans? How are these things used in their uniforms and merchandise?**

Real Madrid soccer team in Spain plays in all white. They are known as the "Meringues" because of this, but I don't know why they chose white.

2 WRITING

A PAIR WORK **Read an essay on creating a new sports team and choosing its colors. What factors are discussed? Which one does the writer claim is the most important, and why?**

It is widely known that there is a strong connection between color and identity – schools, political parties, and sports teams all have signature colors. But what happens when you have to choose a name for a team as well as its colors?

Seattle, Washington, is set to get a new ice hockey team, and the debate over a name is heated. Many names have been proposed – The Whales, The Kraken (a mythological sea creature), The Emeralds, The Metropolitans – but there is no clear favorite among them. Seattle's other sports teams all refer to the town's history as a seaport: The Mariners (baseball) and The Seahawks (football). Some want to keep that tradition alive, but others think it's time for a change.

Though the debate rages on about the name and symbol, there is no disagreement on the team colors. Every proposal uses some version of the signature color scheme of the city's other teams. The distinctive dark blue / forest green / silver-gray combos mirror the landscape of the area and Puget Sound in particular – an inlet from the Pacific Ocean that surrounds the city of Seattle. This shows that color has more power to unite a group than symbols or even names.

B SUPPORT OPINIONS **Read the essay again. What opinions does the writer offer? Note them below. What examples are given to support those opinions? Note them also.**

1 *color – identity connection* ______ *schools, political parties, teams* ______
2 ______ ______
3 ______ ______

WRITE IT

C PLAN **You're going to write an opinion essay of no more than 200 words. With a partner, look at the essay in exercise 2A again. How does the writer start the essay, with general or specific information? What is presented in the second paragraph? In the third paragraph? How does the writer end the essay?**

D PAIR WORK **Look at the two perspectives below. Think of possible groups you could write about and discuss the questions. You can use your phone to find examples to support your ideas.**

FIND IT

Perspectives: It's time for a change. **OR** Traditions should be honored.

- How do the group's colors relate to the culture, geography, or history of the area?
- How much tradition is represented by the current colors?
- Would you like to see such a change? Why or why not? If so, how would you like to change it?

REGISTER CHECK

Use passive voice and *it* constructions to add variety and formality to an opinion piece.

~~*Like most people, I believe …*~~
It is widely believed …
~~*I considered several factors …*~~
Several factors were considered …

E **Working together, choose a perspective and write your essay. Use examples to support your opinions.**

Everyone in our country knows the national soccer team's colors. They are on the flag, in tourism ads, and in the costumes of our folk dancers. Recently, there has been discussion about changing …

F GROUP WORK **In small groups, read your essays aloud and discuss them. Do the examples support the arguments? Do you agree or disagree with the writers? What examples can you give as a counterargument?**

11.5 TIME TO SPEAK
Fly your flag

LESSON OBJECTIVE
- create a flag for a specific group

FIND IT

A **RESEARCH** **With a partner, look at the two flags. Which one is the traditional flag of New Zealand, and which one was proposed as a new flag? What elements are the same? What's different? What do you think the new elements in the proposed design represent? If you can, use your phone to find out more.**

B **The designers of the new flag proposed it because they wanted to better reflect New Zealand's national identity. What elements do you think they considered? Read the list and add at least three more.**

Location: island in the South Pacific

Original people: Maori

National color: black

Biggest industry: sheep farming

History and current relationship with U.K.

____

____

____

C **PLAN** **You and your partner are responsible for designing a new flag for an organization (your city, favorite sports team, a community group, etc.). What will the flag be for? Make a list of the elements you should consider.**

D **PREPARE** **Choose the three or four most important elements from your list to include in your design. Take notes about the reason for each element and give an example to help explain your ideas. If you can, create a visual of your flag to use in your presentation.**

Flag for our school: should include quetzal – our national bird …

E **PRACTICE** **Work with another pair and present your design ideas to each other. Offer suggestions for improvement and listen to their feedback. Then refine your design and your presentation as needed.**

F **PRESENT** **Present your design to the class, explaining why you chose the colors, symbols, etc., and answering any questions. Use visuals if you can to support your presentation. Which designs are the most interesting? Which one would win a referendum, do you think?**

To check your progress, go to page 156.

USEFUL PHRASES

PLAN

If we make a flag for … , it should include …

The flag we make needs to evoke …

I think … is the most important element because …

The color … could symbolize both … and …

PRESENT

Our flag uses the colors … . These are colors that …

To most people, saturated colors convey … , but in our flag, …

That's a good question. … , would you like to take that one?

UNIT OBJECTIVES

- answer job interview questions about change
- talk about places that have changed drastically
- tell a story that you heard from someone else
- write a review of a movie or book
- create a structured story from pictures

THINGS CHANGE

12

START SPEAKING

FIND IT

A **Look at the picture. What is happening? What type of animal is this? Why does it symbolize change? What other transformations occur in nature? Use your phone to find pictures.**

B **Which of the milestones in the box do you think change a person's life the most? Why? Of those you have experienced, which has been the most challenging? For ideas, watch Susanne's video.**

fall in love	get married
have children	leave home
lose someone you love	move to a new place
retire	start a new job
start school	

EXPERT SPEAKER

How has your experience been similar to Susanne's?

12.1 JOB CHANGE

LESSON OBJECTIVE
- answer job interview questions about change

1 LANGUAGE IN CONTEXT

The Job Interview Guru

Episode 3: The change question

Every industry **is undergoing** enormous changes, and companies are acutely aware that **resistance** to these changes is fatal. Without a spirit of **adaptation** and **innovation**, they will be left behind. To meet the challenges ahead, they need to make sure that their staff has a positive attitude toward change.

A 2.44 **Look at the screenshot from an online tutorial. What do you think the "change question" is? Listen and check.**

2.44 Audio script

Host In this episode, we'll talk about the most important job interview question of all.

Guru That's right. Companies today are insisting that recruiters find out as much as possible about a candidate's attitude towards change. The demand that employees be comfortable with handling change is universal, so I strongly recommend that everyone, no matter what the job, prepare a good answer to the question, "How do you handle change?"

Host That seems like a simple question.

Guru Yes, but your answer needs to show that you **embrace** change and see **disruption** as a chance to shine.

Host And how do we do that?

Guru An essential quality of a good answer is that it be practical and specific. Think of an example that clearly illustrates your positive reaction to change – a huge **shake-up** in your life, like a **transition** from one school to another, or a new management system that you **implemented** at work, maybe a policy change that you **facilitated**. Doesn't matter what. The important thing is that it shows you are not afraid of change, nor do you rush in with blind enthusiasm. So, you're aware of the **disruptive** potential of change, but you can evaluate situations objectively, then identify possible obstacles and come up with **innovative** strategies to overcome them.

Host Sounds like a tall order! Let's look at a few examples. …

B 2.44 **Listen again and read. Do you agree that a good answer to the change question is crucial to job interview success? Why or why not?**

INSIDER ENGLISH

a tall order = a lot to ask

2 VOCABULARY: Talking about change

A 2.45 **Look at the bold words in the screenshot and the audio script. Make a chart like the one below and categorize the words according to how they are used. Listen and check. Which words suggest a negative attitude?**

Nouns	Verbs	Adjectives
resistance	undergo	

B **Now go to page 152. Do the vocabulary exercises for 12.1.**

C PAIR WORK THINK CRITICALLY **Read the expressions and discuss them. Do you agree with them? Why or why not? For ideas, watch Susanne's video.**

Change is difficult; not changing is fatal.

The more things change, the more they stay the same.

If it isn't broken, don't fix it.

EXPERT SPEAKER

Do you agree with Susanne, or do you think it's good advice?

3 GRAMMAR: The present subjunctive

A **Look at the sentences in the grammar box. Then complete the rules below. Refer to exercise 1 on page 118 to help you.**

The present subjunctive

Companies today **are insisting that** recruiters **find out** as much as possible.

The demand that employees **be comfortable with** handling change is universal.

An **essential quality** of a good answer **is that** it **be** practical and specific.

1 Use the present subjunctive in *that* clauses after verbs that express a need to act, a request, or a proposal: *advise, ask, demand,* ____________ *, order,* ____________ *, request, suggest.*

2 Use the present subjunctive after nouns that express a strong request or proposal: ____________ *, insistence, recommendation, suggestion.*

3 Use the present subjunctive after expressions containing adjectives that suggest importance: *crucial,* ____________ *, imperative,* ____________ *, vital.*

B **Now go to page 140. Look at the grammar chart and do the grammar exercise for 12.1.**

C PAIR WORK **Look at the situations. Use the words in parentheses ( ) to offer advice using the present subjunctive. Check your accuracy.**

1 A friend is stressed out about an upcoming interview. (I suggest …)

2 A coworker had a heated discussion with his boss. (I recommend …)

3 You need people to understand an important rule. (It is essential …)

ACCURACY CHECK

Be sure to use the base form of the verb in the present subjunctive.

I recommend that everybody ~~prepares~~ an answer. ✗

I recommend that everybody prepare an answer. ✓

The demand that we ~~are~~ on time was repeated many times. ✗

The demand that we be on time was repeated many times. ✓

4 SPEAKING

A GROUP WORK **Look at the job interview questions below. As a group, prepare an answer to one of them. Remember, a good answer should be practical and specific. Try to use the vocabulary from exercise 2A in your answers.**

a Can you tell me about a time when you had to implement a change?

b What changes would you like to see being made in your current situation?

c What has been the most disruptive change in your life in the last 10 years?

B **Think of questions that interviewers might ask in different contexts. What advice would you give about answering them?**

In a job interview, they might ask about past experience. I think **the most important thing is that you be honest** *about what you find disruptive and what you embrace.*

12.2

WHAT ON EARTH?

LESSON OBJECTIVE

- talk about places that have changed drastically

1 LANGUAGE IN CONTEXT

A **Look at the pictures in the article. They show places that were once thriving communities. What do you think happened to them? Read the article. Were you correct?**

INCREDIBLE SIGHTS AROUND THE WORLD

DRASTIC TRANSFORMATIONS

Home News About Sign out

San Juan Parangaricutiro, Mexico

Almost 70 years ago, this tiny village underwent a radical change. It was buried by the birth of a nearby volcano. The lava flowed over the whole village, leaving only the roof and the steeple of the cathedral uncovered. It's an amazing sight, emerging from the black volcanic rock that hardened all around it. Fortunately, no one was hurt. The lava is reported to have taken over a year to reach the village, so the villagers had plenty of time to escape. They eventually built a new San Juan, but of course, they would have preferred to stay in their ancestral homes.

The Aral Sea, Kazakhstan/Uzbekistan

The Aral Sea was once the fourth-largest saltwater lake in the world. More than half a century ago, this magnificent lake suffered a tragic transformation into a desert, with the dried-out bodies of old fishing boats dotted across its sandy landscape. Whole communities were forced to leave, sad to have lost their homes, their jobs, and their traditional way of life. But luckily, this drastic change was not a lasting change. In 2008, a dam was built for the purpose of redirecting water back to the lake, which seems to have worked. The sea has started to return, slowly but surely, marking a gradual but very welcome reversal. The people are moving back, too, glad to have lived to see their beloved Aral Sea come back to life.

2 VOCABULARY: Describing change

FIND IT

A 2.46 **Look at the adjectives in the box. Which are used in the article? Match them to the kind of change they describe. Listen and check. Then think of an example for each kind of change. Use a dictionary or your phone to help you.**

INSIDER ENGLISH

slowly but surely = progressing steadily over a long time

abrupt	desired	drastic	fundamental	gradual
lasting	profound	radical	refreshing	subtle
sweeping	unforeseen	welcome		

1 a change described by its connection to time _____, _____, _____

2 a change that has a large effect _____, _____, _____, _____, _____

3 a small change _____

4 a change that people are happy to see _____, _____, _____

5 a change that was not expected _____

B **Now go to page 152. Do the vocabulary exercises for 12.2.**

FIND IT

C PAIR WORK THINK CRITICALLY **Look again at the description of the Aral Sea. What do you think caused the transformation into a desert? Explain your ideas. Go online if you can to check your ideas and learn more.**

3 GRAMMAR: Perfect infinitive

A **Look at the sentences in the grammar box. Complete the rules below.**

Perfect infinitive

The lava is reported **to have taken** over a year to reach the village.

They would **have preferred** to stay in their ancestral homes.

Whole communities were forced to leave, sad **to have lost** their homes.

A dam was built for the purpose of redirecting water back to the lake, which seems **to have worked**.

The people are moving back, too, glad **to have lived** to see their beloved Aral Sea come back to life.

The perfect infinitive is used to talk about situations and completed actions in the past.

1 It is formed with *to* + ______ + past participle. A modal is followed by *have* + past participle, without ______ .

2 It is used with adjectives such as *glad* and ______ and the verbs *appear* and ______ to comment on something that already happened.

3 It is used with reporting structures such as *it is said / thought /* ______ to indicate information is from other sources, not firsthand knowledge.

B **Now go to page 140. Look at the grammar chart and do the grammar exercise for 12.2.**

C **Look at the pictures of Pripyat, Ukraine, on this page. What do you think happened there? Read the paragraph and complete it using the words in parentheses ( ) in the perfect infinitive. Were you right?**

PRIPYAT, UKRAINE

In April of 1986, a reactor at the Chernobyl Nuclear Station exploded, contaminating a vast area and eventually killing thousands of people. Just three kilometers away, the 49,000 residents of Pripyat were smart [1] ______ (prepare) for this scenario, and their plan seems [2] ______ (work). The evacuation of the town is said [3] ______ (take) only three hours! More than 30 years later and still radioactive, the overgrown remains of the homes, offices, schools, and amusement parks are a ghostly reminder of what life might [4] ______ (be) like before the disaster.

4 SPEAKING

FIND IT

A GROUP WORK **What other places do you know of that have gone through drastic or sweeping changes due to either natural causes or human activity? Discuss the questions. Then use your phone to find out more if you can.**

- What changes took place, and what caused them?
- How were people affected by the changes?
- Were the changes unforeseen or expected? Were the changes welcome?
- Are the changes reversible? Why or why not?

B **Tell the class about the places you discussed in your group. Which place changed the most drastically? Which change had the greatest effect on people?**

My grandparents' little seaside village has gone through a **profound** change. It's now an expensive tourism spot, so they had to leave. They were sad **to have lost** their home, but they were happy **to have** sold their house for a lot of money!

12.3 "AND THAT'S WHEN IT ALL CHANGED!"

LESSON OBJECTIVE

- tell a story that you heard from someone else

1 LISTENING

A **Look at the pictures of celebrity look-alikes. Who are they impersonating? Why do you think they do this? Have you ever seen a professional impersonator?**

B 2.47 LISTEN FOR MAIN POINTS **Listen to Talia and Maggy talking about a celebrity impersonator. Write short answers to the questions on the first line.**

1 Who does he impersonate? ______

______

2 How did he get into it? ______

______

3 What was he doing before? ______

______

4 What is he doing now? ______

______

5 Is he happy with the change? ______

______

C 2.47 PAIR WORK LISTEN FOR DETAILS **Listen again and add details to each answer in exercise 1B on the second line. Compare with a partner. Did you capture the same details?**

D 2.47 LISTEN FOR CERTAINTY **Is Talia confident of the facts she's sharing? Why do you think that? Listen again if needed.**

E GROUP WORK THINK CRITICALLY **What happens to a story when it is told by a second and then maybe a third or fourth person? Think about a story you heard secondhand, or third- or fourth-hand. Would you call it gossip? Why or why not? What's the difference?**

2 PRONUNCIATION: Listening for sound changes in colloquial speech

A 2.48 **Listen. Write the full forms of the underlined words.**

He's British, which is kinda freaky, 'cuz when he's not impersonating Obama, he's got this really thick English accent.

1 ______ 2 ______

B 2.49 **Listen and count the number of words you hear in the colloquialisms. Compare with a partner. Listen again and write down the full sentences.**

1 *6* *Do you want to meet her?* 5 ______

2 ______ 6 ______

3 ______ 7 ______

4 ______ 8 ______

C **Check (✓) the true statement(s). Correct any false information.**

☐ 1 Any word can be shortened or changed if it is said in connected speech.

☐ 2 In informal writing, colloquialisms are often written as they sound.

3 SPEAKING SKILLS

A 2.47 **Complete the expressions in the chart from the conversation in exercise 1B. Put the headings from the box with the correct category. Listen again if needed.**

Skipping details Referring to the original Signaling a retelling

________	________	________
[1] ________ were his exact words, ... In his own words, ... That's [2] ________ he said. I got it straight from the horse's [3] ________ .	To make a long story [4] ________ , ... And the rest, as they [5] ________ , is history.	I can't tell it the way he does. I don't remember/know all the [6] ________ , but ... I can't [7] ________ for him, but ... It's much [8] ________ the way he tells it!

B 2.50 PAIR WORK **Maggy is now retelling the story that Talia told her to Kwan. Use expressions from the chart in exercise 3A to complete their conversation. Listen and check.**

Maggy Well, his name's Sam, and listen to this. He's a professional impersonator.

Kwan What? No way! Who does he impersonate?

Maggy Barack Obama! And he's really good at it, or that's [1] ________________ , anyway.

Kwan How'd she meet him?

Maggy Hmm, I don't know [2] ________________ , but it was through Gael somehow.

Kwan Oh, OK. So, he really looks like Barack Obama?

Maggy Talia says they could be twins. In fact, those [3] ________________ : "They're like twins!"

4 PRONUNCIATION: Reading aloud

A 2.51 PAIR WORK **Listen to the information about Barack Obama and read along. Then practice reading it aloud to each other with the same stresses and word groups.**

Barack Obama was born in 1961. // Although he was the son of an American mother and Kenyan father, // he was raised mainly in Hawaii // but also spent periods abroad. // After graduating from Harvard University Law School, // Obama had a successful career as a lawyer, // showing a special interest in civil rights cases.

B 2.52 PAIR WORK **Read more about Obama's life. Mark the word groups and stresses. Listen and check. Then practice reading it aloud to each other.**

Obama became president of the United States in 2008, having run a campaign based on the need for change and the importance of hope for the future. He was president for eight years, having successfully won reelection in 2012. Among his other achievements, Obama introduced a universal health care program and helped save the auto industry after a financial crisis.

FIND IT

C GROUP WORK **Write a similar paragraph about another influential person, but don't give their name. Use your phone to do research. Divide your text into word groups and mark stresses. Then, in small groups, read your paragraphs aloud and try to guess who the people are.**

5 SPEAKING

A PAIR WORK **Student A: Go to page 158. Student B: Go to page 160. Follow the instructions.**

12.4 "THE NEXT THING YOU KNOW, …"

LESSON OBJECTIVE

- write a review of a movie or book

1 READING

A **Look at the pictures on this page. What famous movies do they make you think of? Why do you think those particular movies were so successful?**

B READ FOR MAIN IDEA **Read the article. What does the author claim is the most important element of any screenplay? What movies does he refer to as examples for his arguments?**

Turning points: the driving force of a screenplay *by Dean Martinez*

Fundamentally, all movies are about change: Someone embarks on a journey to discover the truth, solve a mystery, or learn about love, and they are never the same again. There are many ways to structure a movie plot, but the events tend to follow a three-act progression powered by key turning points.

In Act I, first we learn about normal life in our hero's world, whether that world is a mall in suburban Miami or a space station orbiting Mars. Next, we encounter the *motivator* – something that will push or pull our hero in an unforeseen direction, resulting in profound change or major disruption. The repeated invitations to Hogwarts force a hesitant Harry Potter out of his aunt's house and into an unforeseen magical existence. The discovery of a little green plant in WALL-E's lonely wasteland of trash prompts the arrival of EVE, and robot love is born. We then quickly reach the first major turning point: embracing the challenge. Harry is determined to uncover the truth of his own hidden history. WALL-E makes the abrupt decision to grab onto the spaceship and get EVE back. By choice or by force, our hero now has a mission.

Act II, which makes up most of the movie, begins with the hero rising to the challenge, fully focused on the goal that is now their life's purpose – or so they think. Just as they start to make progress, they encounter setbacks that show the challenge to have been greatly underestimated. The stakes get suddenly higher. The mission expands. It isn't enough that Dorothy and Toto overcome dangerous obstacles and successfully reach Oz. To see the Wizard, she has to kill a wicked witch! And here we find ourselves at the second turning point. The hero accepts the greater challenge, comes up with a plan, and fights the good fight to the end of Act II. There is a win or a loss, which leaves us at the final turning point – What will our hero do now?

Act III, resolution, and all questions are answered. In thrillers, these answers often involve a plot twist – *Who is trying to kill Tony Stark and steal Iron Man? Not who we thought it was. The real villain is revealed to be* – well, I won't give it away. But even with a surprise ending, we and our hero can at last make sense of events and make peace with the outcome. Unless there's a sequel …

Sources: storymaster.com; screencraft.org; www.movieoutline.com

C PAIR WORK ANALYZE CONTENT **Read the article again and complete the chart below.**

START	20–25%		70–80%	END
ACT I: Leaving "normal"	**ACT II:** [3] ______ and setbacks		**ACT III:** [7] ______	
	Part 1	Part 2		
Focus: the [1] ______	**Focus:** rising to the challenge	**Focus:** fighting the [5] ______	**Focus:** making [8] ______ of events; plot twist	
	Turning point #1: Embracing the [2] ______	**Turning point #2:** Higher [4] ______	**Turning point #3:** Win or [6] ______	

D GROUP WORK THINK CRITICALLY **Are you convinced by the author's analysis? Think of a movie you all know well. Map it to the chart above. Does it follow the outline? Do you think it's possible to analyze all stories, not just movies, using this chart? Why or why not?**

2 WRITING

A **Read the movie review. Does the reviewer like the movie? Why or why not? Have you seen it? If yes, do you agree with the reviewer?**

This week's movie review: *A Star Is Born*

This story is so good, they had to film it four times! And the fourth version is just as powerful and dramatic as any of its predecessors. Telling the age-old tale of the transformation from struggling artist to headliner, *A Star Is Born* follows the classic movie structure full of twists and turning points, ending with an inevitable dramatic climax. Ally (played by Lady Gaga) is a small-town singer/songwriter who is discovered by Jackson Maine (played by Bradley Cooper), a country/rock legend on the hunt for new talent. After seeing her perform, Jackson is captivated by Ally's voice and becomes both a mentor and a romantic interest, at once her idol and her biggest fan. As Ally's star rises, however, Jackson's career begins to fall, and the couple faces the inevitable challenges created by the dramatic transitions in their lives.

Some critics claim that the movie is too long and melodramatic. Others say that, while the beginning is enchanting and we are carried along by the romance, the second half is disappointing. Personally, I felt swept up in the amazing performances of both main actors right to the very last minute. *A Star Is Born* is definitely one not to miss!

B CREATE COHESION **Read the paragraph below. Then find the sentence in the review that combines these six simple sentences into one complex sentence. What grammatical changes were necessary?**

A Star Is Born tells an age-old tale. It is a tale of transformation. A struggling artist is transformed into a headliner. It follows the classic movie structure. It has a series of twists and turning points. It ends with an inevitable dramatic climax.

C **How many other complex sentences are in the review? Underline them. Choose one and break it into three or more simple sentences. What grammatical changes are necessary?**

D PAIR WORK **Read the paragraph about another movie. Rewrite it and combine information into complex sentences. Exchange papers with a partner. Did you combine information in the same way? Give and receive feedback on your paragraph. Revise as needed.**

La La Land is a movie about two people. Mia (played by Emma Stone) and Sebastian (played by Ryan Gosling) live in Hollywood. Mia is a struggling actress. She likes old-style Hollywood movies. Sebastian is a struggling jazz pianist. He loves traditional jazz styles. They each have a lot of passion for their dream. This draws them together. They begin a romance.

REGISTER CHECK

Complex, multi-clause sentences are common in written language, especially in reviews of movies, shows, and books, where they condense a lot of descriptive detail into one sentence, giving the reader an overview of the work being reviewed before expressing a judgment of it.

WRITE IT

E PLAN **You're going to write a review. With a partner, find a movie, TV show, or book that you both know well. Review the key plot points together but don't express your opinion about any of it. Then look at the review in exercise 2A again. Where does the writer give the key plot points? When do they express their own opinion?**

F **Individually, write a review of the work you discussed in about 200 words. Use complex sentences to tell the plot and include your opinions.**

G PAIR WORK **Exchange papers with your partner and read their review. Did you choose the same plot points to tell the story in your complex sentences? Do you have the same opinion of the work?**

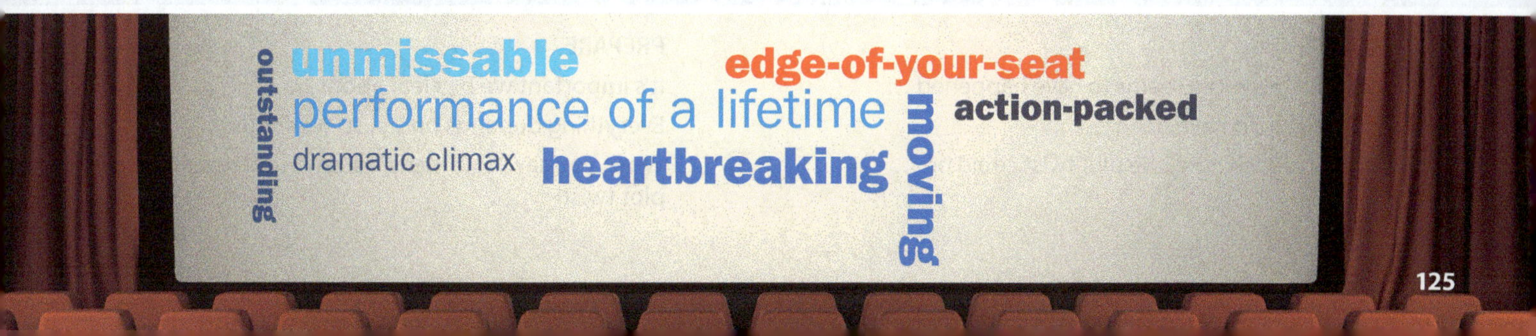

12.5 TIME TO SPEAK
Every picture tells a story

LESSON OBJECTIVE

- create a structured story from pictures

A **RESEARCH** **In a small group, look at the pictures. What is happening in each one? What order should they go in? Could they go in another order? Rearrange them a few different ways. How does the story change each time?**

B **DISCUSS** **Use at least four of the pictures to create a story for a class creativity competition. As a group, first decide on the genre (romance, action, sci-fi, etc.) and the relationships between the characters. Then develop your plot.**

C **PREPARE** **Check your story against the chart on page 124. Does it follow the pattern? If not, does it flow logically? Does your story have a clear beginning, middle, and end? Does it include a plot twist of some kind?**

D **You will have two minutes to present your story to the class, and everyone in your group must participate. Rehearse how you will tell your story and who will deliver which part. Try to maximize the impact of your presentation with clever timing.**

E **PRESENT** **Present your story to the class. Have fun!**

F **AGREE** **Vote on which story is the most creative. (You cannot vote for your own story!) Which story do you think would make the best movie? The best TV series? The best book? The best comic book? Why?**

To check your progress, go to page 156.

USEFUL PHRASES

DISCUSS

Something terrible seems to have happened …

I guess it could have been …

If this one goes here, the plot twist could be …

PREPARE

It's important we be clear about …

Everything depends on … , so we should …

When you say "… ," then I'll step in and reveal the plot twist!

REVIEW 4 (UNITS 10–12)

1 VOCABULARY

A **Circle the best words to complete the conversation about how to market a food product.**

A So, how do you think we should promote this new energy bar?

B Well, first we need to say that it's good for you. Mmm, it's nutritious and … it's [1] *vibrant / wholesome!*

A Yes, that sounds good. And then we should say that the product is green, you know, it's been produced by means of [2]*fossil-fuel / renewable* energy sources.

B Mmm, not sure we need to say that.

A I thought people want everything to be locally sourced with minimal [3]*carbon footprint / solar panels*. You know, like, eco-friendly.

B Yeah, but we can [4]*convey / imply* the message that it's 100% natural with the right image on the logo. Maybe a tree or a green landscape.

A Good! With some soft [5]*bold / pastel* shades, flowers maybe, to [6] *capture / conjure up* the countryside in people's minds. But there may not be room on the wrapper for all that.

B You know, I think the image should be more related to the ingredients, like [7]*appetite / foodstuffs* – you know, wheat fields or a close-up of some [8]*fiber / grains* of wheat.

A I think it should [9]*power / reflect* a natural, simple life. Like a farmhouse that's clearly [10]*off grid / low emission* and disconnected from urban life.

B Or maybe we shouldn't use an image at all – the wrapper is very small.

A So how about just a [11]*muted / saturated* light green color with some leaves drawn on lightly? That would evoke nature and healthy eating, right?

B Great! We've got it!

B PAIR WORK **Think of a product that you know well. How is it marketed? What kinds of images and colors does it use? What do these evoke to you?**

2 GRAMMAR

A **Rewrite the sentences using the words in parentheses ( ).**

1 The time has come to paint the house. (high time)

____

2 I would prefer us to stay in tonight. I'm really tired. (would rather)

____

3 People believe that Pompeii is the greatest Roman ruin. (believed)

____

4 News services have said that the prisoners escaped through a tunnel. (reported)

____

5 The latest statistics show that unemployment is falling. (data)

____

6 The headlines today are all about the train strike. (news)

____

B PAIR WORK **Make sentences that are true for you using the words in parentheses ( ) in exercise 2A. Share them with your partner.**

It's high time I started running again. My knee has felt fine for a while now.

3 VOCABULARY

A **Complete the essay on change with the correct form of the words in parentheses ( ).**

Big life changes are difficult but inevitable. Moving, for example, is said to be one of the most [1] ___________ (disrupt) and stressful things a person can do. [2] ___________ (last) changes, like those that require [3] ___________ (adapt) to new surroundings, can lead to emotional distress, too. Even if the change is a [4] ___________ (desire) one, it's normal for people to feel some degree of [5] ___________ (resist).

My family [6] ___________ (undergo) a really [7] ___________ (sweep) change recently. My company developed this really [8] ___________ (innovate) software, which helped us get an important contract with a Canadian company, and my bosses put me in charge of it. That meant moving my family to Canada immediately. Talk about an [9] ___________ (abrupt) change! We weren't against the idea, but there are always lots of [10] ___________ (not foresee) problems to deal with. My company promised to do whatever they could to make the [11] ___________ (transit) easier for us.

After the shock went away, we decided to see this huge change as [12] ___________ (refresh), a chance to learn about a new place and new culture. We've been in Canada two months now, and it's great!

B PAIR WORK **Do you agree with what the author says about change? Which changes are welcome for you, and which ones are disruptive? Why?**

4 GRAMMAR

A **Complete the sentences with words from the box in the correct form. You won't use all of them.**

be	bring	embrace	facilitate	meet
sell	shake-up	suggest	undergo	win

1 I suggest we ___________ the changes they're making at the office and try to make the best of it all. This ___________ is happening, whether we like it or not.

2 The tour company sent us an email. They recommend that we ___________ clothes for all types of weather. The climate is unpredictable at this time of year.

3 The suggestion from the school board that classes ___________ in the gym during the renovation has not been popular. No one wants to sit on the floor all day.

4 We were so lucky ___________ tickets to that concert. No way could we have afforded to buy them, and the band broke up one month later!

B PAIR WORK **Make sentences of your own using the other words in the box. Read them to your partner. Give each other feedback.**

We were fortunate to have sold our house before the financial crisis started. Real estate prices have really dropped!

GRAMMAR REFERENCE AND PRACTICE

1.1 COMMENTING ADVERBS WITH FUTURE FORMS (PAGE 3)

Using commenting adverbs with future forms

Commenting adverbs with future forms express the speaker's opinion or attitude about the likelihood or desirability of an action or condition. They generally follow the modal *will* or the verb *be* in future expressions.

1 *will* + commenting adverb + (*not / never*) + verb OR commenting adverb + negative contraction (*won't, aren't, shouldn't*) + verb

They ***will undoubtedly become*** *part of everyday life.*

They ***probably won't gain*** *a lot of support among labor unions.*

2 future expressions

- *be* + commenting adverb + *going to* + verb: the action is planned or intended
- *be* + commenting adverb + *about to* + verb: the action will happen very soon
- *be* + commenting adverb + *bound to* + verb: the action cannot be avoided

This ***is inevitably going to cause*** *problems.*

It ***is undoubtedly about to change*** *everything we do.*

They ***are definitely bound to be met*** *with resistance.*

A **Put the commenting adverb in parentheses ( ) in the correct position.**

1 Robotic nurses will become a fixture in all modern hospitals. (inevitably)

2 They are going to take over most of the heavy lifting work from nurses. (undoubtedly)

3 There are bound to be a few problems as medical staff get used to working with a machine. (certainly)

4 They are about to change hospital practices forever. (surely)

1.2 FUTURE PERFECT AND FUTURE CONTINUOUS (PAGE 5)

Future perfect and future continuous

Use the future perfect and the future continuous to describe situations in the future.

1 *will* + *have* + past participle (the future perfect): For actions that will be completed by a point in the future or before another event in the future

Chatbots ***will have taken over*** *from humans by the end of the next decade.*

Will *they* ***have taken over*** *on helplines, too?*

They ***won't have taken over*** *on all helplines.*

2 *will* + *be* + verb + *-ing* (future continuous): For actions that will be, or are planned to be, in progress at a given time in the future

*We****'ll be having*** *real conversations with them.*

Will *we* ***be having*** *real conversations with them?*

We ***won't be having*** *conversations with real people anymore.*

A **Circle the correct form of the verbs to complete the sentences.**

1 If my train's on time, I'll *be knocking / have knocked* on your door at ten o'clock sharp.

2 By the end of the semester, we will *be covering / have covered* most of the material in the book.

3 By this time tomorrow, we'll *be flying / have flown* to Hawaii for a two-week vacation!

4 We'll *be meeting / have met* with the head of Research and Development at the conference next week.

5 I hope I'll *be having / have had* time to read the book before we meet to discuss it.

2.1 USES OF *WILL* (PAGE 13)

Uses of *will*

The modal *will* can be used in many different situations:

1 To make predictions, assumptions, and deductions about the future
*Online personality quizzes **will** always **give** positive, flattering results.*
*In five years, we **will** all **be seeing** much more targeted advertising.*
*By the time you read this, you**'ll have seen** hundreds of quizzes on social media.*

2 To describe typical behavior, habits, and things that are true now or in general
*Personality quizzes **won't** ever **provide** truly valuable information.*

3 To express decisions about the future made at the point of speaking
*I **will** never **take** another personality quiz! This one was totally wrong.*

4 To criticize habits, behavior, and characteristics *Quiz developers **won't admit** to their real motivation.*

5 For making offers, agreeing, and promising *Our site **won't** ever **misuse** or **sell** personal information.*

A **Use the information given to write sentences reflecting the different uses of *will*. Which use does each of your sentences relate to?**

1 My grandmother loves to bake. She has always offered to make cakes for special occasions in our family.
My grandmother loves to bake. She'll always offer to make a cake for a special occasion.
2 Don't bother asking Sylvester to help you. He says no to everything.
3 My father loves to talk about politics, but he told me that he wouldn't do that when my girlfriend's parents come over for dinner next week.
4 You've worked in this building for a year. Do you know that the elevator isn't very reliable? Of course you do.
5 I answered a call from an unknown number, which was just a robocall trying to sell me something. Now I get calls like that all the time. Never again!

2.2 USES OF *WOULD* (PAGE 15)

Uses of *would*

The auxiliary verb *would* is used in many different ways:

1 To refer to past habits and typical, expected behavior *When I was a kid, I **would ride** my bike everywhere.*
2 To make polite requests ***Would** you **help** me with these bags, please?*
3 To express an opinion or judgment politely *I **would think** he'd wear something nicer to a wedding!*
4 To report a statement or question with *will* *He promised I **would get** the job.*
5 To express what someone or something is willing or able to do *The car **wouldn't start**, so I had to walk.*
6 To talk about actions in an unreal situation *What **would** you **do** in that situation?*

A **Rewrite the sentences using *would*. Which use does each of your sentences relate to?**

1 Close the door.
2 That seems like a perfect job for you. What's the problem?
3 He said he was going to arrive at eight.
4 That's so typical of him to say that.
5 In those days, I used to walk for miles.
6 I asked him many times, but he didn't say anything.

3.1 VARIATIONS ON PAST UNREAL CONDITIONALS (PAGE 23)

Variations on past unreal conditionals

Different conditional constructions can be used to talk about past unreal situations. Continuous forms express actions in progress, in both the *if* clause and the main clause. The *if* clause can come first or last in a sentence.

1 To express a situation where both the unreal condition (*if* clause) and the imagined result are in the past, use:

- *if* + *had(n't)* + past participle | *would(n't)* + *have* + past participle
  *If you'**d told** me, I **would have written** it down.*
- *if* + *had(n't)* + *been* + verb + *-ing* | *would(n't)* + *have* + past participle
  *We **would've missed** the announcement if you **hadn't been paying** attention.*

2 To express a situation where the unreal condition is in the past, and the imagined result is in the present, use:

- *if* + *had(n't)* + past participle | *would(n't)* + verb
  *If you **hadn't heard** the announcement, we **would** still **be** at the station.*
- *if* + *had(n't)* + past participle | *would(n't)* + *be* + verb + *-ing*
  *If you **hadn't heard** the announcement, we **would be waiting** on the wrong platform now.*
- *if* + *had(n't)* + *been* + verb + *-ing* | *would(n't)* + verb
  *If you **had been watching** the children, Oliver **wouldn't have** a broken arm now.*
- *if* + *had(n't)* + *been* + verb + *-ing* | *would(n't)* + *be* + verb + *-ing*
  *If you **had been watching** the children, we **wouldn't be cleaning** up this mess now.*

A **Write the correct form of the verbs in parentheses () to complete the sentences.**

1 If he ______________ (pay) attention, he ______________ (notice) that the chair was broken.

2 If you ______________ (wait) as long as I have, you ______________ (complain), too.

3 This ______________ (not happen) if you ______________ (watch) what you were doing.

4 You ______________ (enjoy) the party more if you ______________ (wear) a costume like the rest of us.

5 I ______________ (still sit) on the side of the road if he ______________ (not help) me change my flat tire.

3.2 COMMENTING ON THE PAST (PAGE 25)

Commenting on the past

Use the modal verbs *may*, *might*, and *could* to discuss possible alternative scenarios. Use *should* and *shouldn't* to criticize actions or lack of action. Use perfect forms after the modals when commenting on the past.

1 For a completed action, use *may*/*might*/*could* or *should* + *have* + past participle.
*She **may/might not have heard** the full story.*

2 For an action in progress, use *may*/*might*/*could* or *should* + *have* + *been* + verb + *-ing*.
*You **could have been telling** a story about someone else.*

3 For passive voice, use *may*/*might*/*could* or *should* + *have* + *been* + past participle.
*That information **shouldn't have been shared** with the public.*

A **Complete the sentences with *should* or *shouldn't* and the appropriate form of the verb in parentheses ( ). Use the progressive form where possible.**

I'm really sorry. I really [1] ______________ (check) before taking the keys. I [2] ______________ (pay) more attention, but I was distracted. But you know, you [3] ______________ (not leave) your car keys out in the first place.

I [4] ______________ (not leave) the bike outside, and I [5] ______________ (use) a lock. I was in a big hurry, but I know I [6] ______________ (rush). I [7] ______________ (give) myself enough time. But even so, the bike [8] ______________ (not steal) at all. I can't help it if bad people steal things!

4.1 QUANTIFIERS AND PREPOSITIONS IN RELATIVE CLAUSES (PAGE 35)

Quantifiers and prepositions in relative clauses

To add details in a relative clause, use quantifiers such as *all of, each of, many of, most of, much of, none of, some of.*

1 Use *which* for things and *whom* for people. (When used with a quantifier, *which* cannot be replaced by *that.*) To avoid confusion, place the relative clause immediately after the person or thing it refers to.

Microphotography gives a fresh perspective on everyday objects, ***most of which we usually ignore.***

Microphotographers, ***many of whom are scientists,*** *focus on the tiniest details.*

2 In speech and in most written registers, prepositions in relative clauses come after the verb. In formal or academic writing, you will often see the ending preposition before the relative pronoun.

Special microscopes, ***which cameras are attached to,*** *bring out the delicate details of pollen and dust.*

Special microscopes, ***to which cameras are attached,*** *clarify the structure of the pollen molecule.*

A **Combine the sentences using relative clauses. Use quantifiers where appropriate. Be sure prepositions are correctly placed for an informal context.**

1 I took hundreds of photos on my vacation. Most of my pictures are really awful.
2 We've invited about a hundred people to the party. Many of these guests will have to stay at a hotel.
3 My mother and I both told you about a great book I was reading. It's now available in paperback.
4 I'm working at a restaurant right now. That man over there is the manager of it.
5 This old book is full of words that are very strange to me. I had to look up many of the words.

4.2 NOUN CLAUSES WITH QUESTION WORDS (PAGE 37)

Noun clauses with question words

1 Question words can replace general nouns in noun clauses:

- *what* = the thing / things
- *who* = the person / the people
- *why* = the reason
- *how* = the way
- *where* = the place / location / the point in a process or story

I didn't know ***why*** *you wanted to see me.*

How *eyes adjust to light levels is by expanding or contracting the pupil.*

2 Noun clauses with question words can be the subject or object of the verb.

Subject: ***What we see*** *is a world of grays.*

Object/complement: *Iris scanning proves we are* ***who we say we are.***

3 Noun clauses with question words use statement word order. They are not questions.

I can't remember ***where I left my glasses.*** (not *where ~~did I leave~~ my glasses.*)

A **Replace the bold words with the correct question word.**

1 This is **the reason** I love summer. ________
2 Spending time with my family is **the thing** I like to do more than anything. ________
3 I love **the way** you talk to the kids in your class. ________
4 If I know **the location** you're standing, I can find you on GPS. ________
5 **The way** we see the world is an important part of **the people** we are. ________ ________
6 The man in the hat is not **the person** the police are looking for. ________
7 You need to pay more attention to **the things** your grandfather tells you. ________
8 I can play most of the song, but the chorus is **the point at which** I always have trouble. I don't know **the reason**. ________ ________

5.1 PARTICIPLE PHRASES IN INITIAL POSITION (PAGE 45)

Participle phrases in initial position

Participle phrases at the beginning of a sentence add extra information about the main action or the subject of the sentence. They are often used to avoid repetition and to shorten complex sentences. A participle phrase doesn't contain a subject.

1 Begin with a present participle to describe an action in progress at the same time as the action in the main clause.
__Feeling__ overwhelmed by the crowd, he quickly made his way to the exit.

2 Begin with *Having* + past participle to describe an action that happened before the action in the main clause.
__Having experienced__ the beauty of a desert sunset, she became determined to move to Arizona.

3 Begin with a past participle to describe the subject of the sentence (in the main clause).
__Convinced__ this was his last chance, John dropped everything and ran to catch the train.

Participle phrases in initial position sound formal and are more common in writing than in speech.

A **Rewrite these sentences using participle phrases. Which of these sentences are true for you?**

1 After I finished college, I took a year off to travel.

______

2 Because I live on my own, I mainly eat out.

______

3 I was totally exhausted after a hard week, so I decided to take it easy on the weekend.

______

4 I didn't have a lot of time today, so I took a taxi here.

______

5 I was so relieved that I passed all my exams. I had a big party to celebrate.

______

6 I have almost finished my English course. I'd like to learn another language now.

______

5.2 REDUCED RELATIVE CLAUSES (PAGE 47)

Reduced relative clauses

A relative clause contains a relative pronoun (*which, who, that*) and a verb phrase. When the verb of the relative clause is *be* and there is no subject pronoun, the clause can be reduced by dropping the relative pronoun and *be*.

1 *be* + verb + *-ing* *Tourists ~~**who are**~~ **staying** on the island need to book their hotel room early.*

2 *be* + adjective *Students ~~**who are**~~ **interested in** visiting the sites need to sign up at the office.*

3 *be* + past participle *Areas of the site ~~**that are**~~ **surrounded** by fences cannot be visited by the public.*

4 *be* + prepositional phrase *Requests ~~**which are**~~ **from approved organizations** will be given priority.*

A **Rewrite the sentences using a reduced relative clause.**

1 I've just read a great book that is entitled *Ancient Aztecs*.
2 I thought the man who was walking down the street was my neighbor, but I was wrong.
3 She will be on the train, which is arriving on platform 3.
4 I know a lot of people who are worried about their health.
5 Students who are concerned about climate change should join the environmental action group.
6 People who are familiar with her work say that this piece is one of her best.
7 Buildings that are older than 100 years can be submitted to the Preservation Society for consideration.
8 Conditions that are well suited to one species may not be conditions that another even closely related species could survive in.

6.1 CLEFTS (PAGE 55)

Clefts

Clefts are introductory clauses that are used to emphasize new information or something particularly interesting or surprising. Clefts can take several forms:

1 *What ... + be* ***What she wanted was** a big party!*

2 *The thing (that) ... + be* ***The only thing we wanted to do was** dance!*

3 *The ... (that) ... + be* ***The only guests at the party will be** people from school.*

4 *It + be + that/who/when* ***It was my uncle** who told me the good news.*

***It wasn't until they brought out a cake** that I realized the party was for me!*

A **Use the words in parentheses ( ) to rewrite the sentences with clefts. More than one correct answer is possible.**

1 Some people don't like surprises because they make them feel embarrassed. (thing)

2 My mom loves surprises because life is usually so predictable. (reason)

3 A surprise was on its way, but he didn't know that until he read the card. (it)

4 I really miss the birthday surprises I had when I was a kid. (what)

5 I'd really like to go to the Galapagos Islands on our honeymoon. (place)

6 While we're there, we really hope to see John's cousins. (people).

6.2 QUESTION WORDS WITH *-EVER* (PAGE 57)

Question words with *-ever*

Question words can be changed to pronouns by adding the suffix *-ever* (*whatever, whichever, whenever, wherever, whoever, however,* but rarely *whyever*). They indicate uncertainty or indifference (not a question):

1 To indicate that nothing will change the result

***Whatever** the critics say, I think it's a great movie.* *We'll get there, **however** long it takes.*

2 To indicate that the other person is free to choose *Sleep **wherever** you like. There are lots of free rooms.*

3 To indicate that the details are uncertain or unimportant ***Whoever** told you that was lying. It's not true.*

4 To indicate that the speaker doesn't mind, doesn't care, or has no opinion..

A When should we arrive?

B ***Whenever.** People can come and go as they like.*

A **Add the appropriate question word with *-ever*.**

1 ________________ good their campaign was, I don't think they'll win the election.

2 He says he'd like to get together, but ________________ I try to set something up, he says he's busy.

3 ________________ you want to go for dinner is fine with me. I'll eat anything!

4 ________________ we do to help, they always complain.

5 I'm voting for Sarafina, but I'll help ________________ wins. It's too big a job for one person.

7.1 NEGATIVE AND LIMITING ADVERBIALS (PAGE 67)

Negative and limiting adverbials

To add emphasis, you can start a sentence with a strong adverbial phrase. Negative adverbials include *Never, Never again, Never before, No way, Not until.* Limiting adverbials include *Little, Hardly, Only then, Only when.*

1 When a sentence starts with a negative or limiting adverbial, the word order in the verb phrase changes so that the auxiliary verb comes before the subject.

*Never again **will I** take my family for granted.* *Only then **can we** really understand our own history.*

*Only when everyone is settled and paying attention **am I** starting the presentation.*

2 When the verb is in the simple present or simple past, it expands to include the auxiliary verb *do/does* or *did.* This looks like question order, but the adverbial before it marks it as a statement.

*Not until then **did** I fully **appreciate** their importance.* *Little **do** they **know** what they're going to find.*

A **Rewrite the sentences using the adverbial in parentheses ( ).**

1 I didn't think about the consequences until I got the results. (Not until)

2 We had only just arrived when someone knocked at the door. (Hardly)

3 I didn't tell anyone my news until I got home. (Only when)

4 This was the first time I'd come face to face with my grandfather. (Never before)

5 I didn't suspect there was so much more to the story. (Little)

6 We would never see my aunt's beautiful, smiling face again. (Never)

7.2 FRONTING ADVERBIALS (PAGE 69)

Fronting adverbials

To add dramatic effect, you can bring adverbials of place or movement to the front of a sentence.

1 When the subject of the sentence does not take a direct object, the **subject** and verb of the main clause change position. This is true when:

- the verb is *be* — *In the envelopes are **crisp new dollar bills.***
- the verb indicates place, like *sit* or *lie* — *On the table cloth lies **a stack of red envelopes.***
- the verb indicates movement, like *fly* or *waft* — *From the kitchen wafts **the smell of fresh dumplings.***

2 If the subject has a direct object, the word order does not change.

*In the garden, **she** placed a little ceramic frog near the door for good luck.*

A **Change the sentences so that they have fronting adverbials. More than one correct answer is possible.**

1 A soft breeze floats in through the window every morning.

2 Three generations of the Escobar family waited in the living room.

3 A small boy stands silently between the chairs.

4 The big tree we played in as children is next to the front door.

5 A cold wind blows under the door, warning us all of the coming winter.

8.1 PHRASES WITH *GET* (PAGE 77)

Phrases with *get*

The verb *get* is often used with other verbs to express causation, completion, and changing states.

1 To describe the completion of a task, use *get* + noun/pronoun + past participle.
*How can I **get this paper finished** with all the noise you're making?*

2 To describe a changing state, use *get* + past participle.
*In the second act, the story **gets very complicated** and hard to follow.*

3 To indicate that something or someone is prompting an action, use *get* + noun/pronoun + verb + *-ing*.
*Coffee is the only thing that can **get me moving** in the morning.*

4 To indicate that something or someone else is responsible for an action, use *get* + noun/pronoun + past participle (+ *by* …). (Note: This is passive voice construction using *get* instead of *be*.)
*Our new sofa **is getting delivered** (by the store) this afternoon.*

5 If someone or something else (not the subject) will cause a task to be done, we can use *get* or *have*.
*We're going to **get/have** internet service installed on Tuesday.*

A **Write five sentences about your life using *get* in the five different ways presented in the chart. Which of your sentences can also use *have*?**

8.2 PHRASES WITH *AS* (PAGE 79)

A **Combine the sentences using a phrase with *as*. More than one correct answer is possible.**

1 We learned something in class. Most people can tell the difference between two nearly identical pictures instantly.

____

2 The majority of people say that they trust their gut about entertainment. Here is an example of that.

____

3 First impressions usually turn out to be wrong. That's what our survey results indicate.

____

4 We can all guess the answer. Is it better to marry someone you just met or get to know them first?

____

5 Fairy tales illustrate a lot of basic truths. For example, a person can fool you for a while, but not forever.

____

9.1 REFERENCING (PAGE 87)

Referencing

Referencing techniques make it possible to avoid repetition in a text.

1 To avoid repeating a noun or concept mentioned earlier in the same text, use …

- pronouns such as *it, they, them, this* (the pronoun *it* can also refer forward to a new idea)
- possessive adjectives such as *its* and *their*
- phrases such as *the same* or *similar* + noun

A sedentary lifestyle has harmful side effects. ***It*** *increases the risk of cardiovascular disease.*
It*'s worrying that young children are not getting enough exercise.*
Pedal desks help students focus on ***their*** *studies.*
Schools give children active alternatives. Companies offer their workers ***the same.***

2 To avoid repeating a verb or verb phrase, use an auxiliary verb such as *be, have,* or *do.* Make sure the auxiliary verb is in the same form as the original verb.

The fact that a sedentary lifestyle is bad for you doesn't make for a big news story, but the fact that the sitting disease now affects all ages ***does.***
She doesn't like it, but her parents ***do.***
They haven't tried it, but he ***has.***

A **Complete the promotional announcement with appropriate referencing devices.**

Our sedentary lifestyle is killing us!

But engineers at Hamster Desks have come up with a solution.

[1] ______________'s revolutionary and fun!

No more high cholesterol levels, chronic back pain, or early morning trips to the gym.
With [2] ______________ new office concept, you can exercise while you work.

Hamster wheel desks allow you to walk and work.
[3] ______________ save you time at the gym and keep you focused on work.

Do you want to maximize your time?
Well, there's no better way to [4] ______________ it than with a Hamster Desk!

Be the first to get a Hamster Desk workstation for your office.
Soon all your coworkers will want the [5] ______________.

No doubt about it, [6] ______________ ***is the best way to beat the sitting disease!***

9.2 CONTINUOUS INFINITIVES (PAGE 89)

Continuous infinitives

The continuous form of an infinitive verb emphasizes that an action is in progress over a period of time.

1 *to be* + verb + *-ing*

- Use with the verbs *appear* and *seem* to comment on ongoing actions and situations.
- Use with the verbs *want, would like*, and *need* to comment on intentions and plans.

*We're going **to be looking** at the flip side.*

*We seem **to be packing** way too much into our days.*

*We know we need **to be racking up** at least seven hours of sleep a night.*

2 modal + *be* + verb + *-ing*

- Use with the modals *should, could*, and *might* to criticize or speculate about an ongoing situation.

*You're watching cat videos when you **should be sleeping**!*

A **Rewrite the sentences using the words in parentheses ( ) and a continuous infinitive.**

1 It looks like my daughter is sleeping, but she isn't! (My daughter appears …)
2 It has been suggested that the problem is growing. (The problem seems …)
3 I should run five to ten miles every day if I want to compete in the marathon. (I need …)
4 I was scheduled to meet with my manager right now, but my train was late. (I should …)
5 It's possible that we may drive for 24 hours straight. (We …)

10.1 SIMPLE PAST FOR UNREAL SITUATIONS (PAGE 99)

Simple past for unreal situations

The simple past does not always refer to the past. When used with particular structures or in particular expressions, the simple past can be used to express hypothetical or desirable situations.

1 In unreal conditional sentences, use *if* + simple past.
If we had a more varied diet, we would reduce our negative effect on the environment.

2 To express present wishes, desires, and preferences, use *I wish / If only / would rather* + simple past.
***I wish / If only** people were more careful about what they ate.*
*My parents **would rather** we didn't eat red meat.*

3 To speculate or describe an imaginary situation, use *What if / Imagine (if) / Suppose* + simple past.
***What if** we created a new food product based on insect protein?*
***Imagine (if)** we started a company based on our new product!*
***Suppose** we all stopped eating beef. What would we eat instead?*

4 To make comparisons, use *as if / as though / even if* + simple past.
*We cannot keep ignoring the problems **as if / as though** they didn't exist.*
***Even if** people knew all the benefits, it would still be hard to reduce meat consumption.*

5 To express the need to start doing something, use *It's (about / high) time (we)* + simple past.
***It's time** we started exploring alternatives. Let's make a list.*
***It's high time** we expanded our diet to include insect proteins.*

A **Rewrite the sentences using the words in parentheses ( ) and an appropriate simple past expression.**

1 I don't like it that they're driving here. Public transportation is faster. (I'd rather)
2 A new apartment would be good. We've lived in this ugly place too long. (It's time)
3 Imagine living to be 120 years old. (What if)
4 Just imagine it: All people on earth are vegans, so climate change slows down enormously. (*if* + simple past)
5 I warned you that her dog bites. Stop acting like this is new information. (as if / though)

10.2 *IT* CONSTRUCTIONS (PAGE 101)

***It* constructions**

It constructions make statements more impersonal and objective. They are common in academic writing.

1 To report ideas without stating the source, use *It* + passive reporting verb.
It is said *that renewable energy is our future.*
It has been argued *that climate change is the cause of the increase in hurricanes.*
It was found *that solar batteries can be adapted for use almost anywhere.*

2 When summarizing, speculating about, or drawing a conclusion about an idea, the choice of verb and adjective determines the degree of certainty and strength of the statement.

- *It* + *is* + adjective + infinitive ***It is reasonable to assume*** *a connection between fossil fuels and climate change.*
- *It* + *is/appears/seems* + adjective + *that* clause
It seems unlikely that *social enterprises will replace traditional energy companies.*
- *It* + *appears/seems* + *that* clause ***It appears that*** *this may be a solution to a lot of our problems.*
- *It* + modal + verb (+ noun / verb phrase) + *that* clause
It could be a mistake to assume that *this trend will continue.*
- *It* + modal + verb + adjective
It would seem logical *to start small, but a wider presence is necessary for success.*

A **Rewrite the sentences using an appropriate *It* construction.**

1 Everybody now believes that it's too late to stop global warming completely.
2 According to the research I've done, nobody has figured out how to recycle Styrofoam containers yet.
3 The newspapers have just reported that the government will give tax breaks to companies that use solar energy.
4 There is no indication that cell phone use will decrease in the future.
5 The general feeling is that the people in this neighborhood don't want to put windmills on their houses.

11.1 SUBJECT–VERB AGREEMENT (PAGE 109)

Subject–verb agreement

1 Collective nouns take a singular verb when the focus is on the organization as a whole. They take a plural verb when the context clearly refers to the people in the organization. Some common examples: *association, class, club, community, department, family, government, press, public, school, staff*
The marketing ***department is located*** *on the third floor.*
The marketing ***department are*** *so excited to show everyone the new logo at the meeting.*

2 Singular nouns that end in -*s* take a singular verb. Some common examples: *gymnastics, news, politics*. School subjects that end in -*s* take a singular verb when they refer to a class or subject of study. Some common examples: *economics, ethics, mathematics, physics, statistics*
Good ***news is*** *always welcome.* ***Economics starts*** *at 11, I have lunch, and then* ***physics is*** *at two.*

3 Some words that come from Latin (*datum, medium, criterion, phenomenon*) form the plural with the ending -*a*. Some (*media, data*) take a singular verb. Some (*criteria, phenomena*) take a plural verb.
The ***media*** *never* ***admits*** *when* ***they're*** *wrong about something.*
His team documented ***phenomena*** *that* ***show*** *that color can change behavior.*

4 Words beginning with the prefixes *every-*, *any-*, *some-*, and *no-* take a singular verb. When referring back to them, however, use plural pronouns *they, them*, or *their*. ***Everyone knows*** *that red means stop.*
Nowhere is *the preference for blue more obvious than in the clothing industry.*

5 When the subject of a sentence or clause includes *either* or *neither*, the form of the verb depends on context. When referring back to them, however, use plural pronouns *they, them*, or *their*.
If ***neither of them cares*** *about the color,* ***they*** *should paint it white.* (not one person or the other person **cares**)
Either John or my parents *are going to meet us at the station.* (one person or two people **are**)

6 Monetary amounts take a singular verb when the focus is on the amount as one thing.
A thousand dollars is *a lot of money for one dress!*

A **Complete the sentences with the correct form of the verb in parentheses ( ).**

1 Everybody ________________ (know) that a company like this ________________ (make) a big profit.

2 I think statistics ________________ (be) a difficult subject. The data on unemployment rates that I need for my project ________________ (be) so confusing.

3 Neither the lawyer nor the paralegal ________________ (have) time to see you now. They meet with new clients on Fridays.

4 The news today ________________ (be) all about the elections in Mexico City. Politics ________________ (be) often the focus at this time of year.

5 Nobody ________________ (feel) good about this decision. The committee usually ________________ (vote) one way or the other, but today they ________________ (be) split five to four.

6 Please give! A few cents a day ________________ (be) all that's needed to make a big difference.

11.2 ARTICLES (PAGE 111)

Articles

1 Use a definite article …

- when you both share knowledge of the noun.
  In U.S. weddings, it is common for ***the*** *bride to wear white.*
- when you are giving additional information to identify a specific noun previously mentioned.
  Members of ***a*** *team wear uniforms so people can identify* ***the*** *team on the field.*
- with superlatives.
  This is ***the*** *darkest shade of green I've ever seen in a living room.*
- to talk about things that are unique: *the king, the moon, the equator, the army, the media.*
  People used to say that ***the*** *moon was made of green cheese.*
- with general geographical areas: *the beach, the country, the town, the forest.*
  This color scheme reminds me of ***the*** *beach.*

2 Use no article when a non-count noun or plural noun is being used to make a generalization.
Color *can evoke* ***feelings*** *and* ***memories*** *just like* ***sound*** *can.*

3 Use an indefinite article …

- when the noun is first mentioned, new to the reader, or not specifically identified.
  He used ***a*** *shade of orange that I've never seen before.*
- to talk about jobs and professions or when the noun is part of a category.
  I'm ***a*** *real estate agent, but I'd like to work as* ***an*** *interior decorator one day.*
- when making a generalization using a singular noun.
  Muted yellows and greens work really well in ***an*** *open space, like* ***a*** *kitchen.*

A **Complete the sentences with *a, an, the,* or – (no article).**

Some people would argue that [1] ________ colors are not important in [2] ________ daily life, but if, for example, you're [3] ________ salesperson or work in [4] ________ marketing, your image can be very important. If you dyed your hair [5] ________ strange color one day, [6] ________ clients might be turned off.

Consider also [7] ________ colors you wear. Your clothes are [8] ________ most visible thing about you and [9] ________ first thing [10] ________ people notice. [11] ________ colors you choose say a lot about you.

12.1 THE PRESENT SUBJUNCTIVE (PAGE 119)

The present subjunctive

The present subjunctive is used to lend authority to a speaker's words. It is usually used to refer to demands, suggestions, and recommendations; to describe what should happen; or to identify what is important.

1 Verbs in the present subjunctive do not add *-s* for the third person. The present subjunctive form of the verb *to be* is *be*.
*He insists that we all **be** ready to go at noon.* *I suggest that you **not come** any earlier than two.*

2 Use the present subjunctive with *that* clauses …

- after verbs that express a request or a proposal: *advise, ask, demand, insist, recommend, suggest.*
*He **recommended** that we **allow** extra time for traffic.*
- after expressions containing adjectives that suggest importance: *essential, imperative, important, vital.*
*It is **imperative** that he **complete** the application and **send** it in immediately.*
- after nouns that express a strong request or a proposal: *demand, insistence, recommendation, suggestion.*
*The officer's **demand** that we **pull** the car over and **wait** was surprising to all of us.*

A **Use the prompts to rewrite the sentences with the subjunctive.**

1 Students need to be on time for class. That's a requirement at this school.
The school requires ______________________________

2 He visits his grandma at least once a week, which they say is important for her recovery.
For her recovery, it is important ______________________________

3 The mayor has ordered people to stay indoors during the hurricane for their own safety.
The mayor's order that ______________________________

4 Medical professionals agree that all patients, whatever their age or physical condition, need to do some form of exercise every day.
It is recommended that everyone ______________________________

12.2 PERFECT INFINITIVE (PAGE 121)

Perfect infinitive

The perfect infinitive is used to talk about situations and completed actions in the past.

1 Use *to have* + past participle …

- with reporting structures such as *it is said / thought / reported* to indicate information is from other sources, not firsthand knowledge.
*The hanging gardens of Babylon **are thought to have been built** about 3,000 years ago.*
- with adjectives to describe feelings that resulted from a situation or action in the past.
*We were **relieved to have made** it to the end of the trail before sunset.*
- with the verbs *appear* and *seem* to comment on something that already happened.
*Based on the mess in the kitchen, her dinner party **appears to have happened** after all.*

2 Use modal + *have* + past participle with the modals *should, would, could,* and *might* to criticize or speculate about the past.
*The residents **might not have wanted** to move, but they had to go.*

A **Tell the story behind the headline using your own ideas and perfect infinitives.**

MAYOR LOSES ELECTION AFTER CORRUPTION SCANDAL BREAKS

1 The mayor was shocked … The mayor was shocked to have lost the election.
2 He thinks his defeat might …
3 In a recent newspaper story, he was alleged …
4 Sources say that the mayor is questioning the election's honesty. He is said …
5 Supporters of the opposing candidate believe the mayor should … .

VOCABULARY PRACTICE

1.1 USING ADVERBS TO ADD DETAIL (PAGE 2)

A **Write the appropriate adverb using the word in parentheses ( ). What do you think the development might be?**

1 This is ____________ (question) one of the greatest developments in public transportation in the last ten years!

2 It will ____________ (radical) change the way we move around our cities and ____________ (drastic) cut back on our consumption of fossil fuels.

3 It will ____________ (progress) take over for all traditional modes of transportation.

4 People could ____________ (feasible) save time and money, as well as help the environment.

B **Circle the correct adverbs to complete the paragraph.**

Introducing the new robot surgeon, the radical medical development that is [1]*drastically / gradually* being introduced in hospitals around the world. Currently, the robots are directed by a human and can only perform a limited range of operations. The hope is, however, that they will [2]*increasingly / unquestionably* be able to perform all kinds of major surgery. Researchers expect robot surgeons will [3]*markedly / ultimately* reduce surgical errors, possibly by as much as 25 percent. The robots will [4]*inevitably / progressively* meet with resistance from patients, but they will soon see how effective robot surgeons can be.

1.2 TALKING ABOUT DEVELOPMENTS IN TECHNOLOGY (PAGE 4)

A **Complete the sentences with the correct form of an appropriate word or phrase from the box.**

artificial intelligence (AI)	beta version	computer-generated speech	chatbot
computer translation	facial recognition	image recognition	
operating system (OS)	text to speech / speech to text	virtual assistant	
voice activation	voice recognition	working prototype	

1 Recent developments in ____________ mean that computers are getting better and better at imitating human thought.

2 This new home-security software uses ____________ technology, so your front door won't open until it hears you say it's OK.

3 I can't open any of these work files on my laptop at home. I think my office computer must use a different ____________ .

4 There have been stories in the news recently about ____________ that seem to be laughing at their owners and are refusing to answer their questions!

5 The researchers are currently trying to get a ____________ of their robot ready to show investors. If they get enough funding, they could have a beta version in a year.

B PAIR WORK **Read the needs and decide which type(s) of technology would address them best. Then write four needs and think of the best ways to address them. Compare your work. Can you think of other technology that might address your partner's needs?**

1 You need to identify an object in a photo.

2 Passport machines need to check passenger identity.

3 You need to run programs on your computer.

4 A digital help line needs to answer simple requests for information.

5 You want to dictate a message on your cell phone.

6 You need to check your email, but you're driving.

7 An app company needs to test their new product and find "bugs."

8 A message on a social media feed is in Korean, but you want to read it in English.

9 ____________

10 ____________

11 ____________

12 ____________

2.1 DESCRIBING PERSONALITY (PAGE 12)

A **Complete the sentences with the words in the box.**

accepting	chatty	genuine	insensitive	rigid	self-centered

1 I like that he's so ________________ and sociable, but he has to learn to shut up sometimes.
2 My parents are very ________________. I wish they could relax a little and be a bit more flexible.
3 I thought that question was very ________________. I understand why they were offended.
4 Teenagers tend to be pretty ________________. But they grow out of that and start caring about the rest of the world eventually.
5 I think she'll be a good therapist because she's very ________________ and not at all judgmental.
6 When you're a little child, you're ________________ and honest. You don't hide your feelings at all.

B **Circle the correct adjectives for the context of the paragraph.**

My roommate Selma is amazingly sweet. I've never heard her say a negative thing about anyone! There's this guy in our building who never says hello. I think he's [1]*antisocial / genuine* and unfriendly, but Selma tells me not to be [2]*narrow-minded / sincere*. He's just shy. But there's no reason for him to be so [3]*aloof / talkative*. I may be a little [4]*open-minded / talkative* at times, but "hello" isn't much to expect. Selma says I'm a [5]*rigid / sincere* person who likes to connect with others, which is why it bothers me. I think that's her nice way of saying I'm kind of pushy.

2.2 USING THREE-WORD PHRASAL VERBS (PAGE 14)

A **Complete the sentences with correct form of the phrasal verbs in the box.**

come down to	fit in with	get through to	mess around with	stand up for

1 It's really hard to ________________ him. He has such rigid ideas and doesn't want to listen.
2 I thought he was serious about working this weekend, but he was just ________________ me.
3 I owe her a big favor because she ________________ me when nobody else would.
4 He has good ideas for new products, but they don't really ________________ the rest of the product line. I think he should start his own company.
5 I don't care about fancy brands and fashion. For me, it all ________________ comfort.

B **Match the two parts to create collocations. Then use the collocations in context in the sentences below.**

1 fall back on ___ a people
2 face up to ___ b any nonsense
3 look down on ___ c opposition
4 run up against ___ d established ideas
5 not put up with ___ e (their) mistake

1 They ________________ who don't dress well. I don't like their superior attitude.
2 The bosses at my company are so afraid of taking risks. They always ________________ and never want to try anything new.
3 I wish Mariella ran these meetings. She ________________, and we'd surely finish more quickly.
4 We all wanted her for the job, but we ________________ from headquarters when they saw that she doesn't have a college degree.
5 My son and his friends broke a window at school when they were messing around. They could have run away, but they ________________ and reported it. They even paid for the repairs.

3.1 THOUGHT PROCESSES (PAGE 22)

A **Write the words in the box next to their definitions.**

analyze disregard fixate foresee presume review

1 a be obsessed with a particular idea ______
b think that you know ______
c be able to predict the future ______
d think something is not important ______
e look back over something ______
f examine something in detail in order to understand it ______

dismiss envision evaluate interpret reconsider reject

2 a change your point of view ______
b decide something is not worth considering ______
c imagine a future situation ______
d don't accept something because it isn't good enough ______
e explain what something means ______
f consider the value of something ______

B **Circle the word that is different from the others.**

1 analyze evaluate interpret reconsider
2 disregard dismiss fixate reject
3 envision foresee interpret predict

3.2 DESCRIBING EMOTIONAL REACTIONS (PAGE 24)

A **Complete the sentences with words from the box.**

flustered gracious harmless mellow resourceful spiteful victorious

1 After that truck nearly hit us, I was so ______ that I had to pull over and calm down for a while.
2 John has a very particular way he likes to mow the lawn. It's ______, so I don't try to stop him. Who cares how he does it as long as he does it?
3 With no money for decorations for the play, we had to be ______. We used green paper for the bushes and made flowers from balloons!
4 When our team's design was chosen for the campaign, we walked around feeling ______ for weeks!
5 His coworker was so angry about Pablo's promotion that he started doing little things just to cause problems. His behavior was really childish and ______.
6 During the presentation, I completely forgot to give Sharon credit for her work. I felt awful, but she was really ______ about it. She said everyone makes mistakes when they're nervous.
7 Big parties are OK, but I usually prefer a more ______ gathering, like a small dinner party.

B **Circle the correct adjectives to complete the paragraph.**

What's the most important thing a manager should always remember?

"Don't take it personally."

When people are looking to you for answers, it can feel like they're questioning your judgment, which can easily make you feel [1]*defensive / victorious* about your decisions. Just remember, it's not about you. The workplace can be tense and stressful, which can cause people to blow things out of proportion and become [2]*harmless / hysterical* over the smallest problem. If you stay calm and [3]*composed / resourceful*, people will follow your lead. If you're [4]*melodramatic / spiteful*, you'll only add to their anxiety. But nobody's perfect. If you do lose control, admit it and apologize. People are [5]*flustered / forgiving* when they believe you're sincere.

4.1 DESCRIBING THINGS (PAGE 34)

A **Which adjectives from the box would you use to describe the things? More than one correct answer is possible. Compare your answers with a partner.**

circular	cylindrical	delicate	elaborate	filthy	flaky
mammoth	miniature	multicolored	ridged	stringy	

1 your favorite dessert
2 your favorite athlete's uniform
3 your favorite musical instrument
4 an animal you can see in a zoo
5 a piece of jewelry that you like
6 a machine you have in your home
7 decorations related to your favorite holiday
8 a space ship (real or from a movie)
9 a mountain in your country
10 equipment in a doctor's office
11 the design on the rug or curtains in your room
12 the oldest book you ever saw

B PAIR WORK **Think of common objects from daily life and take turns describing them to your partner using the adjectives in exercise A and others. Don't use your hands when you talk. Can your partner guess the object from your description?**

4.2 EYE IDIOMS AND METAPHORS (PAGE 36)

A **Match the expressions to their definitions.**

1 agree ____
2 be aware of everything around you ____
3 ignore (usually something bad) ____
4 focus on your main aim ____
5 enjoy looking at ____
6 draw your attention unexpectedly ____
7 not caring about the result ____
8 seeing something from above ____
9 very quickly ____
10 currently well-known and in the media ____
11 using imagination ____

a a bird's eye view
b catch your eye
c feast your eyes on
d have eyes in the back of your head
e in the blink of an eye
f in the public eye
g in your mind's eye
h keep your eyes on the prize
i see eye to eye on
j turn a blind eye to
k without batting an eye

B **Replace the bold words with idioms and metaphors from exercise A.**

1 I don't need to **share opinions on** absolutely everything to be friends with someone.

2 If you know that someone is doing something wrong and you **don't do anything about** it, you're just as guilty.

3 This map doesn't give any details. It just gives **a wide-angled perspective** of the area.

4 Long-term goals are more difficult than short-term ones. But no matter what obstacles come up, just **remind yourself how wonderful it's going to be when you've finished**, and you'll get there.

5 Most celebrities prefer that their kids not be **the subject of media attention**, so they have to be careful not to take them places where there's paparazzi.

6 We waited forever for the check. Finally, I managed to **get** the server's **attention** and ask for the bill.

7 Never take your attention off the road when you're driving. An accident could happen **very quickly.**

8 **Get a good look at and enjoy** our showroom full of beautifully restored sports cars from the 1970s!

5.1 DESCRIBING REMOTE PLACES (PAGE 44)

A **Circle the correct words to complete the sentences. Which sentences are true for you?**

1 I love landscapes that are vast and *barren / picturesque* – great empty lands like Patagonia or Iceland.

2 I don't feel comfortable in *deserted / nameless* places, especially if there are lots of *abandoned / anonymous* buildings around.

3 My favorite landscapes are rich, green places that are *hostile / lush*, with different types of vegetation.

4 I like to hike through the forest to a scenic overlook spot on top of the mountain. It has a beautiful view of the *barren / immense* landscape that goes on for hundreds of kilometers!

5 There is a *harsh / vast* area in the center of my country where there aren't many people, only forests and plains. Most people live near the coast.

B **For each group, match the words in the box to their synonyms.**

anonymous   harsh   immense

1 a very large ______
b difficult to live in ______
c unremarkable ______

abandoned   hostile   picturesque

2 a empty ______
b visually attractive ______
c uninviting ______

abundant   isolated   scenic

3 a plentiful ______
b by itself and hard to reach ______
c pleasant to look at ______

barren   lush   unspoiled

4 a not touched by people ______
b with few living things ______
c rich and abundant ______

5.2 TALKING ABOUT INFLUENCES (PAGE 46)

A **Rewrite the ideas in the sentences using words from the box. More than one answer is possible. Compare sentences with a partner.**

consequence   force   impact   implications   influence
motivate   result in   source   stem from   trigger

1 The accountant noticed some unusual items in an expense report and asked the owner of the company about them. Soon, a full investigation of company finances happened.

2 After the government announced it was closing the local school, parents were worried about how this would affect their children's lives.

3 Sometimes a big problem causes you to think about things differently. This can lead to a really surprising or interesting way to solve the problem.

4 Many adult problems exist because of experiences that happened in childhood.

5 When they try to explain their own work, musicians often refer to the music or styles of other musicians that they like or admire.

6 Many factors shape the final design of a product, for example, money, time, target market, and the creativity of the design team.

B PAIR WORK **Discuss the questions.**

1 What (not who) has had the greatest positive influence on your life? What aspects of your life has it impacted?

2 What forces motivate people to make big changes in their lives? Have any of these forces triggered action in you?

3 Imagine you were offered a great job in a country far away. What implications would taking the job have on your family? Your friends? Your current employer?

6.1 USINGS ADVERBS TO ADD ATTITUDE (PAGE 54)

A **Choose an appropriate adverb–adjective combination to complete the sentences. More than one correct answer is possible.**

Adverbs	deeply	genuinely	highly	immensely	incredibly	noticeably	remarkably	utterly
Adjectives	anxious	calm	helpful	popular	shocked	surprised	thrilled	unusual

1 When they announced that they were getting married, I was ______________ ______________ . I didn't even know they were dating!

2 That play was ______________ ______________ . I've never seen anything like it before.

3 It was a tense situation, but she remained ______________ ______________ throughout.

4 The guy at reception was ______________ ______________ and gave us lots of useful tips.

5 I could tell that Max was ______________ ______________ . He kept jumping up and down in excitement.

6 That movie has been ______________ ______________ . There are still lines down the block to get tickets.

7 I was ______________ ______________ when they made me an offer. I didn't think the interview went very well at all.

8 He's been ______________ ______________ these last few days. He still hasn't heard whether his company is going to get the contract. His business really needs the work.

B PAIR WORK **Use the prompts to talk about your experiences. Add attitude with adverbs when you can.**

1 Something that was immensely popular but you didn't like: Why?

2 An experience that made you noticeably anxious: What happened?

3 A time when you were remarkably calm while others were not: What happened?

4 Behavior that utterly shocked you: Why?

5 A product you are highly surprised to find is genuinely helpful: What is it? What does it do? What did you expect?

6.2 USING THE PREFIXES *UNDER-* AND *OVER-* (PAGE 56)

A **Add *under-* or *over-* to the words in the box to match the definitions. More than one correct answer may be possible.**

confident ~~crowded~~ developed estimated paid priced rated whelmed

1 too many people *overcrowded*

2 receiving wages that are too low for the job ______________

3 too expensive for what it is ______________

4 feeling too sure about a result ______________

5 not calculated high enough ______________

6 not able to handle something because it is too much ______________

7 without modern facilities ______________

8 reviewed as lower than it should be ______________

B **Rewrite the ideas in the sentences using *over-*/*under-* words.**

1 The critics gave this movie five stars, but I didn't like it at all.

I think this movie is overrated. It got five stars, but I didn't like it!

2 Even if you think you're perfect for a job, prepare well for the interview. You never know what will happen.

3 I think this phone is a real bargain. People would pay twice as much for it!

4 If you're claustrophobic, don't take the subway between 5 and 7 p.m. There are a lot of people trying to get home after work at that time.

5 In the U.S., servers in restaurants don't have high salaries, so they depend on tips to get by.

6 I have too much work to do this month! It's really stressful.

7.1 TALKING ABOUT ANCESTRY (PAGE 66)

A **Match the words in the box with the definitions.**

adoptive	ancestor	ancestry	ethnic	ethnicity
genealogy	genetic	heritage	inherit	

1 a person related to you who lived a long time ago ______
2 belonging to or relating to genes ______
3 the history and traditions of a particular group ______
4 a person's family going back generations ______
5 get from a parent ______
6 related to a group of people with common origins ______
7 the study of tracing a family tree back in time ______
8 the group of people you identify with biologically ______
9 taking in and accepting as family ______

B **Write the correct form of the word in parentheses ( ). Look at the chart on page 66 to help you.**

We were greeted at the door of the grand old house by an older gentleman. He was well dressed and friendly but walked with some difficulty. He invited us in and gave us a brief tour, sharing stories of his famous family as we looked at the many generations of portraits hanging on the walls. He was deeply proud of his [1] ______ (ancestor) home and clearly enjoyed showing it off.

A young man joined us, and the gentleman introduced him as his son. The son looked very different from his father. In fact, the [2] ______ (heritage) qualities so obvious in the older man's face were nowhere in the son's. We must have been noticeably surprised because the two smiled and explained that the young man was [3] ______ (adopt) from another country, far away.

"He's lucky," the gentleman said. "He'll [4] ______ (heritage) this house, but not my bad knees!"

7.2 TALKING ABOUT CUSTOMS AND TRADITIONS (PAGE 68)

A **Match the verbs with the phrases.**

1 mark / observe ___ a the fight between good and evil
2 honor / pay tribute to ___ b a special day
3 signify / symbolize ___ c a special person or group of people

B **Circle the correct words to complete the paragraph.**

The Indian celebration Diwali is called the festival of lights. To [1] *mark / signify* the occasion, families place lanterns outside their homes to [2] *observe / symbolize* their fight against darkness. Colors are also an important part of the [3] *rituals / significance*. People draw patterns called "rangoli" with colored sand or powders on the floor outside their door. The intricate patterns [4] *observe / signify* the unity of humans and nature and welcome guests to the house. Diwali is a very special occasion, and families of Indian origin [5] *honor / keep* the traditions alive all around the world.

8.1 TALKING ABOUT ATTENTION AND DISTRACTION (PAGE 76)

A **Circle the correct words to complete the conversation.**

A I'm sorry to [1]*concentrate on / interrupt* you, but I need your help.

B That's OK. I could use [2]*a distraction / an interruption.* [3]*I've been / I got* focused on this report all morning, and my eyes are crossing!

A Well, it's about Sam. He's kind of driving me crazy.

B Oh, no! What's he doing?

A Well, talking. Not to me – to himself. It's so [4]*distracting / interrupting.* It's impossible to [5]*be interrupted by / concentrate on* your work when there's someone constantly talking. It's hard enough to [6]*avoid / get focused on* distractions around here.

B I'll talk to him. Maybe we can move his desk to that area by the lobby. Then he'll be the one getting [7]*distracted / focused.*

B **Complete the sentences with the words and phrases in the box. Which of the sentences are true for you?**

avoid	concentration	focus on	get focused	interruptions	stay focused

1 I turn off my phone when I'm working in order to ______________ on my work.

2 I can't get anything done when I work from home because of the constant ______________ in my house: the telephone, my neighbors coming by, sirens from the ambulances, my kids fighting. It's impossible!

3 When I get distracted by something, it's really hard for me to ______________ again.

4 Sometimes you just can't ______________ distractions. It's hard to be disciplined all day!

5 I don't think my powers of ______________ are weaker now. If anything, they're getting stronger!

6 I'm not bad at multitasking, but I prefer to ______________ one thing at a time.

8.2 EXPRESSIONS WITH *GET* (PAGE 78)

A **Look at the expressions with *get* in context. Then match them to the definitions.**

1 What are you **getting at**? I don't understand your point. g

2 I've **gotten** really **attached to** my old car over the years. ___

3 I **got** really **frustrated** in line at the bank. They take so long! ___

4 It took him three tries to put the shelves together, but he finally **got** it **right**. ___

5 We need to **get rid of** that sofa. It's disgusting. ___

6 We **got the go-ahead** from the boss to hire the crew and get construction started. ___

7 I don't think I could ever **get accustomed to** driving on the left. ___

8 I just **got blown away by** how much damage there was. Would we ever get it all repaired? ___

9 Designing a computer program can **get** really **complicated**, so you have to stay focused. ___

10 It's easy to **get lost** on these trails if you don't pay attention to the markers. ___

11 We need to **get something straight**. This is my car, and I'll say who can drive it. ___

a figure out / understand

b feel close to or affectionately about

c be amazed / overwhelmed

d become familiar / comfortable with

e not know your way

f become difficult

g try to communicate

h receive approval

i feel angry or annoyed

j be clear about

k remove forever

B **Replace the underlined expressions with a *get* expression. Make any changes necessary to the structure of the sentences.**

1 When children are learning to ride a bike, they rarely figure it out immediately.
2 I can't understand what you're trying to say.
3 I was totally amazed by the news. I just couldn't believe it.
4 The campus was so big that I couldn't figure out which way to go while trying to find my classroom the first time.
5 It takes a while to familiarize yourself to life in a new country.

9.1 DISCUSSING HEALTH ISSUES (PAGE 86)

A **Match six of the terms from the box to the correct descriptions.**

blood pressure	cardiovascular disease	cholesterol levels	chronic pain
circulation	digestion	immune system	internal organs
joints	posture	sedentary lifestyle	side effects

1 what gives the body resistance to infection and toxins ______
2 the amount of a type of fatty substance in the blood ______
3 what you have if you spend most of your time sitting down ______
4 the position of the body when standing or sitting ______
5 medical conditions that affect the heart ______
6 the process of absorbing nutrients from food ______

B **Use the other words in the box in exercise A to complete the paragraph.**

Research suggests that standing for too long may also have harmful medical [1] ______ ______. It has been suggested that prolonged standing might cause [2] ______ ______ in the hip [3] ______ and lower back, as well as affecting [4] ______ in the legs and feet. Although standing helps relieve pressure on your [5] ______ ______, such as the stomach, liver, and pancreas, it has no effect on your [6] ______ ______ or general heart health. It is important not to stay still in one place for too long, whether you're sitting or standing.

9.2 DISCUSSING (LACK OF) SLEEP (PAGE 88)

A **Match the phrasal verbs to their definitions.**

1 eliminate d
2 go away unnoticed ___
3 slowly relax ___
4 accumulate ___
5 increase over time ___
6 reduce the amount ___
7 gently fall asleep ___
8 make time for an activity ___
9 obtain or achieve to reach a target ___
10 stop someone from going to sleep ___
11 motivate someone to do something ___
12 do a lot of things in a limited amount of time ___

a add up
b build up
c cut back on
d cut out
e drift off
f drive somebody to
g fit something into
h keep somebody up
i pack something into
j rack up
k slip away
l wind down

B **Complete the paragraph with phrasal verbs. Look back at exercise A on page 149 to help you.**

There's no doubt that [1] ______ ______ on screen time before bed and [2] ______ ______ caffeine in the afternoon can help you get to sleep quicker, but there's another problem. We [3] ______ so much ______ our schedules during the week that no matter how hard we try, we just can't [4] ______ the recommended number of hours of sleep. Work commitments [5] ______ us ______ late at night. Family commitments get us up extra early in the morning. Slowly but surely, sleep deprivation [6] ______ ______ until we're barely functioning by Friday.

But there's good news! Some research shows that by sleeping late on the weekend we can actually make up for all those lost hours. Don't set you alarm clock Saturday morning – let yourself [7] ______ ______ and take it easy. Feel the tension and tiredness [8] ______ ______. All that extra sleep will [9] ______ ______ to give you a cheerful Monday morning!

10.1 DISCUSSING GLOBAL FOOD ISSUES (PAGE 98)

A **Write the words from the box next to their definitions. There are three extra words.**

appetite	cattle	cereal	consumption	fiber	foodstuffs	grain
livestock	nutritious	shortage	superfood	supply	wholesome	

1 animals that are kept on a farm livestock
2 cows that are used for beef ______
3 anything people can eat as food ______
4 a substance in certain foods that helps digestion ______
5 wheat, corn, rice, oats ______
6 able to improve your health ______
7 a situation when there is not enough of something ______
8 seeds used to make bread ______
9 the desire to eat food ______
10 how much of something that is available to use ______

B **Complete the story with words from the box in exercise A.**

The açai fruit comes from a palm tree in the Amazon rainforest and has long been popular in Brazil. Now, however, açai is gaining popularity in North America, not only for its flavor, but because it's [1] ______ and [2] ______. It's a great source of dietary [3] ______, keeping the digestive system clean and functioning normally. It is also said to improve skin, boost energy, and increase mental function. For these reasons, [4] ______ of açai has gone up dramatically around the world. People love it!

Try açai for yourself and you'll soon understand why it's being celebrated as the [5] ______ of tomorrow!

10.2 DISCUSSING GLOBAL ENERGY ISSUES (PAGE 100)

A **Complete the story about a social enterprise with words from the box. There are four extra words.**

biofuel	carbon footprint	carbon-neutral	energize	fossil fuel	low-carbon
low-emission	off-grid	power	renewable	self-sustainable	solar panels

Pollinate Energy (PE) is an Australian social enterprise that is improving the lives of India's urban poor by providing them with [1] ______ energy options. Cooking appliances powered by [2] ______ ______ is just one way PE has helped families who live in [3] ______-______ communities and lack access to conventional energy sources. PE provides families with products that can [4] ______ their homes but that are [5] ______-______ because they require only sunlight or wind. If another energy source is needed, PE products are made to use only [6] ______-______ or, better still, [7] ______-______ fuels, as opposed to the different types of [8] ______ ______ previously used in these communities.

B **Circle the best words to complete the sentences.**

1 Social enterprises have the knock-on effect of *energizing / powering* inventors to develop more creative ways to meet people's needs, help the planet, and also make a profit.
2 A *biofuel / fossil fuel* is produced through biological processes, such as agriculture.
3 Livestock farms are bad for the environment due to their *emission / power* of dangerous greenhouse gases.
4 *A carbon footprint / Low-carbon energy* refers to the total emissions caused by an individual, event, organization, or product. The smaller, the better!

11.1 DESCRIBING COLOR ASSOCIATIONS (PAGE 108)

A **Replace the underlined words with a verb from the box in the correct form. More than one option may be correct.**

capture	conjure up	convey	evoke
imply	reflect	resonate with	transmit

1 The strong colors and sharp angles suggest that the artist didn't like the person he was painting.
2 To me, this photograph of an eagle in flight perfectly represents the idea of freedom.
3 The child in the wagon, the ice-cream truck, the women wearing hats – it all communicates a real feeling of nostalgia.
4 I really love her paintings. I grew up near the ocean in western Canada, so her smoky greens and grayish blues really are meaningful to me at a deep level.
5 Looking at old family photos brings back memories of winter nights by the fire with my grandmother.
6 These new designs show the current popularity of pink!

B **Match the descriptions of shades to their definitions.**

bold	muted	neutral	pastel	saturated	vibrant

1 not bright, mixed with gray ______
2 bright and strong ______
3 not strongly any definite color ______
4 pale and soft ______
5 pure, not mixed with other colors ______
6 strong and noticeable against other colors ______

11.2 COLOR EXPRESSIONS (PAGE 110)

A **Circle the correct color to complete the expressions.**

1 My boss gave me the *green / red* light to go ahead with the project.
2 The police caught the burglar *green- / red-* handed as he was leaving the bank carrying a bag full of money!
3 I'm going to vote for the *green / red* party in the next election because they're the only ones with a focus on the environment.
4 Is she OK? She looks a little *green / red* around the gills.
5 I'm worried about my business. We've been in the *green / red* for about three months, and one of our clients just canceled a big order.

B **Rewrite the sentences using an appropriate color expression.**

1 You wouldn't believe all the official paperwork I had to do to open a business in a residential building!
2 Look at this garden! She really knows how to grow plants.
3 I can always tell when my little brother is embarrassed because his face changes color.
4 I'm not sure he's ready for the job. He's still a little young and inexperienced to handle so much responsibility.
5 She shouldn't watch the news. She just gets incredibly angry and is no fun the rest of the evening.

12.1 TALKING ABOUT CHANGE (PAGE 118)

FIND IT

A **Make a word family chart for the words in the box with noun, verb, and adjective forms. Not all words have all forms. Compare your chart with a partner. Use a dictionary or your phone to check your work.**

innovation	disruption	implement	embrace	innovative	disruptive
adaptation	resistance	shake-up	facilitate	transition	

B **Circle the correct words to complete the answer to "the change question" discussed in the unit.**

How do you handle change?

I enjoy working in [1]*a shaken up / an innovative* environment, so I generally [2]*disrupt / embrace* change and see it as an opportunity rather than a threat. Recently, my team [3]*implemented / transitioned* a new communication system across the company. I was chosen to be on the team that [4]*facilitated / underwent* this massive [5]*innovation / transition* because I helped choose it. Well, people didn't like the system at first and showed a lot of [6]*embrace / resistance* to it because they feared that [7]*adapting / undergoing* changes like this during our busiest season was too [8]*disruptive / resistant*. But we went slowly so that it didn't feel like a big [9]*facilitation / shake-up*. And after a few [10]*adaptations / innovations* to align it with our company's processes, people really like it.

Do you think this is a good answer? Why or why not?

12.2 DESCRIBING CHANGE (PAGE 120)

A **Write the type of change described in the examples. More than one correct answer is possible. Discuss your choices with a partner.**

abrupt	desired	drastic	fundamental	gradual
lasting	profound	radical	refreshing	subtle
sweeping	unforeseen	welcome		

1 It was a beautiful day. The sky was blue, and the birds were singing. Then, all of a sudden, big black clouds filled the sky, and it started to pour down rain. ______________

2 We hadn't expected the storm, but the cool water was actually really nice after the blistering heat of the sun. ______________

3 Recent storms have caused a great deal of damage to roads and buildings. Many families have lost their homes, too. ______________

4 They've caused the landscape to change also. When you look at photos from a hundred years ago, for example, you can see that some features are definitely different now. ______________

5 No one predicted the negative effect the storms would have on the local birdlife. ______________

6 Many species have disappeared from the local woods and might not ever come back. ______________

B **Circle the correct words to complete the sentences.**

1 My mom made tacos for dinner last night. It was a *refreshing / sweeping* change from what she usually makes.

2 If you raise your chair a centimeter or two, you won't put so much stress on your wrists and shoulders. Sometimes just a *drastic / subtle* change in positioning can make a big difference.

3 This isn't working! We need to make some *fundamental / unforeseen* changes to the way we do our marketing.

4 He seems to have transformed over the summer. He grew his hair out, got a tattoo, and made a *desired / radical* change in his wardrobe. I didn't even recognize him at first.

PROGRESS CHECK

Can you do these things? Check (✓) what you can do. Then write your answers in your notebook.

UNIT 1

Now I can ...	Prove it
☐ use commenting adverbs to express an opinion.	Use four adverbs from the unit to discuss how useful robots could be in your community.
☐ use commenting adverbs to talk about future probability.	Write three predictions related to technology using commenting adverbs.
☐ talk about changes in technology.	Use four words from the unit to describe a tech item, its functions, and what it is used for.
☐ use future perfect and future continuous to describe future actions.	Write about a future machine and how it will have changed life and what we will be doing differently because of it.
☐ acknowledge arguments and propose counterarguments.	Respond to this argument with two different counterarguments: "Robots will eventually take over the service industry."
☐ write an essay about future possibilities.	Look at your essay from lesson 1.4. Find three ways to make it better.

UNIT 2

Now I can ...	Prove it
☐ describe someone's personality.	Use adjectives to describe the personality of someone you know well.
☐ use *will* to talk about assumptions, deductions, and predictions.	Rewrite the sentence using *will*: They always share their quiz results with friends and are not likely to stop.
☐ talk about labels and their effects on people.	Write sentences using these phrasal verbs: *look down on, fit in with, get through to, stand up for, put up with.*
☐ use *would* in a variety of contexts.	Rewrite the sentence using *would*: I'm not willing to make assumptions about someone based on their age.
☐ compare and discuss similar experiences.	Write two ways to say you had the same experience as someone and two to say you understand their feelings.
☐ write a report based on graphs.	Look at your paragraphs from lesson 2.4. Find three ways to make them better.

UNIT 3

Now I can ...	Prove it
☐ discuss ways to think about past actions and their effects on the present.	Describe a past situation that you regret. What happened? Describe the thought processes that led you to change your mind.
☐ react to past situations.	Write three sentences about your hindsight situation proposing different actions and results. Use *if* constructions.
☐ describe emotional reactions.	Describe a past situation in which you reacted emotionally. What happened?
☐ comment on the past.	Respond to the situations using the prompts: "I ran out of gas." (should / pay attention) "I can't find my passport." (could / leave)
☐ describe a negative experience and offer sympathy and reassurance.	Write three different ways of showing sympathy and offering reassurance to somebody who has had a bad experience.
☐ write a short story based on a set of facts.	Look at your story from lesson 3.4. Find three ways to emphasize the coincidences more.

PROGRESS CHECK

Can you do these things? Check (✓) what you can do. Then write your answers in your notebook.

UNIT 4

Now I can ...	Prove it
☐ describe things.	Describe something in your home but not in the classroom to a partner. Can they guess what it is? Take turns and describe five things.
☐ use quantifiers and prepositions in relative clauses.	Write four sentences about eyes using quantifiers and prepositions in relative clauses. For example, "My cousins, *all of whom* have their father's green eyes, also have their mother's dark skin."
☐ talk about how eyes function.	Write three expressions about eyes in context.
☐ use question words in noun clauses.	Use your expressions in sentences with question words. For example, "We have never seen eye to eye, so in planning meetings *what we mostly do* is argue."
☐ use expressions to clarify points or highlight problems.	Think of an issue with different viewpoints. Write three sentences clarifying your own perspective. For example, "The *truth of the matter is* ..."
☐ write a personal statement for a résumé.	Look at your profile statement from lesson 4.4. Find three ways to make it better.

UNIT 5

Now I can ...	Prove it
☐ describe remote places and landscapes.	Think of two very different remote landscapes you have seen pictures of. Use adjectives to describe them.
☐ use participle phrases in initial position.	Write four sentences about the above landscapes using initial participle phrases. For example, "*Looking at the lush forest,* I ..."
☐ talk about influences and how they have affected your life.	Choose three things that have influenced your life choices and describe them. Then think of three personal habits and think of possible reasons for them.
☐ use reduced relative clauses.	Combine sentences you've written above using reduced relative clauses. For example, "Anyone afraid of snakes should not travel there."
☐ discuss the pros and cons of working from home.	Write two responses to signal a cause and an effect. 1 Working from home is gaining popularity. 2 Some remote workers feel lonely.
☐ write a company profile.	Look at your company profile from lesson 5.4. Find three ways to make it better.

UNIT 6

Now I can ...	Prove it
☐ discuss different reactions to unexpected events.	Write five adverb–adjective combinations. Use one of them to talk about something that surprised you recently.
☐ use clefts to make sentences more emphatic.	Write three things that you like and give reasons why using clefts. Use *reason, thing, it,* and *what* one time each.
☐ use words with the prefixes *under-* and *over-* to modify descriptions.	Give your opinion on six things that you think are not fair or accurate in some way. For example, "I think most pro athletes are *overpaid* because ..."
☐ use questions words with *-ever* to show uncertainty or indifference.	Write four questions and responses with question words with *-ever*. For example, "What time should we leave?" "*Whenever* you want."
☐ add emphasis in different ways in a discussion.	Write one example sentence for each emphasis technique: Adverb–adjective combination, cleft, adverbial (*even, at all*, etc.), auxiliary *do*.
☐ write a paragraph drawing from multiple sources.	Look at your paragraphs from lesson 6.4. Find three ways to make them better.

PROGRESS CHECK

Can you do these things? Check (✓) what you can do. Then write your answers in your notebook.

UNIT 7

Now I can …	Prove it
☐ talk about ancestry and genealogy.	Write down five terms related to ancestry. Use them to write a few sentences about your family history.
☐ use negative and limiting adverbials for emphasis.	Rewrite the sentence starting with *no way*, *never*, and *little*: I thought her presentation would be boring, but it was interesting.
☐ discuss cultural celebrations and preserving them.	Write four verb–noun collocations associated with customs and traditions (mark an occasion, e.g.). Use them to write about a tradition that you observe.
☐ use fronting adverbials to add dramatic effect.	Describe the look of a celebration with fronting adverbial phrases. For example, "*Around the fence* hang strings of colored lights."
☐ share an anecdote about traveling and also comment on it.	Write a short conversation about a recent trip. Comment on your own story and respond to it.
☐ summarize a topic with information from different sources.	Look at your paragraph from lesson 7.4. Find three ways to make it better.

UNIT 8

Now I can …	Prove it
☐ talk about attention and distraction.	Write five phrases related to attention. Use them to write about an experience in which your concentration was tested.
☐ practice causative structures with *get* and *have*.	Write four sentences using expressions with *get* + verb. Could you also use *have* + verb?
☐ use *get* expressions to talk about actions and reactions.	Write five expressions with *get*. Use them to write how you feel about the digital age. For example, "I *get frustrated* when …"
☐ refer to information with *as* phrases.	Why do we use phrases with *as*? Give three examples.
☐ describe selling points and best features of products.	Think of an app and write a few ways to present its best features and main selling points, and then its specific selling points.
☐ create effective presentation slides.	Look at your slides from lesson 8.4. Find three ways to make them better.

UNIT 9

Now I can …	Prove it
☐ discuss health issues.	Write about three physical effects of some aspect of modern life on health.
☐ use referencing techniques to avoid repetition.	Using different types of referencing, write a paragraph based on your sentences from the previous task.
☐ use complex phrasal verbs.	Write sentences using the phrasal verbs *cut back on*, *drift off*, *pack something into*, *fit something into*, and *wind down*.
☐ talk about actions over a period of time with continuous infinitives.	Complete the sentence using the continuous infinitive: "My career ______________ nowhere, but I don't know what to do about it."
☐ ask questions and buy time when answering them.	Imagine that you want to press a local government official on an important issue. Write three probing questions you could ask.
☐ explain how an initiative works.	Look at your paragraph from lesson 9.4. Find three ways to make it better.

PROGRESS CHECK

Can you do these things? Check (✓) what you can do. Then write your answers in your notebook.

UNIT 10	Now I can …	Prove it
	☐ talk about rethinking issues around food production.	Write five words associated with food production and use them to talk about foods that are popular where you live.
	☐ use the simple past to imagine possibilities or pose scenarios.	Complete the sentence about something wished for: Some people ________ ________ we ________ ________ plastic at all.
	☐ talk about rethinking energy options for the future.	Write five expressions related to energy issues: two with a negative connotation and three with a positive connotation.
	☐ use *it* constructions to present information.	Write three sentences on topical issues or trends using *it* constructions. For example, "*It would appear* that beards are back in fashion."
	☐ defend my opinion and allow others to give theirs.	Write a short conversation about using plastic. Use expressions to defend an opinion and conclude a speaking turn.
	☐ write a summary of one side of a debate.	Look at your summary from lesson 10.4. Find three ways to make it better.

UNIT 11	Now I can …	Prove it
	☐ talk about what colors represent.	Think of one color you like and one you dislike. What does each represent for you? Use different verbs in your answer.
	☐ make sure different types of subjects agree with their verbs.	Do the nouns usually take a singular (*S*) or plural (*P*) verb? *company* ___ , *data* ___ , *everyone* ___ , *criteria* ___ , *news* ___
	☐ talk about color idioms.	Write three color idioms that you learned in this unit. Use them in a sentence in an appropriate context.
	☐ use articles correctly in different contexts.	Write about your favorite color as a child. Do you still like it? Use *a*, *an*, and *the* correctly.
	☐ respond to questions in different ways for different purposes.	Write one sentence to buy time while thinking, one to pass the question to someone else, and one to clarify your understanding.
	☐ write an opinion essay.	Look at your essay from lesson 11.4. Find three ways to make it better.

UNIT 12	Now I can …	Prove it
	☐ discuss change and my experience with it.	Think of two nouns, verbs, and adjectives related to the action of changing. Use them to write about changes in your life.
	☐ use the subjunctive to present a call to action or important information.	Rephrase the statements as advice using the subjunctive: 1 Be adaptable. 2 Companies want open-minded people.
	☐ talk about different types of changes.	Write five adjectives that combine with *change* and describe a situation that captures each one of them.
	☐ use the perfect infinitive to talk about completed actions in the past.	Write three sentences about a change in the past using the perfect infinitive – with a modal verb, a reporting verb, and an adjective.
	☐ retell a story.	Write a conversation about a story you heard from someone else. Use expressions to signal retelling, to refer to the original story, and to skip details.
	☐ write a review.	Look at your review from lesson 12.4. Find three ways to make it better.

PAIR WORK PRACTICE (STUDENT A)

3.4 EXERCISE 2C STUDENT A

FACTS:

- Two people with the same name turn up at a hotel.
- Both made reservations on the same day at the same time but on different booking sites.
- They live in different cities, but their street addresses are the same.
- There's only one room booked under the name.

5.4 EXERCISE 2C STUDENT A

1 **Read about two companies.**

Company A: Educational publisher

This company decided to create online products only and avoid traditional paper-bound books. Only executives and marketing staff work in-house, but there are teams of freelance workers who produce the digital content and design it using online platforms. Freelance project managers oversee the whole process.

Company C: Expat retailer

This company sells typically American products, everything from food to clothes, to Westerners living in Hong Kong and Singapore. They decided to close their brick-and-mortar locations and operate online only. Their payroll (money paid to employees) has been cut drastically, but shipping costs have increased greatly.

2 **Choose one of the two stories and summarize the information for your partner.**

6.1 EXERCISE 4A STUDENT A

A **Read a post on a social media group for fathers and take notes.**

So most of you know my youngest daughter, Hannah, graduated from high school last week, and that I'd been struggling to come up with a way to celebrate other than the usual, boring graduation party. She had a difficult year and worked really hard, so I wanted to do something incredibly special for her. But what? She loves traveling and learning languages. And she's always been a very adventurous eater – she'll try almost anything, especially seafood – so I thought about getting her a trip abroad somewhere on the coast. But then, I thought "No, that's been done. I want to do something *really* different." And I wanted it to be something she'd never expect but would remember for the rest of her life.

Well, I'm happy to say, I totally nailed it! We just got back from the trip of a lifetime to Arches National Park in southern Utah. I'd never been, but some coworkers had told me about it, and it sounded like the perfect surprise for Hannah. It was just amazing. If you've never been, you have to go. It's just this remarkably beautiful desert landscape with bare, red rock formations. I've never seen anything like it. And the wildlife! We saw little desert foxes and bighorn sheep. Coming from the city, it was just awe-inspiring.

But the best part was that she didn't expect a thing! I told her to pack her bag for the airport, but I didn't tell her where we were going. You wouldn't believe how surprised she looked when she figured out where we were headed! Seriously: Best. Trip. Ever.

B **Share key information from the post with your partner. Then do exercise 4B on page 55.**

7.4 EXERCISE 2C STUDENT A

Read one perspective on the value of writing things by hand, and take notes.

A recent study claims that writing notes by hand helps us process and retain more information than typing notes on a keyboard. Researchers at Princeton University and UCLA conducted tests on students. Half were asked to take notes by hand as they watched a TED talk, while the others took notes on a laptop. All answered factual follow-up questions well, but the hand writers were significantly better at answering abstract questions.

The researchers argue that writing by hand forces students to process and synthesize the material, as they can't write down every word. Typers could record more information, but they did not retain it as well.

PAIR WORK PRACTICE

6.2 EXERCISE 4B STUDENT A

1 **Read about another famous upset.**

Crash wins Best Picture Oscar against all odds.

Crash won the Best Picture Oscar at the 78th Academy Awards in 2006, controversially beating the critically favored *Brokeback Mountain*. A thriller set in LA, *Crash* was only the second film ever to win the Best Picture Oscar without being nominated for any Golden Globe Awards. Many felt that *Crash* won because some judges were uncomfortable with the subject matter presented in *Brokeback Mountain*. Even *Crash* director Paul Haggis said in a 2015 interview that he did not believe that his film deserved to win Best Picture. In this case, the underdog was not the popular favorite.

2 **Tell your partner about the story. What do your two stories have in common? Which one do you think is more surprising? Why?**

3 **What factors might have contributed to this situation? Were people overconfident that *Brokeback Mountain* would win, or was *Crash* perhaps underrated?**

7.4 EXERCISE 2C STUDENT C

Read one perspective on the value of writing things by hand, and take notes.

Have you ever noticed that hand-lettered motivational quotes fill the walls of trendy cafés, coffee shops, and hotel lobbies? A simple search online will confirm the current popularity of calligraphy – the art of drawing letters. This love of lettering is becoming a popular hobby. Fans say that they enjoy the focus and discipline of this ancient art. There are long waiting lists for classes in trendy studios around the world – London, Wellington, Los Angeles. And online calligraphy tutorials are viewed by millions.

People are also making a living from the art, charging a high price for handwritten wedding invitations and promotional posters.

12.3 EXERCISE 5A STUDENT A

1 **Read a story about how life changed in an instant.**

Leila's story

I used to be afraid of flying. I mean, terrified. Then my best friend asked me to be in her wedding – in Australia! So, no choice, I had to get on a plane.

Waiting at the gate, I was feeling very nervous. Someone said it was going to be a really rough flight – bad weather or something. Great! I was taking deep breaths, trying to calm myself, when I noticed this old guy a few meters away also breathing deeply. He looked even more scared than me, and for some reason that made me feel calmer.

We boarded the plane, and his seat was near mine. I swapped with the person next to him and sat down. I introduced myself and told him that I'd seen him before and how his fear had actually lessened mine, so I thought maybe we could get through this experience together. He was all for it. We talked all through the flight, which was horrible, by the way. There was so much turbulence! We just gripped the armrests and kept talking.

We said goodbye at baggage claim, and I said I hoped his flight home was better than this one. He said, "Well, it can't possibly be worse." And that really struck me. He's right, I thought. We were on the worst flight ever, but we were fine! And I realized in that moment that my fear of flying was gone. Poof!

2 **Retell the story to your partner as if a friend had told it to you. Use expressions for retelling a story in your conversation. Which story do you find more interesting? Why?**

PAIR WORK PRACTICE (STUDENT B)

3.4 EXERCISE 2C STUDENT B

FACTS:

- A woman lost a ring on the beach.
- Six months later, she finds the ring in a secondhand shop 200 kilometers away.
- The woman in the shop was on vacation at the same beach at the same time.

5.4 EXERCISE 2C STUDENT B

1 **Read about two companies.**

Company B: Architecture firm

This company closed its office, and employees now work remotely. They meet regularly online to discuss current and future projects. Without an office, employees must travel to their clients and bring along whatever is needed. For this reason, any new employee or freelancer must live near where their projects are based.

Company D: Food delivery cooperative

The small restaurants on one street joined together to centralize their delivery services. Instead of each restaurant taking orders and delivering, all orders go through one app. The restaurants split the costs evenly, regardless of which restaurant gets the most orders day by day. They had to hire a few employees to manage the service, but they need a lot fewer freelance delivery people.

2 **Choose one of the two companies and summarize the information for your partner.**

6.1 EXERCISE 4A STUDENT B

A **Read Hannah's email to her friend and take notes.**

Soooooo… I just got back from that surprise graduation trip with my dad and… I don't even know where to start. Seriously, WHAT is wrong with him? He told me to pack a bag for a four-day trip, but he wouldn't tell me where we were going. Since I'd been studying Spanish, I figured maybe we were taking a trip to Mexico – Cancun or Playa del Carmen or some other beautiful coastal town. He knows I've always wanted to go to those places. And a week just relaxing on the beach? Yes, please!

Anyway, we get to the departure gate at the airport and they announce, "Now boarding for the 8:30 flight to Salt Lake City, Utah." My dad's like, "Surprise! We're going camping in Arches National Park." Camping… in the desert. I packed a swimsuit and flip-flops! I tried to look excited, but I think my dad could tell I was annoyed.

Things just got better and better once we got to Utah. The first day, I almost stepped on a rattlesnake. I'll bet you could have heard me screaming from halfway across the park. And that night I could hear wolves – actual wolves – howling outside our tent.

I mean, don't get me wrong, it was beautiful. And, yes, it was really great to spend some quality time with my dad. But it was my graduation trip… I just wish I'd had a chance to take a shower!

B **Share key information from the email with your partner. Then do exercise 4B on page 55.**

PAIR WORK PRACTICE

6.2 EXERCISE 4B STUDENT B

1 **Read about another famous upset.**

Uruguay beats Brazil in the 1950 World Cup against all odds.

The 1950 World Cup tournament was held in Rio. In the final match, the Brazil team just needed a draw to secure its first trophy. Brazil had outscored opponents 21 to 4 in their previous five matches and had beaten Uruguay 5 to 1 in the previous year's South American championship, leaving Brazilian media and fans certain they would win. But underdog Uruguay utterly shocked the crowd by beating their host 2 to 1. In this case, almost nobody was cheering for the underdog.

The match became known as the *Maracanazo* (*Maracanaço* in Portuguese), after Maracanã stadium where the match was played. The "Phantom of '50" lives on in Brazil's collective imagination, and each time the two countries play, the story is retold.

2 **Tell your partner about the story. What do your two stories have in common? Which one do you think is more surprising? Why?**

3 **What factors might have contributed to this situation? Was one team underestimated or overrated, for example?**

7.4 EXERCISE 2C STUDENT B

Read one perspective on the value of writing things by hand, and take notes.

In the age of computers and smartphones, why are we still asking schoolchildren to suffer through hours of painful penmanship lessons? Is handwriting really a life skill that is needed in the twenty-first century? In today's digital workplace, no one cares if your handwriting is neat, or even legible, because no one writes by hand anymore. Think about it. When did you last write out a full sentence?

Reports, memos, even shopping lists, are all tapped out on keyboards and keypads these days. It's far more important that children learn how to communicate effectively using the digital channels at their disposal than it is to impress their teacher with pretty penmanship.

12.3 EXERCISE 5A STUDENT B

1 **Read a story about how life changed in an instant.**

Manny's story

My first year as a doctor was terrifying. There I was, an emergency room doctor but totally green and scared to death of doing something wrong. I had no confidence at all.

Then, this one night, the ER was understaffed, just one other doctor and me. Things were going OK – some minor injuries, and the flu was going around. But then we got word that there had been a big accident on the highway. Ambulances were on their way.

The next thing we knew, the ER was a madhouse – so many people with so many different injuries! I was standing there, frozen, when I felt a hand on my arm. I looked down and saw this old lady lying on a stretcher. She smiled at me and said, "Young man, do you know what the most comforting words in the world are?"

Shocked and confused, I finally sort of sputtered, "No, what?"

She pulled me closer and whispered, *"It's all right. I'm a doctor."*

I didn't get it at first, then it clicked. These people needed a doctor – a strong, decisive doctor. I nodded at her, took a deep breath, and got to work.

After that, everything changed. The ER became my home. And the first thing I do when a sick or injured person arrives is look them in the eye and say, "It's all right. I'm a doctor."

2 **Retell the story to your partner as if a friend had told it to you. Use expressions for retelling a story in your conversation. Which story do you find more interesting? Why?**